LAW AN...
NEIGHB...

Nick Yapp was born in 1938 and read law at King's College, London. He taught from 1961 to 1988 and is now a full-time writer and broadcaster.

LAW AND YOUR NEIGHBOURS

NICK YAPP

ROBERT HALE · LONDON

© Nick Yapp 1989
First published in Great Britain 1989

Robert Hale Limited
Clerkenwell House
Clerkenwell Green
London EC1R 0HT

British Library Cataloguing in Publication Data

Yapp, Nick
    Law and your neighbours.
    1. England. Real property. Disputes. Law
    I. Title
    344.2064'3

    ISBN 0-7090-3611-6
    ISBN 0-7090-3531-4 Pbk

Photoset in North Wales by
Derek Doyle & Associates, Mold, Clwyd.
Printed in Great Britain by
St Edmundsbury Press Ltd, Bury St Edmunds, Suffolk.
Bound by WBC Ltd.

Contents

PART II: AN OUTLINE OF THE PROBLEMS

PART III: THE NEIGHBOURLY MINEFIELD

PART V: THE WAY AHEAD

Chapter 24   Where Do We Go From Here?   **233**

Acknowledgements

I should like to thank the many people – lawyers, local officials, members of the police, researchers and voluntary workers who helped me in the compilation of this book, for their time and interest, for allowing me access to research reports and for showing their concern about problems between neighbours.

I should particularly like to thank Vivien Fletcher of the Laws Library, King's College, London, for allowing a very poor graduate to return to his Alma Mater and hopefully use the library to better effect this time.

Lastly, I should like to thank my neighbours, for being a constant source of inspiration in so many ways.

Introduction

Recent research suggests that around thirty per cent of the population of Britain feel that they have a serious problem with their neighbours. Probably a further thirty per cent have some slight trouble with their neighbours from time to time – the odd complaint, the occasional snappy word, a brooding resentment. This means that well over half of us believe that we don't get on well with the folks next door.

This may be cold comfort to you if you're in this situation. It's a frightening figure. We all like to think that home is safe, secure, comfortable, free from worry, somewhere we can do what we like without fear of criticism or censure. And we all like to think that those around us will either keep themselves to themselves or be pleasant and understanding in any communication they have with us.

In practice, it seems, life is very different. The incidence of neighbour disputes seems on the increase. The variety of bones of contention between neighbours is staggering, ranging from banging doors to flooding of a neighbour's property, from abusive language to heavy breathing, from noisy parties to unpruned greengage trees. In some cases we are faced with a mere minor irritation, in others with a major catastrophe. A few people are driven to such despair by neighbour problems that they commit suicide. Many more feel constrained to move house. The vast majority suffer in silence.

If you are in dispute with your neighbour, don't despair. There are legal remedies to cover most problems, and there are many agencies outside the legal profession who can help. There are also clear signs that the idea is rapidly growing that something must be done about neighbour problems. Several universities have embarked on research programmes; there are initiatives from the Home Office; voluntary groups connected with the Quakers and other Churches have set up counselling and mediation services.

The problem has become so big that it can't be ignored.

PART I

AN OUTLINE OF THE LAW

1   The Problem

The biggest single cause of trouble is noise: doors banging, washing-machines, children playing on the walkways of estates, hi-fis, parties, cars revving, dogs barking, DIY drills and hammers, rows, music practice, matrimonial discord, babies crying, TVs, dancing on the ceiling, CB radios, abusive language, drunken revelry, airlocks in water pipes, lawnmowers, pet canaries, hyperactive burglar alarms. Most complaints by one neighbour against another contain a 'noise' element. Our environment is getting noisier and noisier. We have more and more machines capable of making and spreading noise. We now have twenty-four-hour-a-day television. The number of dogs in the country is increasing, as is the number of power tools. More and more houses are being converted to multiple occupation – we are living on top of (and underneath) each other.

In towns and cities there is increasingly a problem of lack of space. One Environmental Health Officer I spoke to said that, where houses had been converted into bedsits, providing multiple occupation, there were a great many problems among neighbours simply because, living so close to each other, they were conscious of every slightly irritating aspect of each other's behaviour. For people living in blocks of flats, there is clearly a premium on space where children can play. This leads to children playing in areas where some residents feel they shouldn't. This in turn leads to complaints and arguments. Most families now own a car, but most families have nowhere to park the car. Some blocks of flats have built-in car-parks or areas set aside for off-street parking. Arguments arise when access to such areas is obstructed. Occupiers of houses without garages tend to see the patch of road opposite their house as theirs when it comes to parking. If a neighbour repeatedly occupies that space, trouble may well arise. In fact, it's often this persistent aspect of a nuisance or an annoyance that makes a minor irritation into a major conflict, and makes that conflict so difficult to resolve.

The number and variety of problems that can arise in towns and cities seem almost limitless. Sometimes they're short-term problems, such as the clearance of a site where fleets of lorries may be rumbling to and fro, eight hours a day, carting rubble away. This may not sound like a short-term problem, but it does have an end. Other problems are timeless – our neighbour had a neurotic, noisy and extremely unpleasant dog which died last summer. Within days it had been replaced by another, more energetic and noisier than its predecessor. But maybe we're lucky. We don't live near a pub (closing-time noises and whoopee and slamming car doors every night) or a factory or a minicab office or a disco.

In rural areas different problems arise. There may be plenty of space, but each bit of it is precious. Boundary disputes arise, fences are replaced in the wrong position, hedges grow too big, tree roots invade subsoil, the branches of trees block out light. And still there is noise – hay-balers, combine harvesters, crop-spraying helicopters, dogs, shooting-parties, children.

We live in an age where there is a growing disparity in the lifestyles of the employed and the unemployed, the haves and the have-nots, the young and the old. This leads to grating disharmonies, suspicion, resentment, fear, misunderstandings, insensitivity, even outright jealousy. Old people are often set in their ways and feel they are entitled to expect the rest of the community to respect this.

Young people have very different expectations from life and are prey to the glamorous (and frequently noisy and flamboyant) images served up by the media. Old people want peace and quiet; young people want fun and noise.

Everyone wants a decent place to live. Where people are living in poor or substandard housing, the number of disputes between neighbours increases, especially where there is resentment against a neighbour who has been lucky – 'Why should that lot at No. 10 get things done? They do nothing but cause trouble. That dog barks all day, and their kids run wild,' etc. (Next to noise, dogs and children are the most common causes of complaint among neighbours.) The problem also tends to be worse in blocks of flats – the bigger the block, the worse the problem – where communication between families is likely to be minimal and reserved entirely for when things go wrong. Noise is again the main cause for complaint, although most purpose-built blocks of flats are supposed to have sound insulation.

Everyone I spoke to in the preparation of this book (police, Environmental Health Officers, staff at Citizens' Advice Bureaux, Housing Officers, solicitors) agreed that we tend to tolerate – or, more accurately, suffer – neighbour trouble for far too long. They all had tales to tell of people putting up with a neighbour's noise or litter or thoughtlessness for over thirty years before complaining to a third party. Quite what this indicates in us all, I don't know, but the advice of all the experts is that we shouldn't be so patient. Their general feeling is that the moment we are inconvenienced by a neighbour we should do something about it. And they are of one mind as to what that 'something' is – we should speak to our neighbour.

Of course, this makes a lot of sense. It is quite possible that our neighbour has no idea that he or she has done anything wrong as far as we're concerned. Until it's brought to our neighbour's attention, there's little likelihood that he or she will stop doing whatever it is that's causing annoyance.

There's no doubt that some neighbours, once they were made aware of the situation, would apologize and mend their ways. On the other hand, it's equally certain that some neighbours would do nothing of the sort but would give us an earful of abuse and repeat their anti-social behaviour with relish and renewed vigour. One of the troubles is that too many of us assume that that is how our neighbour would react if we complained. Because we think our neighbour is at fault in the first place, we tend to assume that he or she is bad or awkward or rude or thoughtless in every way. We make this assumption partly because few of us have much to do with our neighbours, except when things go wrong. Increasingly we live our own lives, isolated even from those who live next door to us. We may be gregarious animals but we seem to have lost that tribal feeling that some other societies have. We move house more. Communities are shaken up. Yuppies move into traditionally working-class areas, townies into rural hamlets, young people into streets populated mainly by the middle-aged or elderly. It often means that we regard the people next door as 'not our sort'. Owner-occupiers don't expect council tenants who move into their area to 'fit in'. The spectre of racial hatred may raise its ugly head. Few people welcome the arrival of squatters.

What sort of neighbours we do have is purely a question of luck. Estate agents may lavish their prose on garden, bedrooms, fitted kitchen, closeness to amenities etc. They say nothing about neighbours. Some of us, when showing potential buyers round our own house, hope fervently that our neighbours will be out. Few of us would be so honest as to say to a potential buyer: 'Of course, the bloke next door's a right noisy bastard who'll punch your face in if you say anything to him.'

Which brings us to a reason often given for reluctance to complain about a neighbour – fear of reprisal or retribution. Occasionally such a fear may be well grounded; usually it isn't. We make assumptions about groups of people – all young people are into drugs and sex, all dog-owners are happy to let their dogs mess in the streets, all football fans are hooligans, all noisy neighbours are likely to turn violent if you complain. My wife and I have consistently failed to get on well with our neighbours. My wife is braver than I am and has complained directly to our neighbours whenever the occasion demanded. There has never been any violence – even when we lived in a cottage in the country next door to a man whose living-room walls were covered in guns and knives, whose garden was always full of alsatians and whose temper was always on a very short fuse.

So perhaps it is wrong to assume that thoughtlessness and violence go hand in hand, and perhaps the best way to approach a problem that you have with your neighbour is to tackle it the moment it arises, reasonably, politely and constructively. You may be agreeably surprised.

Complaints and Offenders

People who have to deal with neighbour disputes grow wary of accepting that the person who complains is always in the right. Some of us do complain about very tiny issues. Some of us appear obsessed with something our neighbour does that is quite harmless and can hardly be said to constitute a nuisance. In more than half the cases where the police or council officers become involved, some fault seems to lie with both complainant and alleged offender. Often someone against whom a complaint is made will retort, 'Well, she's got nothing better to do all day than stand by the window looking for something to moan about.' Life isn't simple.

Certain patterns emerge about complainants and offenders. Women are far more likely to be complainants. Men are far more likely to be offenders. Nearly half the complainants are elderly people, i.e. over sixty-five years of age. Nearly half the offenders are young people, i.e. under nineteen years of age. There doesn't seem to be any particular ethnic factor in neighbour disputes, except that black people are far more likely to be the victims of racial abuse than white people.

The classic situation for a neighbour dispute, then, would seem to be a block of flats where a male youth is doing something noisy that upsets an elderly woman. Like most generalizations, however, this grossly over-simplifies the problem. In the last few years an interesting and important development has taken place in attempts to help solve neighbour disputes. In many parts of the country mediation centres or agencies have been established which seek to bring warring neighbours (complainants and offenders) together to talk, to negotiate and, hopefully to settle such disputes (see Section 97, How Mediation Centres Work). In mediation the attempt is made to help neighbours meet and not only to find a resolution to the apparent problem that is amenable to both parties but also to bring in the other, underlying issues that have created a hostile atmosphere or led to frequent misunderstandings, resentment, bitterness or suppressed rage in the past. The emphasis in this sort of approach is on working together to solve a problem – it isn't seen as a question of A being right and B being wrong – and there seems little doubt that such an approach is appropriate to many neighbour problems.

Mediation seems, at the moment, the most helpful way of trying to solve a great many neighbour problems (though there are clearly some situations where it isn't appropriate). The bulk of this book assumes that there is a right and a wrong side to any dispute being discussed and, for the most part, assumes that you (or 'we') are in the right.

It's more comfortable that way.

Note: It may be helpful, whatever the problem, to refer to the chart below from time to time. It isn't like a board game: you don't always have to start from point 1, but, generally speaking, this does hold out the best hope of a real and long-lasting solution to your neighbour problem. Things get slower, meaner and more expensive the further into the chart you proceed.

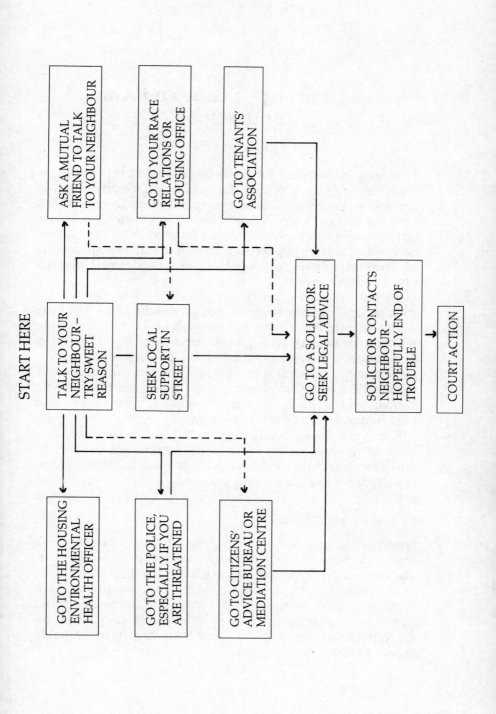

START HERE

TALK TO YOUR NEIGHBOUR – TRY SWEET REASON

ASK A MUTUAL FRIEND TO TALK TO YOUR NEIGHBOUR

GO TO YOUR RACE RELATIONS OR HOUSING OFFICE

GO TO TENANTS' ASSOCIATION

SEEK LOCAL SUPPORT IN STREET

GO TO A SOLICITOR. SEEK LEGAL ADVICE

SOLICITOR CONTACTS NEIGHBOUR – HOPEFULLY END OF TROUBLE

COURT ACTION

GO TO THE HOUSING ENVIRONMENTAL HEALTH OFFICER

GO TO THE POLICE, ESPECIALLY IF YOU ARE THREATENED

GO TO CITIZENS' ADVICE BUREAU OR MEDIATION CENTRE

2 Purpose, Scope and Aim of the Book

This book is intended for the general reader. It is not a law book aimed at specialists but a guidebook for all of us. We are said to be gregarious animals, but there seems to be a limit as to how closely we wish to live together. If our territory, our defensible space, is invaded – by noise, animals, children, vegetation, smoke or any one of dozens of other interlopers, we may feel threatened. Certainly, we often become angry.

Recent surveys carried out by the Home Office and various universities suggest that over half of us feel that we have problems with our neighbours or with people who live near us or with people who visit us (for business or pleasure). To feel uncomfortable or threatened in our own home is a dreadful thing – home is our sanctuary, our escape from what may seem the hostile world of work, shops, buses, trains, traffic, school, anywhere and everywhere, anyone and everyone.

But is our home really our castle? The purpose of this book is to show what we can do, where we can go, to whom we can turn when we wish to raise the drawbridge or sally forth to charge at the enemy.

1 A WORD OF CAUTION

Some of the remedies or strategies outlined in this book are very time-consuming and can be expensive. It is always worthwhile trying to establish good relations with your neighbours, a fluent and regular practice of communication, so that, when things do start to go wrong, there is a chance that a solution can be found by diplomatic means. A good neighbour is a most valuable asset to a happy life.

Even if you don't have such a relationship with your neighbour, it is always a good idea to try to settle disputes, problems or arguments by mutual agreement. Don't race to a solicitor or the police at the first sign of trouble – the first wisp of bonfire smoke, the first unwelcome and uninvited visit from next door's alsation or the first time you are aware of late-night DIY with a hammer drill. Try to talk to your neighbour. Live for as long as you can with the hope that sweet reason will prevail. Similarly, if your neighbour approaches you with a complaint, try to listen. Try to see if he or she has a valid point. Try to see the problem from your neighbour's point of view. Police, Housing Officers, Citizens' Advice Bureaux and solicitors all say that, in ninety per cent of the cases they deal with, there are two sides to every complaint. We may all feel that we are the perfect neighbour. It is never our fault. As far as this book is concerned, if we have a problem, it isn't our fault. But, consciously or unconsciously, there is a great deal of tit-for-tat in dealings between neighbours. You park your car blocking my drive, and I couldn't care less if my late-night party keeps you awake.

So try to settle matters amicably. Be bold. Knock on your neighbour's door – ring his bell before you want to wring his neck. Don't let minor irritations become major upsets before you seek a remedy. And always try the cheapest and the quickest remedy first – an appeal to reason.

2 A FURTHER WORD OF CAUTION – THE LAW

Perhaps it hardly needs to be said that, wherever we have dealings with the Law, we face not only delay and expense but also unpredictability and (frequently) what seems like downright irrationality. The Law often doesn't make sense or is apparently unfair.

Don't be put off. If you are being unfairly treated, harassed, abused, intimidated or grossly inconvenienced by your neighbour, the Law wants to be on your side. But the Law has some very ancient components and holds certain old-fashioned concepts very dear. In all moral, logical and common-sense terms, you may be in the right.

Legally, however, you may be on very shaky ground. In the last resort only a court can decide, but one of the aims of this book is to help predict what the outcome of going to court might be, by looking at cases involving neighbour disputes and Acts of Parliament that regulate dealings between neighbours. At the very least, it's possible to inform you of some of the situations where it is already well established that the court would *not* help.

It's also worth bearing in mind that, even where you are legally in the right, there are some things a court simply cannot do. One solicitor I interviewed in the preparation of this book said: 'You can't do anything in court, or in any judgment of the court, to make two people who dislike each other and can't get on, change.'

So, check – even if you get judgment in your favour in court, will it solve the problem? It may, in matters such as boundary disputes, statutory nuisance or industrial pollution. But in terms of the everyday quality of living, of give-and-take, of your neighbour not blocking your exit again, it may not. The Law cannot lower the animosity that exists between two people. Only the people themselves can do that. It may be better to try false smiles and rank hypocrisy before approaching the majesty of the Law.

If you feel there isn't just one problem with your neighbour but that the whole of life is shot through with difficulties, harassment, misunderstandings, moans and ugly scenes, you may be forced to consider moving. It's a desperate action, but some people do get into desperate situations. One Housing Officer I spoke to saw the option of moving house as being one of the great advantages the owner-occupier has over the council tenant. It's worth considering, but only if things are very, very bad.

3 Neighbours

The first thing to do is to find out ...

3   WHO IS YOUR NEIGHBOUR?

At first glance, this is a silly question. Your neighbours are
the people who live in the houses on either side of your
house or in the flats above and below you. What about the
people who live in the house that adjoins the bottom of
your garden? Well, of course, they're your neighbours,
too. And next door but one? And the people over the
road? What about No. 10? Admittedly three doors away,
but it's his bonfire that ruins the washing most Sundays in
the autumn and his dog that keeps fouling your front path
at all times of the year. Is he your neighbour? Come to
that, what about the people in No. 9, who complain
whenever you park outside their house. That's on the
other side of the road – do you have a neighbourly
responsibility towards them? Should they have a similar
responsibility towards you?

The Neighbour Principle
Over the last fifty or so years, the Law has evolved a kind
of formula to decide who is your neighbour. It began with
a case in 1932, *Donoghue v Stevenson*. In his judgment in the
Appeal Court, Lord Atkin said: 'The rule that you are to
love your neighbour becomes, in law, you must not injure
your neighbour; and the lawyer's question, Who is my
neighbour? receives a restricted reply. You must take
reasonable care to avoid acts or omissions which you can
reasonably foresee would be likely to injure your
neighbour. Who, then, in law is my neighbour? The
answer seems to be – persons who are so closely and
directly affected by my act that I ought reasonably to have

them in contemplation as being so affected when I am directing my mind to the acts or omissions which are called in question.'

An enormous number of subsequent cases have hinged on this decision, although judges have been careful not to let the floodgates of liability open too widely.

In the case of Donoghue and Stevenson (a drinks manufacturer), the facts were these: A friend of Mrs Donoghue bought a bottle of aerated ginger beer from a café in Paisley. Mrs Donoghue drank some of it and then found the bottle contained the remains of a decomposing snail. As a result, she suffered from shock and severe gastro-enteritis and sued for damages, alleging negligence on Stevenson's part. Mrs Donoghue was successful. As far as the House of Lords was concerned, Stevenson owed a duty of care to Mrs Donoghue, even though it was the friend who had bought the ginger beer. It's worth quoting at length from another judgment in that case, that of Lord Macmillan, as the principles established by *Donoghue v Stevenson* cover many of the unhappy dealings between neighbours.

> In the daily contacts of social and business life human beings are thrown into, or place themselves in, an infinite variety of relationships with their fellows: and the law can refer only to the standards of the reasonable man in order to determine whether any particular relation gives rise to a duty to take care as between those who stand in that relation to each other. The grounds of action may be as various and manifold as human errancy; and the concepts of legal responsibility may develop in adaptation to altering social conditions and standards. The criterion of judgment must adjust and adapt itself to the changing circumstances of life. The categories of negligence are never closed. The cardinal principle of liability is that the party complained of should owe to the party complaining a duty to take care, and that the party complaining should be able to prove that he has suffered damage in consequence of a breach of that duty. Where there is room for diversity of view, it is in determining what circumstances will establish such a relationship between the parties as to give rise, on one side, to a duty to take care, and on the other side to a right to have care taken.

Note: We have just 'cited' (referred to) our first case – *Donoghue v Stevenson*, and we need to take time out for an explanation of a little legal jargon. Although civil (non-criminal) cases are written as '*Donoghue v Stevenson*', they are spoken of as 'Donoghue *and* Stevenson'. The first named (in this case Donoghue) is the person or company or club or Government department or local authority that has brought the action, and is always referred to as 'the plaintiff'. The second named (Stevenson) is the person against whom the action is brought, and is referred to as 'the defendant'. When a case reaches the Court of Appeal or the House of Lords, it means that a previous loser is dissatisfied with the result in the lower court and wants to try again. In these cases, the previous loser is known as the 'appellant' and the previous winner is known as the 'respondent'. I just thought you might like to know.

4 WHAT DOES IT ALL MEAN?

Like many key cases in law, you have to rummage through the words to pluck out the principles laid down. What Lord Atkin said was: anyone who is likely to be affected by your acts or omissions is regarded (in law) as your neighbour, as someone whom you must consider.

In terms of our social and community relationships, this may seem straightforward. If No. 10 leaves the dog out all night, and it barks from dusk to dawn, anyone within earshot is inconvenienced and, if the nuisance persists, may well have a legal remedy. Furthermore, No. 10 certainly should be aware that anyone within earshot would be affected by his omission (failing to take the dog in). The law would regard everyone within earshot as a neighbour.

Similarly, if No. 10 lights a bonfire, and acrid smoke blows the length of the street and beyond, it's obvious that not just the families at No. 8 and No. 12 will be affected. But suppose you decide to put up some shelves one morning – there you are, happily drilling, sawing and hammering away, when there is an abrupt knock on your door and there stands a gummy-eyed but furious neighbour who is on night shift this week, returned home at 6 a.m. went to bed at 8 a.m. and had just dozed off when you began your DIY. Should you have anticipated that he was likely to be affected by your act?

In the first place, if you had known that your neighbour was on night shifts, that might have made a difference. You might have warned him, consulted him, negotiated with him, fixed a time when he wouldn't mind noise – maybe in the afternoon, after he'd slept. This comes back to the importance of keeping in touch with your neighbour: there really isn't any substitute for communication.

What Lord Atkin and Lord Macmillan ruled was that, where we should foresee that our acts or omissions are likely to affect people and where those acts or omissions cause hardship, nuisance or, more particularly, damage, we may be held liable in law. It's not possible to put it stronger than 'may be'. Few things are absolutely certain in law (except cost and delay), and for the thoughtless act of a neighbour to constitute a legal wrong, it has to fall within one of the defined categories laid down by the law – of which more later.

This isn't to deny the importance, socially and morally, of what Lords Atkin and Macmillan said in *Donoghue v Stevenson*. The general principle that we should consider how those around us may be affected by our acts or omissions provides a sound basis for what the Americans used to call 'a good neighbour policy'.

5   MORE RECENT DEVELOPMENTS

Despite appearances to the contrary, the law doesn't stand still; it hasn't totally solidified. In the fifty or more years since Lord Atkin's judgment in the above case, other cases have attempted to explain, modify or limit the principle he laid down.

In 1965, in the case of *Weller & Co v Foot and Mouth Disease Research Institute*, the Institute had imported a virus for use in experimental work on foot and mouth disease. Because some of this virus escaped, cattle in the vicinity of the Institute became infected. Local cattle markets had to be closed. The plaintiffs (Weller & Co) were cattle auctioneers and were temporarily unable to carry on part of their business. They lost money. They didn't win the case either, as the court ruled that the defendants shouldn't necessarily have foreseen a duty of care to the cattle auctioneers, though they should have to cattle-owners. There was an important distinction between the 'neighbouring' cattle-owners and the physically remote auctioneers.

Against this we may set *SCM (UK) Ltd v W.J.Whittall & Son Ltd* in 1970. Here the defendants cut through an electric cable which deprived the plaintiffs' factory of power. It was held that, although the cable didn't belong to the plaintiffs, the defendants were in breach of duty of care which they owed to the plaintiffs not to damage the cable, because they knew it supplied electricity to the plaintiff's factory. There wasn't the remoteness between plaintiff and defendant that existed in *Weller & Co v Foot and Mouth Disease Research Institute*.

Also in 1970, the House of Lords stressed that any act causing foreseeable damage to another (or his property) should prima facie be liable for compensation in negligence unless there was good reason to the contrary. In *Dorset Yacht Co Ltd v Home Office*, a group of Borstal boys escaped from a boat at night and damaged a nearby yacht. Their Lordships ruled that such a possibility should have been foreseen, especially since the three officers in charge of the boys had retired to bed.

In 1984, in the case of *Peabody Donation Fund v Sir Lindsay Parkinson & Co Ltd*, the House of Lords warned against the dangers of treating statements in judgments as definitive. Lord Keith said: 'A relationship of proximity in Lord Atkin's sense must exist before any duty of care can arise, but the scope of the duty must depend on all the circumstances of the case.'

In 1985, in the case of *Tutton v A.D.Walter Ltd*, a deputy High Court judge held that the defendants owed a common duty of care to neighbouring bee-keepers, whose bees were killed by insecticide sprayed by the defendants on their own flowering oil rape seed, since

(a) they knew of the bees' presence in the neighbourhood;

(b) they had knowledge of the danger to bees of spray
in the flowering period;

(c) they had the bee-keepers in their contemplation
before they began spraying.

The important thing for us to notice here is that what
seemed very clear after Donoghue and Stevenson seems
less clear now as a matter of principle, because on top of
the notion of foreseeability and damage we now have the
notion of 'proximity' to deal with, and the House of Lords
has muttered warnings about opening the floodgates of
litigation to those of us who feel we have grounds for legal
action against our neighbours. On the other hand, there
are more cases already judged to which we can turn, to get
some idea of the way the courts are moving.

6   THE NEIGHBOUR DILEMMA

When our neighbours feel they have a complaint against
us, we want each case to be judged on its own merits. We
are never intentionally unreasonable. We want all the
circumstances of the case to be taken into consideration. If
we had a noisy party last Saturday night, ending with
much merriment and slamming of car doors in the road at
3 a.m., that's because it was Linda's twenty-first birthday
party. A fracas such as that won't occur again for years,
not until she gets married or Steve has his twenty-first or
some other cause for legitimate celebration arises.

On the other hand, when we feel aggrieved, when our
neighbours have upset us, that's when we want definitive
statements. Never mind about Lord Keith and 'the scope
of duty must depend on all the circumstances of the case',
we agree with Lord Atkin: a duty is owed to *anyone* who is
likely to be affected. Never mind special circumstances,
special pleading. We want a decent night's sleep.

Herein lies the dilemma for the Law and all the agencies
involved in trying to keep the peace between neighbours
and sort out their problems. Each complainant wants each
complaint dealt with immediately and wishes to establish

a general principle, binding on the offender so that he or she never offends again. Even anarchists, deprived of a night's sleep or having trodden in dog mess, become advocates of a rigid system of law, strictly and unerringly imposed.

The law wants to be just and reasonable. It hopes others want the same.

Note: Several of the cases quoted above come from the House of Lords, via the Court of Appeal and the Queen's (or King's) Bench of the High Court. These are awesome, solemn and prohibitively expensive places. Don't panic – should you go to litigation, you are most unlikely to end up there. The vast majority of disputes between neighbours never go to court. Many of the small number that head that way are settled out of court, the remainder go to county courts, or, in some instances, magistrates' courts, which are much, much cheaper and far more homely. But always remember: even if you obtain judgment, you are unlikely to change your neighbour's heart, soul and attitude towards you or even blunt his or her propensity to annoy.

7   THE LAW OF OBLIGATIONS

Recently, another way of looking at the question of 'Who in the law is my neighbour?' has been in terms of obligations. The idea here is to provide the fabric of legal control without which social life would be impossible, and it may serve as a useful model for dealing with problems that arise between neighbours (i.e. those living in a 'neighbourhood').

For the purposes of this book, the most likely area that concerns us is interference with land, which may take one of two forms:

1. Direct interference. This physically impinges on the land itself. Here we are concerned with the Law of Trespass (see Section 32).

2. Indirect interference. This doesn't affect the land itself but reduces its value or utility. Here we are concerned with the Law of Nuisance (see Section 28).

There are, of course, certain criteria that have to be applied. If you are the complainant, then, firstly, the interest you seek to protect must not be too sensitive. You may well be annoyed at the way branches from next door's trees tap against your garden shed but wanting to go to court over such a matter is classic sledgehammer-and-walnut stuff. (What you do here is prune the offending branches and hand the cuttings back to your neighbour.)

Secondly, you can't really complain if the damage to your land is normal where that land is. If you live next to an industrial estate, you must endure more noise than if you lived in a leafy suburb – be it Beckenham, Solihull, Dewsbury or Arcadia. A hundred years ago, the law was more assuredly snobbish about all this. In 1879, in the case of *Sturges v Bridgman*, Lord Thesiger said: 'What would be a nuisance in Belgrave Square would not necessarily be so in Bermondsey.' It's not hard to see where Oscar Wilde got a lot of his material.

In *Sturges v Bridgman*, Bridgman was a confectioner who had for more than twenty years used a pestle and mortar in his back premises in Wigmore Street. These premises abutted those of a physician, Sturges, who lived in Wimpole Street. For twenty years the noise and vibration were not felt to be a nuisance by Sturges and were not complained of. But in 1873 he erected a consulting-room at the end of his garden, and then the noise and vibration became a nuisance to him. Sturges won his case.

So you can point out to your neighbour that it's no good his saying that you've put up with his noise for twenty years, so you're stuck with it. And if you've newly moved into your house, it's no good his saying that you should have found out what sort of a neighbour he was before you moved in.

On the other hand, if you choose to go and live next door to industrial premises (which can be anything from a small panel-beater's or garden centre to a giant glue factory or nuclear power station) and are subject to pollution, the owners of the industrial premises cannot defend themselves by saying that you *came* to the nuisance, that you should have known what you were letting yourself in for and that you have only yourself to blame. It would be interesting to know where that leaves anyone living within a five-mile radius of Heathrow.

8 DIFFERENT SORTS OF NEIGHBOURS

All of the foregoing should give some idea of how widely the law is prepared to interpret the notion of 'neighbours'. In any inner city, provincial town or leafy suburb, there are dozens of people whose acts or omissions can interfere with our quiet enjoyment of our own home. Similarly there are dozens of people whom we can upset by our acts and omissions. The law holds out at least the hope of remedy against all these people and against business premises, public institutions, Government agencies and local authorities – as well as those exasperating people at No. 10.

In many ways, you may be better placed if the source of your upset is a commercial firm than you would be if it was a private individual, because, in the case of the former, you are far more likely to have the support of an Act of Parliament, known in law as a statute.

More about that in the next chapter.

4   An Outline of English and Scottish Law

A Note about Scotland
When lawyers talk about English law, they really mean English and Welsh law, which are one and the same. Scotland is different. In legal matters, Scotland has always been different. they have different courts, different types of lawyer (attorneys, sheriffs, procurators fiscal) and, most importantly, different laws.

9 SOURCES OF LAW

There are three main sources of English Law: Common Law, Statute Law and Case Law.

Common Law is a kind of traditional (often, but not always, 'common sense') body of law which has existed for centuries and has been unchanged by either Statute or Case Law. It's a kind of law by memory, not written down, but of great importance. For a long time there was no Act of Parliament that said, 'Thou shalt not kill' – it was simply the accepted practice, part of the province of Common Law. Because it deals with such fundamental matters and because it is so venerable and ancient, Common Law is very important and very powerful. It takes a lot to overthrow it, but, because of the encroachment of Statute Law coming from Parliament, and the increasing volume of Case Law coming from the courts, the Common Law is a constantly dwindling source of law.

Statute Law is the law as enacted by Parliament, ever since that august body first met. Over the centuries, Statute Law has codified, clarified (hopefully) and ratified much of the Common Law, as well as having plugged loopholes and brought the law up to date (also hopefully). The England of the Black Death (1348) may have needed a Public Health Act, but there wouldn't have been much point in passing one as there was no machinery to put it into effect. On the other hand, while there was no need for a Town and Country Planning Act in the fourteenth century, 600 years later there was.

Many statutes affect the rights and responsibilities of neighbours and cover relations between them. These will be dealt with in Part III. For the moment, here are some of the more obvious examples: Prevention of Damage by Pests Act, 1949; Occupiers' Liability Act, 1957; Control of Pollution Act, 1974; Local Government (Planning and Land) Act, 1980; Litter Act, 1983.

Like Common Law, Statute Law is very powerful indeed. Technically speaking, it can do anything to anybody in legal terms – change their sex, deprive them of their home, conscript them into the Armed Forces, make them chop down trees, prevent them from chopping down trees – anything.

Case Law, as its name implies, is law that arises out of the cases judged by the courts – the higher the court, the more powerful the case as a precedent, as a model for subsequent cases of like situation. (See Section 11, The Hierarchy of the Courts.)

Case Law works like this. A judge (or several judges, depending on which court is involved) makes a decision in a case where there may be a small gap left by Statute or Common Law or where there is a debatable point of interpretation. It may be that any statute or part of Common Law is too outdated to be fairly applied. As far as the judge is concerned, the facts in front of him (it's nearly always a 'him') are novel – they haven't previously been before a court. He can use the novelty of this situation as a basis for his decision, called in law his *ratio decidendi*. Once that decision has been made, it has implications for all subsequent similar instances of dispute. Where the facts are similar, this case will be cited as a precedent, i.e. used as a powerful argument to decide subsequent cases the same way.

Suppose your next-door neighbour, No. 10, has opened a private zoo. We have also to assume that he or she has obeyed all the rules and regulations regarding control of the animals, noise, smell, prevention of escape, land usage etc. and has obtained all the necessary licences. The only trouble is, the proximity of his beasts of prey has given your budgies (or pigeons or ducks or whatever) such palpitations of the heart that they have all folded their wings and died. No statute covers this situation. Neither does the Common Law, private zoos being a comparatively recent phenomenon.

If you went to court, and you would almost certainly be advised not to, the decision made by the judge in your case might well become a precedent, a reference point for any later actions brought by other sorrowful budgie-owners. You would become part of the great body of English Case

Law, and your name would be remembered by law
students for generations to come – sadly, without any
gratitude whatsoever.

10   CIVIL AND CRIMINAL LAW

English and Scottish Law are both divided into two
branches: civil and criminal. It's important to know the
differences between these, as they have separate courts,
different procedures, and you may not be able to seek a
civil remedy for a criminal deed. You certainly can't seek a
criminal punishment for a civil wrongdoer.

Most disputes between neighbours fall under the Civil
Law, where a 'defendant' is 'sued' by a 'plaintiff' in a civil
court – usually a county court.

Only if the police are involved and a crime has been
committed (for example: breach of the peace) will a
defendant be 'prosecuted' and the action be heard in a
criminal court – at first instance always a magistrates'
court.

Few disputes between neighbours involve the Criminal
Law. This has important implications for all of us
regarding where we should turn to when we want a
remedy. It's no good phoning the police at 2 a.m. and
expecting them to break up a noisy party, to arrest the
owner of the portable disco and cow the other
merrymakers into silent submission. Noise isn't a crime.
Sometimes, against their will and with great reluctance,
the police do respond to complaints about rowdy (rather
than noisy) parties, because they well understand that – at
2 a.m. – no one else will. But there's little they can do.
They can *ask* the organizers of the party to quieten things
down, but that's all. And once the police go away, the
party will almost certainly return to its cacophonous glory.

If the party is getting out of hand, however, spilling out
onto the pavement or heading towards an alcoholic
punch-up, that's a different matter. A breach of the peace
threatens, and here the police can act, because a crime
may be committed. Similarly the police have powers to act
is they have reason to believe that there are drugs on the

premises where the party is being held. There has to be the reasonable expectation of some crime.

The cynical conclusion is that, if you want to stop a noisy party, the thing to do is phone the police and say you think a breach of the peace is likely to occur or that you smell the heady scent of 'grass' on the summer air, whether you do or not. The police are wise to this, however, and will probably want your name and address. If you won't give it, they won't bother to go round to the party. If you do and there isn't a threat of breach of the peace or all they can find is high-quality joss-sticks, you may be in trouble yourself.

An alternative is to threaten to create a breach of the peace yourself, thereby seeking to force the police to attend, but there are drawbacks to this course of action. If you do create a breach of the peace, you will almost certainly be charged with the offence. If you don't create a breach of the peace, you may well be charged with some other offence such as wasting police time.

One of the main differences between Civil and Criminal Law, therefore, is in who can commence proceedings. Anyone can bring a civil action: only the Crown, through the Director of Public Prosecutions and the police, can prosecute for a criminal offence. There is an exception here: criminal actions brought by private individuals. They are very rare and very risky. You would need extremely strong advice from a solicitor and possibly considerable financial backing, or the promise of a great deal of legal aid, to consider taking a private criminal prosecution, but it has been done.

11   THE HIERARCHY OF THE COURTS

It hardly seems appropriate to describe anything to do with the Law as 'humble', so perhaps it's better to start with what we may call the least haughty court and work upwards.

At a local level, any dispute between neighbours that doesn't involve criminal proceedings will start at the county court. Your nearest county court won't be far away

– you can look it up in Yellow Pages, under 'Courts'. If you are the complainant, whether or not you'll have to attend will depend on several factors. You may not have to if, for example, you are not the plaintiff but have persuaded your local authority (Environmental Health or Housing Department) to act on your evidence but in their own right. People often don't like to confront their neighbours in a court of law. It tends to sour relationships for a long time, and it's hard to nod a cheery 'Good morning' at the garden gate to someone you last saw glaring at you across a courtroom. The chances of subsequently borrowing a lawnmower are slim.

If you are the defendant, if you're the one that other people are complaining about, you still may not have to attend. It could depend on what sort of action has been brought. A great many actions are settled out of court in the nick of time, simply because people don't want to go through with what seems a ghastly ordeal once they get to the court. At the time when your neighbour upset you, you were in no doubt that you'd do anything to stop what the law calls the invasion of your 'quiet enjoyment' of your property. It takes many months for an action to reach the courts, however, and you may be then have had second, third and fourth thoughts.

It's not a bad idea, if you have the time, to visit your local county court just to see the law in action. Don't believe everything you see in films or on television.

County Courts

County courts can hear a wide variety of cases, including most actions for torts (see Section 19, Crimes and Torts). These include many of the disputes that arise between neighbours, involving trespass, negligence and nuisance. County courts can also hear actions involving land, houses or buildings, where the rateable value does not exceed £1,000 (or £1,500 in Greater London). This limitation will obviously have to be revised as and when the system of rates is replaced by a Poll Tax.

Few courts of law in Britain are truly informal, but much has been done in recent years to make it easier for the private individual to conduct his or her own case in the county court. These courts were set up (in 1846) in the hope that they would prove an accessible forum in which small claims could be settled.

There are two types of county court action:
1. Fixed Date Action. This is any claim other than for the payment of money.
2. Default Action. This is any claim for the payment of money.

The High Court
Occasionally a row goes further – to the High Court, in London. This is a dread and very expensive place. You can almost hear the lawyers licking their lips when a High Court action seems in the offing. The likelihood is, therefore, that you or your neighbour would go to such lengths and expense only if a considerable sum of money was involved or the right to a piece of land, or, exceptionally, an important point of law that lawyers were keen to explore or on which they wished to have a ruling.

The High Court is divided into three divisions: Queen's Bench, Chancery and Family. The Chancery Division deals with cases arising out of trusts, tax questions, probate and the interpretation of wills, bankruptcy and partnership cases, but it has also dealt with many cases involving neighbour disputes, as the Chancery Division can dispense the appropriate remedies. Since the Family Division deals only with defended divorce cases, and cases relating to separation, custody, adoption, mainten-ance and wardship, it's unlikely that neighbours would end up here. However, the Queen's Bench Division could be involved if the issue was financially important enough or, of course, if either party wished to complain about or appeal against a decision of a lower court – say a county court.

An example of the sort of issue that might go to the High Court would be that of the Stonehenge Peace Convoy and their right (or not) to camp on farm land as they moved about the country, or what is otherwise considered a long-running trespass, such as that of airspace over someone's land. Most people do not realize that they have a right in law to the airspace above their property. If building land is being developed next to you, and a crane swings round over your property, you may well be able to sue the aerial intruder. But don't go for British Airways or the RAF. In 1977 Lord Bernstein of Leigh sued Skyviews & General Ltd, a firm who had flown over his estate, taking photographs without his permission. He brought an action for trespass of airspace. The court held that the rights of an owner of land in the airspace above the land extended only to such height above the land as was necessary for ordinary use and enjoyment of that land and the structures on it, and above that height the owner had no greater rights in the airspace than any other member of the public. Skyviews & General had, in this case, flown several hundred feet above Lord Bernstein's estate. the court also held that, even if there had been trespass to airspace, Lord Bernstein was precluded from bringing an action by Section 40 of the 1949 Civil Aviation Act. So leave Pan Am alone and, if your neighbour starts to fly motor-driven model airplanes over your back garden, it might be better to complain on the grounds of noise and bring an action for nuisance (see Section 28, Nuisance).

Another example might be a boundary dispute. It is surprising how many fences, walls, paths and even hedges move if property is left unoccupied for any length of time. And moving a boundary can make a great deal of difference to the value of a piece of property or the extent to which it is enjoyed. We may all regard such actions as stealing but, if you can get away with it for long enough without challenge, the law legitimizes such acts after a certain length of time, usually twelve years. Even where the land is registered and there are plans with the local authority showing where the boundary between two properties should be, it may be difficult to claim back land you have lost. Plans are drawn to scale, usually a very small scale, and the thickness of a boundary line drawn on a map could represent ten metres or more.

The Court of Appeal

Obviously, once a case has reached the High Court and thousands of pounds have been spent, the outcome of any case matters a great deal to both parties. The losing party may not wish to accept defeat and let the matter rest there. The next move would be an appeal to the Court of Appeal – a place more awesome, more dread and even more expensive than the High Court. The Court of Appeal is presided over by the Master of the Rolls (nothing to do with the car he drives), and the judges in the Court of Appeal are called Lords Justice of Appeal. You don't have to get special permission to appeal to the court, but it will be extremely expensive. You and your neighbour would be embarking on an experience that neither of you would ever forget.

The House of Lords

If either party really wants to go for broke, then, failing satisfaction in the Court of Appeal, the ultimate move is to the House of Lords. This doesn't mean every duke, earl, viscount, marquis and bishop in the land. It means the Law Lords – a very select group who, although they forsake the wigs and gowns of the lower courts and wear plain old suits, don't come cheap. (Although the judges in the House of Lords are usually called Law Lords, their official title is 'Lords of Appeal in Ordinary'.)

Unlike the Court of Appeal, you do have to get permission to appeal to the House of Lords, and this permission can be granted only by the Court of Appeal or the Appeals Committee of the House of Lords. Usually the case must involve a point of law of general public importance. That rules out most rows between neighbours, though many of the cases relevant to neighbour disputes are decisions of the House of Lords.

You are unlikely ever to reach these higher courts. Your own lawyer would advise against such action ninety-nine times out of a hundred. You would have to find a lawyer who felt you stood a very, very strong chance of getting a judgment in your favour, and you would have to have almost unlimited time and money at your disposal. It would have to be a remarkable dispute.

12   THE HIERARCHY OF SCOTTISH COURTS

The Sheriff Court

This is described as an inferior (a word *never* used in the context of an English court) but very useful and important court. Scotland is divided into six sheriffdoms based on the grouping of local government areas: Lothian and Borders; South Strathclyde, Dumfries and Galloway; Glasgow and Strathkelvin; North Strathclyde; Tayside, Central and Fife; Grampian, Highlands and Islands.

Each sheriffdom is divided into several sheriff court districts centred on towns where the sheriff courts are held and has a force of several sheriffs who are qualified and experienced lawyers permanently resident in the principal towns of the sheriffdoms.

In civil business, the sheriff court is both a court of first instance and a court of appeal (to the Sheriff Principal). This allows for an appeal being heard locally without undue expense. The courts have a wide jurisdiction, wider than the county courts in England. They can deal with actions of damage without any pecuniary limit whatever. Thus they deal with cases involving thousands of pounds.

The Court of Session

This is a superior civil court that sits in Edinburgh, in Parliament House. It can be used as a court of first instance. The court is divided into two parts:

The Outer House is where junior Lords of Session sit singly, sometimes with a jury, to determine cases at first instance. Their jurisdiction is extensive and they hear all kinds of civil claim.

The Inner House is used mainly as a court of appeal. Three judges sit together, reviewing judgments of the sheriff court or the Outer House of the Court of Session.

The House of Lords

This is where Scottish and English and Welsh (and Northern Irish) systems merge. The same House of Lords hears cases from all parts of the British Isles.

It is worth noting the following, however. Scottish lawyers take it much unkindly that English Lords of Appeal in Ordinary, with no experience of Scottish Law, can overturn decisions taken by the expert lower courts up in Scotland.

'The House of Lords has been responsible for some of the worst misunderstandings and confused law in the Scottish books; over and over English doctrines have been forced into Scots law by English Law Lords who did not know or realize the fundamental differences of principle and reason which frequently underline apparent similarities of result, as where remedies are granted in circumstances similar to those justifying the corresponding remedy in English Law.' D.M.Walker, *The Scottish Legal System* (W.Green & Son Ltd. 1981).

13 PERSONNEL IN ENGLISH LAW

There are only three types of lawyer in England and Wales – not the Good, the Bad and the Ugly but judges, barristers and solicitors. The difference between barristers and solicitors is fairly simple: barristers are specialists who are allowed to wear natty wigs and gowns and present a case in court.

Before reaching any court, however, most people will have seen a more accessible professional lawyer – a solicitor. There are about 45,000 solicitors in Britain and, since they too are in Yellow Pages, they're not hard to track down. Most of their work is in conveyancing or helping people draw up their wills, but solicitors do get involved in disputes between neighbours and, if you've tried sweet reason and all the other avenues and agencies (Housing Officers, police, Citizens Advice Bureaux etc – see Part IV), they're the people to go to.

The first question that comes to anyone's mind when they have to see a solicitor is: 'How much will it cost?'

This is a difficult question to give a precise answer to, but don't be deterred from obtaining the services of a solicitor if you feel something must be done about your neighbour. It isn't prohibitively expensive to get a solicitor

to write a letter to your neighbour, giving details of the
matter you're complaining about and, maybe, hinting at
what might happen if the neighbour continues with the
nuisance or whatever. At the time of writing, your first
consultation with a solicitor, lasting say half an hour, will
cost approximately £20 – about the price of three bottles of
gin. It may prove more helpful and calming to the nerves
in the long run.

14   THE LEGAL AID SCHEME

If you intend to apply for help under this scheme, you
must first check that the solicitor you wish to consult is a
member of the Legal Aid Scheme – sometimes called the
Green Form Scheme. Often you can ascertain this from a
sign in the solicitor's window – if not, you can ask.

The Law Society (the body which registers and
supervises solicitors in England and Wales) has established fifteen area committees of barristers and solicitors,
and a network of local committees to administer the Legal
Aid Scheme. If you wish to apply for legal aid, you have to
submit a detailed application to your local committee. You
can get help with this from your local Citizens' Advice
Bureau.

The local committee has to decide whether or not you
have reasonable ground for taking, defending or being a
party to the proceedings contemplated. If the committee
decides, by 'applying the standard of a reasonably
prudent man of moderate means', that legal aid should be
granted, they issue a legal aid certificate. If this is refused,
you can appeal.

You can't get legal aid for an action for defamation
(slander or libel). If your neighbour is spreading malicious
gossip about you, it will cost you to take the action to
court, unless you are successful – and if he or she can pay.
Always bear this point in mind. You may win a case in
court, but it's a hollow victory if you aren't awarded costs
and if your opponent isn't in a position to make
recompense. Fortunately, in most neighbour disputes, all
you may want is for him to shut up or clear up. The

general advice, in matters where your neighbour is being abusive, even to the point of defamation, is to keep calm and wait for things to quieten down.

If you're successful in your application for a legal aid certificate, you will be examined by an assessment officer of the Department of Health and Social Security (DHSS). This is to discover your 'disposable income' and 'disposable capital'. If you want to know how these figures are arrived at in your particular case, you need to consult the Legal Aid (Assessment of Resources) Regulations, 1980. Briefly, to qualify for completely free legal aid, you must have a disposable income of less than £2,555 pa, and disposable capital of less than £3,000. * If you have a disposable income of more than £5,415 (after payment of tax, mortgage or rent, basic bills, food etc) and disposable capital of more than £4,710, legal aid is not normally available. In between these sets of figures, it's a sliding scale with varying contributions payable.

Once all this has been sorted out, you get an offer, setting out what you'll have to contribute and how you'll have to pay. You then have twenty-eight days to make up your mind whether or not to accept the offer.

If you do accept, you are then invited to choose a solicitor from the panel of names kept by the local Legal Aid Committee. You may have already done so when you checked whether or not the solicitor you wished to act for you was a member of the Legal Aid Scheme. Under the legal aid scheme, solicitors get only ninety per cent of what they'd normally get – this is because the system pays promptly and isn't a bad debtor. It makes you wonder what solicitors' ordinary clients are like.

15   LEGAL ADVICE AND ASSISTANCE

The Legal Aid and Advice Act of 1949 made provision for a legal advice service alongside the Legal Aid Scheme. It's known as the Green Form Scheme (guess why). Solicitors

---

* Check these and all following figures, in case they have changed since publication of this book.

can give you advice or do work (such as writing a stinking letter) up to a value of £50, at the expense of the Legal Aid Fund, so long as you qualify for assistance. The idea is to enable advice and assistance to be given straight away, without the delay involved in the formalities of applying for legal aid (see Section 14, The Legal Aid Scheme).

Financial qualifications for this scheme can be found in the Legal Advice and Assistance (Financial Conditions) Regulations, 1985. Once again, you are subject to a kind of means test. Eligibility for the scheme depends on having a disposable income and disposable capital of not more than £114 pw and £800 respectively. Free advice is available to those whose income is less than £53 pw.

16   LOCAL LAW CENTRES

If you're very lucky, you may live in an area that has a local Law Centre (Yellow Pages again). These are confined mainly to inner urban areas, often the less salubrious districts as far as estate agents are concerned. There are only some sixty Law Centres in the whole of England and Wales, funded by public and charitable bodies. They are very busy places, and some of them say that they will be able to help in disputes between neighbours only where there are what they regard as special circumstances, such as an element of racial harassment.

17   PERSONNEL IN SCOTTISH LAW

In Scotland the legal profession is divided into three branches, as in England – judges, advocates and solicitors. Just as no one in England or Wales can be both a barrister and a solicitor, so no one in Scotland can be an advocate and a solicitor. Advocates are the Scottish equivalent of barristers, specialists or consultants. Solicitors are general and primary advisers.

Solicitors were formerly known as 'writers' or 'law agents'. They are easy to find, as there are Yellow Pages in Scotland too. Scottish solicitors are governed by the Law

Society of Scotland, which controls the Scottish Legal Aid
Scheme, under the Solicitors (Scotland) Act, 1980.

Procurator Fiscal Service
This is a body of lawyers (a few advocates but mostly
solicitors) employed full time as civil servants and located
at the various sheriff courts throughout Scotland, and
responsible for investigating and initiating proceedings
for criminal offences within their districts and for
presenting cases in court. They would become involved if
your neighbour attacked you or committed some other
crime towards you. (See Section 19, Crimes and Torts.)
The more serious crimes (if your neighbour murdered
you) are reported to the Crown Office for the
considerations and instructions of Crown Counsel.

18   LEGAL AID AND ADVICE IN SCOTLAND

There has been free legal aid in Scotland for the poor since
1424, putting the English system to shame. The poor had
to produce certificates of poverty, and the Faculty of
Advocates annually appointed a number of their members
as counsel for the poor. (You may recall that, in the case of
Donoghue v Stevenson, the bottle of ginger beer with the
decomposing snail was bought in a café in Paisley,
Scotland. Mrs Donoghue was officially a pauper – maybe
the case could never have been brought in England.)

A modern Legal Aid Scheme was introduced in
Scotland in 1950, to make legal aid more readily available
to persons of small and moderate means. It's now widely
available for proceedings in almost all Scottish courts. As
in England, applicants go to a solicitor within the scheme
and have to declare their 'disposable income' and
'disposable capital'. (See Sections 14 and 15, The Legal Aid
Scheme and Legal Aid and Assistance.)

Note: An unsuccessful legally aided litigant is responsible for any award of expenses made against him or her,
though the court must have regard to his or her means
when they make such an award. Even if you're successful,
some money may be docked from your award to make up

any sums that aren't covered by the award against your opponent.

As in England, the Scottish scheme is really to *assist* litigants and is not intended to be free.

19   CRIMES AND TORTS

Since English law has a dual system of courts (see Section 10, Civil and Criminal Law), it's important to understand the distinction between a crime and a tort (not a sort of cake, though 'tort' is a French word, but the lawyers' word for a 'civil wrong'). A cynical way of distinguishing between crimes and torts might be to say that 'crimes' are wrongful acts that get into the papers no matter who commits them, while 'torts' are wrongful acts that get into the papers only if someone famous commits them. Or, to continue the gastronomic analogy, the proof of the pudding is in the eating. You need to look at the remedy to a wrong to decide whether the wrong was a crime or a tort.

'Tort' derives from the Norman-French for 'twisted' or 'wrong'. As far as lawyers are concerned, torts are wrongs remedied by civil actions as distinct from criminal proceedings. The remedies obtainable are, therefore, civil ones also. You cannot hope that your neighbour will be sent to prison for committing a tort. Remedies against torts are damages or injunctions.

The law of torts is the product of the ever-increasing activities of members of society, who, through their acts or omissions (there we go again), cause harm to the legally recognized interests of their fellow human beings. As well as crimes, other wrongs that need to be distinguished from torts are breaches of contract. Few things in law are simple, so it may come as no surprise that some wrongs can be crimes, torts *and* breaches of contract.

The classic example of this is the wayward taxi-driver who crunches into a lamp-post. He has more or less scooped the jackpot of legal depravity, since his action may lead to:

(a) liability in tort to his passenger,

(b) liability in tort to the person from whom he has hired the taxi (if the cab belongs to a company),

(c) liability in tort to the council, who own what's left of the lamp-post,

(d) liability for breach of contract to the passenger, who never reached his or her destination, and

(e) criminal liability under the Road Traffic Acts if the accident was the result of reckless, negligent or dangerous driving or if the taxi-driver had been drinking.

You might like to have a little fun imagining how many different wrongs your neighbour could commit at any one time. Or maybe you've already had to do that.

In a profoundly solemn profession, there is one legal joke that arises from the distinction between a crime and a tort. It is still common to see notices stuck up on building sites and industrial premises and in the rolling hectares of farmland stating that 'Trespassers will be prosecuted.' This is said by lawyers to be a 'wooden falsehood' (that is supposed to be the joke), since you can 'prosecute' only for a crime, and trespass is not a crime. Trespassers can only be sued (or, as it nearly says in the prayer, forgiven). For trespass is a tort, and to gain recompense or satisfaction in a civil action for trespass, you will have to prove that you have suffered some kind of damage. As far as this aspect of the law is concerned, your own children may safely and happily nip over the fence to retrieve their ball or frisbee from your neighbour's garden. Sadly, your neighbour's children may, of course, do likewise if their playthings land in your garden. Only if the visits over the fence cause damage (to plants, flowers, equipment, fish in your pond, garden furniture etc) or become unbearably frequent can you seek a remedy. (See Section 32, Trespass.)

Examples of torts are:

Conversion (trespass to chattles)	Malicious Harm
Dangerous Property	Defamation (Trespass to the Person)
Dangerous Things	False Imprisonment
Assault and Battery	Conspiracy
Negligence	Deceit or Fraud
Nuisance	

Where relevant, and it is profoundly to be hoped that neither you nor your neighbour gets embroiled in an action for false imprisonment, each of these will be examined in Part II.

Crimes

This isn't the place to attempt an exhaustive list of crimes. Most shouldn't be applicable in neighbour disputes. If you really fear that your neighbour is attempting to murder you, you should go straight to the police or move or both.

Unless you live in an area where cattle-rustling and ranch warfare are still the order of the day, the only crimes your neighbour is likely to commit against you will be theft or one or other of what are known as offences against the person. These include assault (attempting or offering to apply physical force to another person in such a way as to cause reasonable fear in the mind of the person that the wrong will be committed) and battery (the actual application of force to the person of another).

There is also one of criminal damage, which is largely the province of the Criminal Damage Act, 1971. There are three main offences:

(a) destroying or damaging property, which may be aggravated by the addition of 'with the intent to endanger the life of another person' or 'with reckless disregard of such danger'. An example of this would be if your neighbour decided – in a fit of frenzied landscaping – to blow up or burn down his garden shed without any consideration of whether or not he would be endangering you or your family.

(b) threatening to destroy or damage property – certainly a possibility in neighbour disputes, and

(c) possessing anything with intent to destroy or damage property – less likely to be relevant, but still a possibility.

20   FREEHOLD AND LEASEHOLD OWNERSHIP OF LAND

Another important distinction in law, relating to property, is that between freehold and leasehold ownership. People who own the freehold of their property usually regard themselves as in a stronger position than someone who owns a lease. Legally, this isn't always the case.

A freeholder can do almost what he or she likes with property, provided:

(a) it doesn't become dangerous or verminous;

(b) the use of it isn't changed (e.g. from residential to industrial);

(c) any alterations, extensions etc are made within building and planning regulations (see Chapter 17);

(d) it doesn't become a brothel – although, should you have the misfortune to live next to such premises, it might be wiser to let the police handle the problem;

(e) it isn't a listed building, in which case there are all sorts of restrictions about maintenance, decoration, renovation etc.

A freeholder can sell a house to whom he or she likes, when he or she likes. You, as a neighbour, have absolutely no say in the matter. The only exceptions here might be if the house was part of a fairly new development, part of an estate where the properties where regarded as having some sort of corporate identity or integrity. More about this in Section 36, Restrictive Covenants.

A freeholder's rights in property exist in perpetuity – that means for ever.

A leaseholder has the right to enjoy the property for the length of time specified in the lease – whether that is a formal or informal document. There may also be limitations on the extent of the leaseholder's enjoyment.

Leases may run from a week to 999 years. The latter may seem as good as a freehold and are held to be for the purposes of buying and selling property, but there may still be important differences. (See Section 36, Restrictive Covenants.) Ninety-nine year leases are almost as valuable as a freehold at the beginning of their term but become less and less valuable as their term nears its end.

If you own a freehold, the only person looking over your shoulder with a financial interest in the property is a Building Society or bank if your property is mortgaged.

If you own a leasehold, even a 999-year one, somewhere

you have a landlord.

In most neighbour disputes it doesn't matter whether you are freeholder or leaseholder.

21 LANDLORDS, TENANTS AND NEIGHBOURS

There are, of course, many occasions where two neighbours may have a common landlord – most obviously and commonly in the case of local authority housing. This may simplify matters. If, for example, you are being racially harassed by your neighbour, it is quite possible that the local authority landlord would seek to rehouse your neighbour. Seeking, however, isn't necessarily 'doing'. How far the local authority is able to rehouse your neighbour and therefore remove him or her from the scene (the ideal solution in your eyes), will depend on how far there is alternative local authority housing available. In some areas there is very little. In other areas there is none.

Nevertheless, it is clearly not in the interests of local authorities to have neighbouring tenants at each other's throats, and in such a situation you could well find your landlord a valuable ally, as someone who removes a lot of the burden of finding a solution to the problem from your shoulders. The first person to contact would almost certainly be your Housing Officer. (See Chapter 22, Housing Officers.)

Disputes between local authority tenants can lead to some strange legal situations. Suppose you and your neighbour are both local authority tenants, and you wish to complain about the state of your neighbour's property – it is verminous or a hazard to health. Ultimately, responsibility for the state of your neighbour's property rests with the local Environmental Health Department. You complain to your landlord, the local authority, through your Housing Officer, and you and your neighbour sit back, while one department of your local authority sues the other. In practice, of course, it seldom comes to that.

5   General Legal Principles

The Law goes to considerable lengths to define certain concepts and constantly seeks to establish and proclaim comprehensive definitions of these concepts, so that it may be clear how they are to be applied in any particular case. Cynics may argue that the Law makes a pretty poor job of this, or that lawyers seem to do just the opposite, but that really isn't their intention. No system of law can operate without a reasonable level of predictability.

So if we are going to look closely and in detail at the rights, duties, responsibilities and liabilities that exist between neighbours, it's first necessary to examine some of the relevant abstract notions of law: justice, rights, duties, privileges, liability, reasonableness and privacy.

It's not easy to describe exactly how these notions or principles apply to any individual case or situation, but there are discernible patterns. Once we have some idea of the origins of any particular statute or regulation, we may be able to understand what sort of wrong, injustice or unfair situation it was intended to correct. That way we can tell what the law is trying or hoping to achieve, and where it will be most widely applicable.

Every case may be judged on its own merits, but there is a clear structure that the law seeks to impose on society so that we may all bask in what has been called 'quiet enjoyment', modern parlance for 'An Englishman's Home Is His Castle.'

This book has already been peppered with words that have special legal meanings – such as 'rights', 'duties', 'privileges' and 'responsibilities' – and others – such as 'inconvenience', 'unfair' and 'unnecessary' – that don't. To be in as strong a position as possible to foretell whether or not we have a just complaint against our neighbour, we now need to look at some of these concepts.

22   JUSTICE

Pick up any general guide to the Law in a bookshop or
your public library, look in the index, and the probability
is that you won't find an entry under 'justice' (except
perhaps under 'Justice of the Peace'). And yet 'I want
justice' or 'I demand justice' or 'Let justice be done' are
cries that have echoed and re-echoed down the corridors
of legal history and are still repeated, albeit a little
archaically, today. They may even have sprung to your
own lips – or at least entered your own thoughts.

What is 'justice' supposed to mean as far as lay people,
us ordinary folk, are concerned? A dictionary definition is:
'The quality of being (morally) just or righteous; the
principle of just dealing, just conduct; integrity, rectitude.'
This probably does cover what we mean by justice –
putting something right that has gone wrong to our
detriment. As far as the law is concerned, however, all
'justice' means is enforcing the law as it stands. Which
means it's no good going to law to stop your neighbour
having his regular Sunday afternoon bonfire if there's
nothing in the law that says it's illegal. What is just is what
the law says is just. 'Let justice be done' simply means 'Let
the law run its course.'

23   RIGHTS AND DUTIES

Another famous, echoing cry is: 'I want my rights.'

It's easier to find books written for the general reader
that go into the subject of 'rights', though your own legal
rights may be hard to quantify accurately or precisely.
Basically, you have a right wherever someone else has a
duty towards you. If that duty has not been discharged, a
wrong has been done, and you have a right to recompense
or to an injunction enforcing the person who owes you the
duty to carry out that duty.

An example may help. As the occupier of property, you
have a duty to make sure that your property is safe for
visitors, even if the visitor is someone you don't like and
don't want to visit you – even, indeed, if the visitor is there

without your knowledge or is a burglar. If there's a large pothole in the driveway leading up to your front door, and your visitor falls into it and is injured, clearly you have not discharged your duty and have infringed your visitor's rights. A wrong has been done. Your bruised and battered visitor (or burglar) now has another right: to sue you for the injuries he or she has received. (More about all this in Section 34, Occupiers' Liability.)

Rights and duties have been called correlatives in law. It's a bit like Love and Marriage in the Frank Sinatra song – you can't have one without the other.

What we all have to remember is that we don't all have the same rights and that our own rights may vary from time to time and from situation to situation.

24 PRIVILEGES

Summoning up what little Latin we may have, we can just about work out that 'privi-leges' are 'private laws'. The suggestion is that the ordinary balance of fairness – in children's eyes often the notion that everybody should have the same – is shifted. One person is deliberately placed in a more favoured position than another. As a landowner, therefore, you have the privilege of ejecting trespassers from your property. You don't have a duty to let trespassers stay; correspondingly, they have no right to stay. You could say that a 'privilege' is the opposite of a 'duty'.

To take another example. We are all under a duty not to defame people by slandering or libelling them. Members of the House of Commons, while speaking in the House, and judges in courts of law, are not under such a duty. They have the privilege of saying anything they like about a person.

25 LIABILITIES

Some people find it easier to describe 'liabilities' in terms of what they're not – in much the same way as we can describe a tort as being a wrong that isn't a crime.

Liabilities arise out of power, out of people being in positions of power. If you have the power to affect someone's legal rights, you have a liability towards them. We can go back to *Donoghue v Stevenson* and the (by now completely decomposed) snail in the ginger-beer bottle. Again to quote Lord Atkin: 'A manufacturer of products ... with the knowledge that the absence of reasonable care in the preparation ... of his products will result in an injury to the consumer's life or property, owes a duty to the consumer to take reasonable care.' The defendant in *Donoghue v Stevenson*, the man who made the ginger beer, didn't take reasonable care, and so he was liable for the damage – the shock and gastro-enteritis – that ensued.

A great deal of liability is rooted in Common Law, but, increasingly, Statute Law creates new areas of liability or tidies up old ones, such as under the Occupier's Liability Act, 1957 (of which more in Section 34).

To return to the opening sentence of this section – liability is the opposite of immunity. If you do not have immunity from prosecution in a criminal matter or from some other legal action in a civil matter, a legal liability exists, *where the law holds it to be reasonable*.

26   THE MEANING OF 'REASONABLE'

The word 'reasonable' has already cropped up several times, as it does repeatedly in many arguments and disputes between neighbours. What is meant, legally, by 'reasonable'? Well, that's precisely the sort of concept the law has agonized over, and it is of vital importance.

If the residents of a whole street or block of flats were asked to say what they regarded as reasonable behaviour among neighbours, although there might be some maverick responses, the probability is that there would be a considerable consensus. At an elementary level, we all want much the same in terms of 'quiet enjoyment' of our homes. We all want peace and quiet. We none of us want other people's rubbish dumped on our property. We don't want other people's dogs messing in our garden. We don't want our night's sleep to be disturbed. We don't want our washing coated in soot and smoke from somebody's else's bonfire. We don't want our own exit blocked by another's parked car. We don't want to be threatened, insulted, harassed or abused.

On the other hand, we reckon it's reasonable to have the occasional bonfire. How else can we get rid of clippings from the hedge, offcuts of wood from a bit of DIY, weeds from the rosebed? And you can't have a bonfire without making a bit of smoke. Similarly, surely to goodness we can have a late-night party once in a while? Or aren't people ever allowed to enjoy themselves? And we've got to park the car somewhere, haven't we?

What it amounts to is this: I think my bonfires are reasonable, but I don't always think yours are. The crucial question is: what does the law think is reasonable?

Perhaps the fairest answer is: the law isn't quite sure. Many words have been solemnly uttered, many judgments awesomely pronounced in the search for a definition of 'reasonable'. 'Reason,' wrote Lord Jowitt, 'is the foundation of all our laws.' Well, if so, the temptation is to say that all our laws rest on somewhat shaky foundations, since nobody seems certain what is or isn't reasonable.

In 1851 the then Lord Chief Justice told a jury that if 'reasonably' meant anything else than 'in good faith', it meant 'according to his reason', as contradistinguished from 'caprice'. Try applying that thinking to the problem of whether or not your noisy neighbour's party was reasonable.

In 1945 the Court of Appeal said: 'The word "reasonable" has in law the prima facie meaning of reasonable in regard to those existing circumstances of which the actor [or omitter, presumably], called on to act [or omit] reasonably, knows or ought to know.' This suggests that your neighbour's noisy party is unreasonable if he ought to know that the circumstances of his party include keeping you awake. The staggering reality is that (apparently) few noisy party-givers have the least awareness of the effects their party may be having on the neighbourhood. They are creatures of little imagination.

In 1960 the Lord Chancellor said that a 'reasonable man' denoted ' ... an ordinary man capable of reasoning who is responsible and accountable for his actions, and this would be the sense in which it would be understood by a jury'. So if your neighbour is a bit thick and therefore not perhaps accountable for his actions, he can have as many noisy parties as he likes without being unreasonable.

What lawyers have done, especially judges, is try to define 'reasonable' as it relates to specific legal concepts: reasonable care, reasonable cause, reasonable time, diligence, doubt, excuse, price, satisfaction, security.

In 1951 the House of Lords, in the appeal case *Bolton v Stone* (a case where, during a cricket match, a batsman hit a ball which struck and injured Mr Stone, who was standing on a highway adjoining the cricket ground) said: 'The fact remains that, unless there had been something which a reasonable man would blame as falling beneath the standard of conduct that he would set for himself and require of his neighbour, there has been no legal duty.' For an act to be negligent, there must be a reasonable possibility not only of its happening but also of injury being cause thereby. What happened in this case was that Stone was hit by a cricket ball while he was a hundred yards away from the cricket pitch. The ball had cleared a fence seventeen feet above the level of the pitch, a feat achieved only six times in thirty years. The House of Lords decided, therefore, that the risk of injury to a person on the highway resulting from hitting a ball out of the ground, was so small that the probability of such injury *would not be contemplated by a reasonable man*; and the appellants (the cricket club) were not liable to the respondent (poor bruised Stone).

Even less helpful is a remark made by the Court of Appeal in 1956: the ' ... fair and reasonable man ... represents after all no more than the anthropomorphic conception of justice ... ' (*Davies Contractors Ltd v Fareham UDC*, 1956). Quite where this places smoky bonfires, yelping dogs, unpleasant odours or Heavy Metal at 4 a.m., it's difficult to see.

We have to turn to Scotland to get a clearer explanation.

In 1943 the Scottish Appeal Court ruled: 'The standard of foresight of the reasonable man ... eliminates the personal equation and is independent of the idiosyncracies of the particular person whose conduct is in question' (*Glasgow Corporation v Muir*, 1943). Here we are on happier ground. The awful neighbour at No. 10 can't defend his dreadful actions by saying that that's the way he is or that's what he's always done and you'll have to like it or lump it. Both he and those that have the misfortune to live near him will have to take into consideration what may be generally perceived as reasonable.

We are back where we started this section. The safest way of defining what is reasonable in law is to say that it's whatever the judge says is reasonable. It's a case of finding some average behaviour, neither too robust nor too timid. 'The reasonable man is presumed to be free both from over-apprehension and from over-confidence' (*Glasgow Corporation v Muir*).

Another case spells this out more clearly for the law relating to neighbours. 'A balance has to be maintained between the right of the occupier to do what he likes with his own land, and the right of his neighbour not to be interfered with.' In *Sedleigh-Denfield v O'Callaghan* 1940, the cause of concern was a blocked drain. On the defendant's land was a ditch with a pipe to carry off rainwater. The defendant hadn't installed the pipe – it was there when he bought the land – but he knew of its existence. He also knew of its condition and the fact that it could be blocked by leaves since it didn't have an adequate grating to prevent this. It did become blocked, and water consequently flooded the plaintiff's adjoining land (they were neighbours). The House of Lords held that O'Callaghan was liable for the damage caused. He ought to have foreseen what would happen.

The vital point to remember is that, if you bring an action against your neighbour to court, one of the tests that will be applied by the court is that of reasonableness. And what is considered reasonable will depend on the nature of the nuisance or interference of which you complain, the nature of the premises (yours and your neighbours) and the surroundings, and how and to what degree the subject of your complaint is interfering with the quality of your life. It's still true that, if you live next door to a sewage works, no court will uphold an action for nuisance because of the smell. We are back to Lord Thesiger and his distinction between Belgravia and Bermondsey.

27 PRIVACY

The concept of privacy in our law is nothing like as wide or all-embracing as you might expect. There are no statutes dealing with the matter, and few cases. Nor is there any Common Law right to privacy. Those dreadful people at No. 10 can put in new windows directly overlooking my garden, or any part of my house, and there's nothing I can do about it – unless the windows or the extension are in breach of a restrictive covenant. (See Section 35, Restrictive Covenants.)

Neighbours can even more obviously intrude on privacy. They can take photos of you with a telephoto lens, provided the photos are not used in a defamatory way. It's really up to you not to give your neighbours any reason for wanting to take photos of you. To this end, it may be of at least some little comfort to know that your neighbour cannot object to anything he or she sees through the telephoto lens.

The reason why we have no general right to privacy on our own property is because the law still sees property as land on which buildings happen to be. This explains why, in disputes between neighbours, the law is much clearer where problems relate to land or cutting down trees or moving boundary walls or where livestock is involved. The law clicks into action on such issues as though certain of the appropriateness of its involvement. There is a sense of the stability that we are led to believe existed before the Industrial Revolution and the urbanization of Britain. There may be an almighty legal wrangle as to who owns which piece of land, but at least the law is happy to be called upon.

PART II

AN OUTLINE OF THE PROBLEMS

6 The Subjects of Disputes

The broad sub-headings that categorize neighbour disputes are: nuisance, rights of way, public rights of way, rights of light, trespass, squatters, occupiers' liability, restrictive covenants, positive covenants, rights of entry, defamation, intimidation and harassment, racial harassment, and negligence.

28 NUISANCE

A 'nuisance' as far as the law is concerned is something that has gone too far. Nobody expects life to be so ordered and structured that neither you nor your neighbour can ever do anything to upset or annoy each other, but the law does admit that people can be too noisy, too inconsiderate, even too dirty.

There doesn't have to be any malice behind nuisance. To take a simple example: home-improvement and DIY are all very well (and your neighbour's DIY may well add to the value of your property by improving the general 'tone' of the neighbourhood), but you may consider that banging nails into the wall at three o'clock in the morning is going too far, and that's where the Law of Nuisance comes in.

A nuisance is something that your neighbour does on

59

his or her property that prevents you from enjoying your property (or, inconceivably, since you're an ideal neighbour, vice versa). So noise obviously isn't the only category of annoyance and upset that fits here. Smoke, smells, vibrations, airborne seeds, wandering animals – many things emanating from your property and ending up in your neighbour's – may constitute nuisance.

In fact, there are so many varieties of nuisance that they are divided into three divisions: public nuisance, private nuisance and statutory nuisance.

Public nuisance laws are concerned with such matters as obstruction, interference with the navigation of streams, pollution with fumes (not bonfires), emission of noise from steam hammers or fairgrounds or – exceptionally, even if you live in Streatham – the fact that your next-door neighbour is keeping a brothel. Public nuisance, you may deduce from this, is very hard to establish. It is really concerned only with very special and hopefully rare circumstances.

Private nuisance laws stem from legal precedents, cases that have been heard by the courts and under certain statutes, such as the Control of Pollution Act, 1974. This Act applies wherever there is noise nuisance. Full details will be given in Chapter 8, but the crucial point is that the Act empowers local authorities to take action against an individual or group of individuals or a company who are making excessive noise. It removes the necessity for the private individual to have to take legal action. Indeed, the Act is very strongly worded, for it says that, where the local authority is satisfied that a noise nuisance exists, it must take action, by serving a notice on the person creating the noise, requiring its abatement. Details of an appeal against such notice will be given in Chapter 8.

The third category of nuisance is statutory nuisance. The idea behind this category is that there were obvious limitations inherent in the law of private nuisance and that remedies were slow and costly to obtain. Among the effects of urbanization and industrialization has been the need to provide neighbours with remedies that are more easily accessible. So certain matters are defined as statutory nuisances, and a summary procedure is prescribed for dealing with them. They can be dealt with in the magistrate's court and are open to local authorities and private individuals (Public Health Act, 1936 sections 92-9). The private individual's Common Law rights are not affected.

There are six basic classifications of statutory nuisance:

1. Any premises in such a state as to be prejudicial to health or a nuisance.

2. Any animal kept in such a place or manner as to be prejudicial to health or a nuisance.

3. Any accumulation or deposit which is prejudicial to health or a nuisance.

4. Any dust or effluvia caused by any trade, business, manufacture or process and being prejudicial to the health of, or a nuisance to, the inhabitants of the neighbourhood.

5. Any workplace which is not provided with sufficient means of ventilation, or in which sufficient ventilation is not maintained, or which is not kept clean or not kept free from noxious effluvia, or which is so overcrowded while work is carried on as to be prejudicial to the health of those employed therein.

6. Any other matter declared by any provision of the Public Health Act 1936 to be a statutory nuisance.

These various categories will be examined in more detail in Part III.

For our purposes, what this means is that, under the Public Health Act of 1936 and various subsequent Housing Acts now consolidated in the Housing Act of 1985, local authorities can take proceedings against a landlord where there is what is known as a statutory nuisance. In general, this means where property is in such a bad, dilapidated or verminous condition as to constitute a risk to health, or where there is a defect in the common or shared parts of a house or block of flats causing harm in the tenant's property. (See Chapter 14.)

It's already been said that the law isn't always as rigid as we imagine. This is a mixed blessing. It may mean that it can, therefore, be interpreted and enforced in what seems a generally just and fair way, but it also may mean that we can't foretell what the outcome of any particular considered legal action may be. In matters of alleged nuisance, what is unacceptable in a quiet residential street may be held perfectly reasonable in an industrial area. A noise that keeps people awake at night may be deemed unfair; the same noise, gratingly unbearable to a nursing mum during the day (after many a broken night), may be deemed fair and permissible. It all depends on the facts of the case and what is thought to be reasonable.

What can be said with more certainty is that, to show nuisance, you have to establish an appreciable interference with the way you use your property. Every case has to be treated on its own merits – all are 'one-offs'.

There may also be a time factor involved. Don't delay too long before pushing your case if you think you are suffering from an unfair interference with your enjoyment of your property. It has been well established that people who cause a nuisance for long enough, without a complaint being made, may end up with a legal right to continue the nuisance. Besides, as a general principle, the sooner you take steps to deal with a neighbour dispute, the less likely you are to be *in extremis*, and the more likely it is that the problem may have a satisfactory solution.

Many things that you may describe as appalling nuisances in real life do not constitute nuisance in law. Your neighbour may have a horde of revolting and hyperactive children. They may scream, shout, argue and whoop it up all day long. They may kick their footballs over the fence every other minute. You may be driven to thoughts of multiple infanticide, out-Heroding Herod, but this situation still doesn't constitute nuisance in law. don't despair – see Sections 32 and 41 on Trespass and Negligence.

29   RIGHTS OF WAY

It's common for the owner of one piece of land to have a right of way across his neighbour's land. A frequent example of this is where A has to cross part of B's land to reach a shed or garage. Rights like these are known as 'easements' (see Chapter 15) and may be general or limited. A general right of way gives A an unlimited right to cross and re-cross B's land for all purposes and at all times. A limited right of way may specify that the right can be exercised only in the daytime or during certain hours, or may have limitations as to who can exercise the right: only A, not A's cows or sheep or Rolls or Land Rover.

It's also common for gas, water and electricity supplies to be brought through one person's land or garden to reach another's house. the person getting this supply has no authoritative right over the other person's garden but has another example of an easement.

Similarly, if you and your neighbour share a drive, one half is yours, the other half is your neighbour's, but you don't have to drive down your side of the pathway only, scraping your vehicle along the wall at the side in a desperate attempt to avoid even one wheel touching your neighbour's half. In this situation each of you has a right of way over the other's half. The right of way amounts to permanent permission to encroach on each other's property. You should note, however, that it doesn't give permission for either of you to block the driveway, even if you are blocking only your half.

30 PUBLIC RIGHTS OF WAY

Public rights of way differ from private rights of way in that they are routes that any member of the public may use, for a journey or simply for recreation. If you live next door to people grand enough to have a public right of way over their land, you will almost certainly be able to get help with any problems you have in exercising that right of way from such bodies as the Open Spaces Society and the Ramblers Association (addresses in Appendix I). Fifty years ago, in the case of *Jones v Bates*, it was established that the ways over which the public walks and rides in the countryside are legally protected rights of way, not privileges granted by kind landlords.

So if your neighbour ploughs up public footpaths, or demolishes bridges over which you and the rest of the public have a right of way, or festoons his land with barbed wire, or patrols the paths with gun and mastiff, you will have many allies, advisers and supporters in any legal action you contemplate.

31   RIGHTS OF LIGHT

Stories and poems for children and adults abound in phrases about 'leafy glades' and 'cool shade'. It is a fact of nature that trees and their leaves block sunlight; in fact, they block any sort of light. This is pleasant enough on a hot summer's day but isn't so good if your house or garden becomes gradually and permanently darker and darker and it appears that your much-loved and much-watered tomatoes have no chance of ripening this side of Christmas, and your house plants have completely given up the ghost. But there is no automatic right to have enough light coming over someone else's property and in through your windows or onto your garden.

There are, however, situations where such a right has been acquired by long usage. You may have seen the notice 'Ancient Lights' on the walls of old buildings. This signifies that such a right does obtain and serves as a warning to neighbours that they are not to block that light. But even this light may be eroded. At best, all anyone is entitled to is a *reasonable* amount of light – here we go again. No one has the right to an uninterrupted view. And no one has the right to screening from an unpleasant or undesirable view. If your neighbour plants rapid-growing laylandii or laurels or Russian vine on his property and your beautiful prospect of Christchurch Meadows or Flatford Mill is destroyed, it's tough luck. Similarly, if your neighbour hacks down his or her centuries old boxwood hedge to reveal Sizewell 3 in all its throbbing, nuclear glory, there is nothing you can do about it – except move, which is why it really is a good idea to try to keep on good terms with your neighbour.

On the other hand, there is always the chance that you could protect your property against a development that would block your view or your supply of light, by persuading the local authority to refuse planning permission (Chapter 16).

New Estates
This is another situation where it isn't easy to give precise guidelines. It may be that on new estates the deeds of the houses acknowledge rights to light. On such estates, there are often clauses in the initial conveyances to the first owners limiting such rights, so that the building won't be prevented from making further developments and further profits near your property. (See also Section 35, Restrictive Covenants.)

There are a few cases that may shed a little more ancient or modern light on this subject. In one case, the owner of a greenhouse was said to have a right to direct sunlight. The greenhouse was very old and had occupied its site for a long time. It isn't known how far this principle might be extended today to cover new greenhouses, home extensions, conservatories or solar panels, but see Chapter 15. If you can, it's a good idea to talk to your neighbour before embarking on any such structural project on your own home, letting him or her know about delivery dates and times of materials, roughly how long the work will take, what sort of noise might be made. A great many people who complain about noise or other nuisance arising from building work say they wouldn't have done so if only they had had some idea of how long they were going to have to endure the noise or other inconvenience.

It may seem a little unfair that, if your neighbour builds near your property with a window opening in your direction, he has the chance of becoming entitled to an easement of light. In the old days, when subtlety took a back seat, the way to avoid such an easement was to throw up some temporary structure that immediately blocked your neighbour's light. You probably couldn't do that now, because of planning restrictions, but you could try putting a notice in the Public Register. This has the same legal effect as previous direct action and may seem less spoil-sporty.

Enjoying Light

There is also a legal concept that says, if you have enjoyed light coming from your neighbour's land (which may sound too much like a concept from a Steven Spielberg film) for upwards of twenty years, you can insist that you continue to enjoy that light – though not necessarily the same amount. Ever watchful for a chance of argument and litigation, the law here looks for what may be considered a reasonable amount.

There are, however, restrictions even on this. If you enjoy the light with your neighbour's permission, you don't have the same degree of protection. Nor do you if there is a clause in the deeds of the property that says you cannot protest at anything of this nature done on the neighbouring property. (See note on New Estates, above.)

32   TRESPASS

Most people regard trespass as the actual presence of a person on your land or property when he or she is not entitled to be there, but the concept is more complicated than that. Animals can also commit trespass, and so can trees and shrubs by root or branch. Indeed, trespass has a wide scope. It can include throwing articles onto someone's land, leaning a ladder against their land or erecting scaffolding that overhangs their property.

A couple of years ago, a firm of sub-contractors were stripping the tiles from the roof of our house. To do this, they had erected scaffolding, several poles of which stuck out over the passageway to the side of our neighbour's house. I hadn't foreseen that this would happen. The sub-contractors hadn't asked my neighbour for permission. The first indication I had that anything was wrong was when I discovered my neighbour, extremely angry, wielding a fourteen-pound sledgehammer and threatening to bring four storeys of scaffolding to the ground. Technically he was within his rights. The sub-contractors had indulged in an orgy of trespass, for they had also entered his garden without permission (so that they could remove some panels of wood, also without his permission) and had thrown a good many old slates from my roof into his garden. Two years later, neither my neighbour nor I has quite recovered.

To be a little more formal – there are three kinds of trespass: (a) to land, (b) to chattels, (c) to the person.

When we talk about trespass in everyday terms, we usually mean trespass to land. Any unlawful entry upon land or buildings in the possession of another (even in wrongful possession) is actionable as a trespass. Further, a person who has authority to enter another's land for a particular purpose becomes a trespasser if he or she goes beyond that purpose. If your postman starts helping himself to apples from your front garden, he becomes a trespasser and is also guilty of theft.

Trespass to chattels consists of a direct or unlawful injury to, or interference with, a chattel in the possession of another. It has been applied to driving away another person's cattle, wrongfully keeping a jewel which had been handed over merely to obtain a valuation, and negligently sinking a Mail ship.

Trespass to the person may consist of assault and battery or false imprisonment, and as such in neighbour disputes is more likely to be considered under Criminal Law and complaint made to the police. (It is a crime by virtue of the Offences Against the Person Act, 1861, Section 1.)

The law lays down clear instructions as to what you should do when confronted by a trespasser. Remember, trespass isn't a crime (except in the case of trespass to the person, where it is both crime and tort). You mustn't, therefore, treat the trespasser as a criminal or you may end up committing a crime yourself. The first thing to do with a trespasser is to *ask* him or her to go away, to leave your property. The second thing to do is to *tell* him or her to leave your property. If he or she doesn't, you are entitled to use the minimum necessary force to get him or her off your property by the shortest possible route.

Try to avoid even this. Force often leads to more force and sometimes ends in a punch-up. Sadly there's something about trespassers that frequently enables them to win punch-ups.

If the trespasser has done some physical harm or damage to your property (picked fruit, broken windows, trampled plants, damaged a lock), you may bring an action for trespass if that physical harm has a cash value. Crushed grass leaves probably won't qualify, nor wounded pride. There is also the problem of identifying a trespasser – finding out who they are and where they live, though this doesn't arise if it's one of your neighbours.

In general, it's no good summoning the majesty of the Law to deal with someone peacefully taking a short cut through your garden, but if they repeat the trespass regularly, you may well be able to get a court order to restrain them. The police are concerned with trespassers only where there is a likelihood of a criminal offence taking place. If you are having to resort to force, there is always the chance of a breach of the peace, or it may be that the trespasser is contemplating theft. In such cases, the police may be prepared to take a hand.

Trees and Plants
Whether the invasion of your property is by root or branch, you are allowed to prune at the point where the offending limb invades, i.e. crosses from your neighbour's land to yours. The cuttings that you take are not yours, however. You must either hand them back over the fence – carefully, so as not to cause damage – or give your neighbour the chance to come round and collect them.

Note: Some trees are subject to preservation orders under the Town and Country Planning Act, 1971. Such trees may not be lopped, topped or felled without consent from the local authority.

The same, sadly, applies to fruit on your neighbour's tree. No matter how far your side of the fence the luscious pears, plums or peaches may dangle, they are not yours. They belong to your neighbour, and you mustn't pick them, even if they are about to rot on the tree. What you can do is sit under the tree (like Isaac Newton) on your side of the fence and wait for the fruit to fall into your greedy hands. Once the fruit falls, your neighbour is deemed by the law to have abandoned it. It's yours – but no shaking the tree.

Beware of trees that are growing in your garden. Your trees could cause damage to one or other of your neighbours in a variety of ways. Yew leaves are poisonous. In one case, a neighbour's horse ate yew leaves from an overhanging branch. The horse died, and the owner of the yew tree was held responsible and had to pay compensation. On the other hand, if livestock wander from your neighbour's land into your garden and they eat something poisonous, you are not liable, unless you deliberately planted the noxious plant or unless it was your duty to see that the fence was kept in a strong enough condition to keep the livestock out.

Roots can also cause problems. There are restrictions as to how near a house you may plant a tree. This is because the roots spread and suck water from a wide area, causing the land to dry out. If the roots lie in heavy clay soil, that clay will contract as it dries, with subsequent cracking of, say, the foundations of a house when the soil subsides. It could be very expensive for you if your neighbour could prove that you were responsible for his house subsiding through your negligence in planting a tree too near his house. Even where you have insurance cover against this, it is possible that the insurance company would not pay the full cost.

It is no defence to say that the tree in your garden was there before you were, i.e. planted by someone else, nor to say that the tree was wind-sown. You cannot plead ignorance of the botanical situation, and it is no defence to say that the damage was caused by 'natural growth'. On the other hand, if your neighbour's house is built in a silly position, the court may decide that your neighbour is not in a position to claim damages.

Note: You or your neighbour can claim here only for money loss. You can't, for example, claim for damage to your lawn by roots from your neighbour's trees.

Animals
If your animal wanders onto your neighbour's land, this doesn't necessarily constitute trespass. Your neighbour

has to show that you intended your animal to go on his or her land, or that you were negligent in failing to take steps to prevent it happening. You are unlikely to be caught urging your Dobermann Pinscher over the fence into your neighbour's garden, but if your dog squeezes through a gap in the fence, and it is *your* fence (i.e. it is your responsibility to keep the fence in good repair), this may well amount to a trespass, and you will be liable for any damage the dog causes – killing or injuring pets or livestock, damaging plants, biting members of your neighbour's family. This could prove very expensive and extremely upsetting.

Note: This doesn't mean that you can force your neighbour to keep any dog or cat on his or her property. Pet-owners have no duty to keep them out of other people's gardens. All the law says is that they may be liable for any damage they do if they stray.

In rural areas, there are obviously more occasions where trespass by animals takes place, and several more types of trespass. If a hunt crosses land without permission, in pursuit of fox or stag, the owner of that land may well have grounds for an action for trespass. In 1985 the League Against Cruel Sports brought an action against a local Master of the Hunt and others. The League owned unfenced areas of land on Exmoor to provide sanctuaries for wild deer when hunted. They refused to allow the local hunt permission to enter their land. After seven incursions onto the League's land in 1982 and 1983, the League brought an action, seeking an injunction restricting the Master of the Hunt, his servants, agents and hounds from entering their land. The League won the case. The court said that, if the Master insisted in hunting in the vicinity of the prohibited land knowing that he couldn't stop his hounds entering it, 'His indifference to the risk of trespass could be construed as an intention that the hounds should trespass.' The question of the Master's intention or negligence was to be inferred from his conduct in all the circumstances of the case (remember Lord Keith?). The League received £180 in damages and, more importantly, an injunction in respect of one particular piece of land which had been persistently trespassed by hounds.

Children

If your neighbour's children keep barging into your garden, you mustn't smack their heads. Tell your neighbour and ask him or her to keep them under control. If they cause damage, that is a different matter. The first approach would be to ask your neighbour to pay for the damage. Failing that, the law holds young people responsible in negligence (provided they're not too young) and says they may be sued in court. There isn't a lot of point in suing a child, because he or she won't be able to pay any compensation, but you can sue your neighbour if you can show that there was a failure to take reasonable care to see that the child did not cause harm to others.

Other Types of Trespass

Suppose the fence between your property and that of your neighbour is dilapidated, in much need of repair. It is important that, when it is repaired, it follows the same line as the old fence. So, if your neighbour repairs his or her fence and in doing so alters the line of the fence, perhaps moving it only a few centimetres into your garden, that is a trespass. Your neighbour may feel he or she has a good reason for moving the line of the fence – maybe it makes it much easier to get the car in and out. This makes no difference.

Faced with such a situation, there are several things you can do. You can pull the fence down. You can apply for a court order for your neighbour to remove the fence, or you can apply for an order for damages for any money loss you have incurred. The important thing is to do something, because, if you take no action, the effect can become permanent. After twelve years, the law regards the new line of the fence as being the true line.

Note: In matters of trespass between landlords and tenants, the general rule is that a landlord can sue for trespass only if he or she can show injury to what is called the 'reversionary interest', e.g. injury of such a permanent

nature that it affects the interest that returns to the
landlord at the end of the tenancy. (See also Section 35,
Occupiers' Liability, and Section 37, Right of Entry.)

33 SQUATTERS

Legally, when faced with the problem of squatters, you
are on better ground, though obviously a squatter in your
house is far more upsetting than a mere trespasser on your
land. The vital thing is to secure your house whenever you
leave it, even if you're only going down the road to the
shop for five minutes. A door left open can make a very
important difference in law to the position of a squatter, a
difference that works entirely and possibly catastroph-
ically to your disadvantage.

By way of definition, a squatter is someone who comes
into your house as a trespasser while you are away (even if
only for five minutes) and then keeps you out. By virtue of
the Criminal Law Act, 1977, Section 7, such a person
becomes guilty of a criminal offence the moment you ask
him or her to leave.

If you're unlucky enough to have squatters on your
property, again, as when dealing with trespassers, the first
thing to do is to ask them to leave. If they do not, then,
unlike trespassers, they are committing a criminal offence,
in which case (if you feel up to it) you can evict them
bodily yourself. Those of us of a more wimpish disposition
can enlist police help. It's probably better to do this
anyway, as it's never a good idea to put yourself in a
position where the outcome is going to depend on brute
force and violence. Direct action may not be the best
move. Squatters may be peaceable enough folk on the
whole, but remember – you are seeking to take away what
is probably their only home. Most people take unkindly to
that, whatever the circumstances. Also, the law won't be
on your side. You don't have any right to evict or threaten
people who are squatting on property other than your
own.

A much trickier problem may arise if squatters move in
next door to you. The difficulty is that only the owner of

the property can legally order squatters out. Suppose the house next to yours is empty. Suppose people who regard themselves as epitomizing the spirit of freedom, selflessness and true love – but whom you regard as a load of disgusting layabouts – arrive one day and within a very short space of time have taken over. There isn't a great deal you can do about it. It is up to your real neighbour, the true owner of the house, to ask them to leave and then take the necessary action if they won't. If you are able to contact your neighbour, you may be able to persuade him or her to take this action. If you can't, or if you don't know who is the true owner of the house in question, the squatters may look forward to making themselves very comfortable.

The 1977 Act covered situations only where people occupied buildings or land adjacent to a building (such as a garden). It didn't cover the actions of such groups as the Stonehenge Peace Convoy, who wandered the lanes of the English countryside seeking suitable venues for their festivals. Between 1977 and 1986 they were able to take advantage of what some regarded as a loophole in the Act, and set up temporary camps in farmers' fields – land not adjacent to buildings.

Things began to hot up in 1986 with such cases as that of *Wiltshire County Council v Frazer and others*. Here a group of what were described as 'nomadic, gipsy-like squatters' had moved onto farmland. They had been issued with an order for possession of land (in favour of the landowner) and had then gone away, but at least some of them had returned, their numbers swelled with newcomers. It was held that, where an order for possession of land had been obtained, a writ of restitution could be issued to recover the land from occupiers who were neither party to the original proceedings nor dispossessed by the possession order, provided there was a plain and sufficient 'nexus' between the order for possession and the need to effect further recovery of the same land. (Nexus = bond, link or connected group.)

The simplest way to explain this is to imagine that you and I agree to park our cars at meters in, say, the same square, and that at a fixed time we will swop meters. The law is seeking to stop squatters, or hippies or Peace Convoys or nomads or gipsies, or whatever we like to call them, from playing the same kind of game by swopping fields to camp in, so that any possession order is always one jump behind them. Since then the law has been changed, and farmers in Wiltshire may sleep more easily in their beds at the approach of the summer solstice.

Note: Even more difficult to deal with is the situation where a group of people whom you regard as undesirable buy the house or flat next to yours. Here there really is nothing you can do about it. A couple of years ago a group of Hells Angels bought a house, and, it was said, began running it as a kind of club for other Angels. The people in the neighbouring house felt obliged to move, but perhaps fortunately, did not sell their house. Eventually, it was the Angels who sold, and the neighbours were able to return to their original house.

34 OCCUPIERS' LIABILITY

The law distinguishes three types of visitor to your land: those you have invited, those you have not invited and those who have a legal right to be on your property even without your permission. To all three, as occupier of the property, you have certain duties, more to some than others.

The category of those you invite onto your land or into your house obviously includes guests, friends and relatives. Less obviously, it includes people whom you haven't specifically invited but who are judged to be there with your permission: the postman, dustman, milkman, girl delivering newspapers etc. Those you haven't invited will include trespassers, thieves and burglars. Those who may legally be on your property whether you want them there or not will include representatives from the Gas or Electricity Board, who have come to read your meters; police officers (if chasing a suspect to make an arrest, or with a search warrant); a bailiff to seize goods to pay overdue rates or an unpaid debt (Perish the thought! What will the neighbours say!) and health officials. If you rent a television set or video recorder, it is quite possible that the small print on the rental agreement gives the company you rent from the right to send a representative into your house to make sure their set is still there. Various local authority inspectors may also have the right to enter your property – if certain infectious diseases are suspected or to see that standards are observed if you let rooms (e.g. adequate facilities and no overcrowding) or to make sure that there is no contravention of planning control.

There is perhaps a fourth category: casual callers, not specifically expected but generally tolerated. This is really a sub-category of the first group and would include political canvassers, carol singers and Jehovah's Witnesses. You can, however, forbid their presence on your property by a suitably worded notice at your gate or on your front door, the traditional 'No Hawkers, No Circulars' type of thing. If you do display such a notice, these hitherto 'tolerated' people fall into the class of trespasser. Your own responsibility then, so far as they are concerned, is to see that you do nothing positive to harm them, such as laying traps – appealing though the thought may seem to open your front door and espy a pit full of Jehovah's Witnesses and policitical activists.

The law says that you owe a common duty of care to almost everyone who enters your property and that you may owe a higher standard of care than this 'common' one to some people, e.g. children. The Occupier's Liability Act, 1984, deals with your liability towards persons other than visitors or those with a legal right to enter your premises, by which is largely meant trespassers and burglars. The duty owed to such people is defined in Section 1(4) of the Act: '... to take such care as is reasonable in all the circumstances of the case to see that the person other than his visitor does not suffer injury on the premises by reason of the danger concerned.' The occupier is liable if he or she is aware of the danger or has reasonable grounds to believe that it exists or that the unwelcome person is in the vicinity of the danger, and if the danger is one that he or she ought reasonably have been expected to protect the unwelcome visitor from.

This means that, although there is a lesser duty owed to trespassers, burglars and the like, there are limits on the precautions you may take against unwanted visitors. You are entitled to fit burglar alarms, but you can't lay fiendishly cunning traps or put 20,000 volts through the door handle at night (it has been done, but you mustn't). Generally any trespasser has to take things as he finds them, and he can't blame the owner if he gets hurt, but the law does draw the line at crafty traps and ambushes. That kind of cunning would make you liable for any injuries the trespasser or burglar received. If your neighbour is in the habit of annoying you by making frequent trips onto your property, you may not attempt to ensnare or electrocute him.

There are thus two variables that have to be taken into account when dealing with Occupier's Liability: the nature of the premises, and who the visitors to it are likely to be. Surprise, surprise, the general principle laid down by the law, is that you must do what is reasonable in the circumstances.

If small children are likely to play in your garden, even if they just wander into it, you may have to take precautions to make sure that they come to no harm. If, for example, there is a steep, unguarded drop in your garden, it would be insufficient putting up a notice warning little children, because they may not be able to read it. You would probably have to erect some kind of guard rail. The same may be true of garden ponds, particularly a pond in your front garden. It is amazing how many small children do not see ponds. A neighbour of ours, across the road, brought her small son round one afternoon. We were sitting in the back garden, morosely watching the weeds grow, when the small son trotted happily down the passage at the side of the house, beaming ecstatically (presumably at the thought of seeing us) and walked right into the pond. We hauled him out immediately but, had we not been in the garden and had we negligently left the side gate open, the incident could have ended most unpleasantly.

What the law requires is that you take the steps any prudent householder would take to keep property in a reasonably safe condition. You should repair worn stairs, fill potholes in your path or driveway, make sure you have no loose stair carpets or excessively slippery floors and clear ice from your front path in the winter. You are not expected to carry out regular professional surveys to search for any hidden weaknesses in the building but, if you knew that dry rot had weakened the supporting timbers of your floors, and your visitor plunged through ('dropped in', as it were), you may well be liable for any injury the visitor suffered.

In 1987 the duty of care owed to visitors was made very apparent by the High Court in Exeter, where a family was ordered to pay £35,000 compensation to a dustman for back injuries received when he tried to lift a bin full of building rubble. This was the first time a householder had been ruled responsible for injury to a dustman. Perhaps we should be especially thoughtful towards dustmen, since their Union (the TGWU) began operating a good neighbour scheme during the 1987 Christmas period, checking that elderly people, whom they knew to be living on their own, were warm and comfortable. Initiatives such as this could do a great deal to induce a neighbourhood spirit and hence cut down on the number of neighbour disputes.

It's important to note here that the liability in a case involving an injury can be financially heavy and out of all proportion to momentary thoughtlessness or cost of a neglected repair. I shall not forget being hauled out of bed very early one soaking wet Saturday morning by a neighbour knocking on the door to tell me that he had noticed that one of the slates on our roof was loose. My initial reaction was to thank him, curtly, and return to bed, fuming and muttering vitriolic sentiments about 'nosey parkers'.

As the morning wore on and the rain pelted down, it did occur to me that, if the slate slipped from the roof and sliced the postman's head off, I should be in all sorts of trouble – especially since I now knew of the danger. I constructed a weird, Heath Robinson, extending-arm contraption from pieces of wood, which enabled me to lean out of the attic window and slide the slate into the gutter, where it would be safe for a while. It didn't make me love my neighbour any more, but it did give me peace of mind.

Apart from attending to current maintenance of your property, the only sensible precaution you can take is to insure. Cover against liability to visitors is a normal part of comprehensive household insurance policies. It's best to check, however.

Landlords and 'Occupier's Liability'

A landlord can be liable for injury occurring on premises that are let, if it occurs because of a repair that should have been done under the terms of his arrangement with the tenant. If, under the terms of a lease, it's the landlord's duty to repair and maintain a part of the flat or house and if failure to do so results in a visitor's being hurt, it's the landlord who is liable.

In many cases there doesn't have to be a term in the lease. The Occupiers' Liability Act, 1957, section 2, states that the occupier of premises owes to all visitors a common duty of care, to see that any visitor will be reasonably safe in using the premises for the purposes for which he or she was invited or permitted by the occupier to be there. Where a house is divided into flats or where there is a purpose-built block, there may well be areas of shared usage – hallways, stairs, lifts etc. The landlord is regarded as the 'occupier' of these common areas and therefore owes the common duty of care to visitors.

Similarly, the Defective Premises Act, 1972, section 4, imposes a general duty on landlords to all persons who might reasonably be expected to be affected by defects in the state of the landlord's premises, to ensure that such persons are reasonably safe from personal injury and damage to their property. (Note the two 'reasonablys' in that last sentence.)

35 RESTRICTIVE COVENANTS

This is one of those legal terms the mind runs away from, convinced that it must be beyond comprehension, but it's not as complicated as you may fear. A restrictive covenant is just what it says: a covenant to restrict someone from doing something. The simplest example is one that enables the owner of one piece of land to prevent his or her neighbour using their land in a particular way. There may be a restrictive covenant that prevents your building on your land, using it for business or commercial purposes, keeping animals on it or using it in an illegal or immoral way. Details of such restrictions would be on the deeds of the property, and you may well be bound by agreements former owners made before you came along.

New Estates
Some developers impose restrictions to preserve a homogeneous character on the estate, to maintain the 'tone' of the development. There may be restrictions against building extensions to your house or otherwise getting out of step. Think what the background to the opening credits of *Brookside* would look like if all the houses were not of a kind.

Large Landed Estates
The former owner of the estate, maybe a squire of bygone years, may have wished to maintain the character of the neighbourhood in which he still held a lot of property.

Building Plots
Someone who sells off a part of their land as a building plot may wish to stipulate that only one house is to be built on that plot or that part of the plot mustn't be built on at all, to preserve a view that he or she enjoys.

Trade Restrictions
To prevent local competition, there may be a restrictive covenant on your property that says you can't carry on a

certain trade or profession on the premises. My wife and I once lived in a small cottage in the country, whose deeds said we mustn't carry on the business of a corn chandler. It didn't matter – for some unfathomable reason neither of us has ever wanted to be a corn chandler. A lot of restrictive covenants on older property may have little application to modern life.

What binds these four types of restriction together is the notion that they are all supposed to restrict one property for the benefit of another. You can't simply impose a restrictive covenant for the hell of it or just to be mean. There has to be a real benefit for another identifiable property. The original person to benefit may be dead, but the benefit is said to pass with the property, and the current owner still has the right to enjoy whatever benefit the restrictive covenant confers. In law, the covenant is said to 'run with the land', which means that anyone happening to own the 'dominant' land (land that gets the benefit of the restrictive covenant) can enforce it at any time and that the owner of the 'servient' land (land subject to the restrictive covenant) will always be bound by it.

On some estates, such as new 'integrated' developments (above), all the owners may be said to benefit, so each one has the right to enforce the restrictions.

A restrictive covenant has to be negative in nature. This is obviously the case where the covenant forbids building an extension or carrying out a certain trade. In such cases there is a purely passive obligation. What you can't have is a negatively worded covenant that imposes a positive obligation. For example, a covenant 'not to let property fall into disrepair' is not a restrictive covenant, because it imposes a duty on the servient owner to do something, to spend money or to take action or both.

Since many restrictive covenants were created a hundred or more years ago, a lot of them may be out of date (there isn't a lot of call for corn chandlers these days), and the original reason why the covenant was imposed may no longer apply. A large Victorian house, built as a private dwelling, may be eminently suitable as office accommodation. A field that was once in the heart of the country may now be a small island of green in the pebble-dashed sea of suburbia. In such a case, the servient owner – the person against whom the restrictive covenant acts – may apply to the Lands Tribunal under the Law of Property Act, 1925, section 84. This tribunal can modify or discharge restrictive covenants on various grounds, particularly that of obsolescence, although the servient owner may have to pay compensation.

To succeed in such an application, you would have to show:

i. that there has been a change in the character of the neighbourhood making the restrictive covenant out of date, e.g. that corn chandling, tanning or brewing no longer has to be a protected occupation, or,

ii. that the restrictive covenant is an unreasonable restriction on the use of property for private or public purposes, or,

iii. that all former beneficiaries of the covenant now agree to cancel or alter it – maybe the entire cast of *Brookside* fancies stone-cladding.

36 POSITIVE COVENANTS

Since we have seen that restrictive covenants can only be negative (can only stop people doing things, rather than make them do things) it may come as no surprise that there are also positive covenants. But don't get excited.

There is nothing in law that can compel a neighbour to keep his property in good order, neat and tidy, regularly repainted, ablaze with wallflowers in the early spring, festooned with delphiniums and geraniums in the summer. This is true even when there is a degree of sharing in the property, e.g. a pair of semi-detached houses or a terrace row. I am here assuming that you are the one who wishes to keep the street looking at its best – of course, if you are the Avenue Slob, this will come as good news.

It is possible for you and your neighbour to enter into a private agreement to maintain and repair (the roof, the guttering, the façade of both dwellings), but the problem is that such an agreement would not 'run with the land'. If your neighbour sold his house, and the new neighbour didn't want to honour the agreement, he would be under no obligation so to do. The legal principle to be drawn from this situation is that you cannot enforce a positive covenant against the freehold.

One way out of this problem is not to grant a freehold in the first place, and this is, indeed, one of the reasons why many new properties over the past twenty years or more have been sold as 999-year leasehold, for a positive covenant (such as that suggested above) can be enforced by a landlord against a tenant. It seems sensible, for example, that, where a large old house is divided into flats, there should be a way of ensuring that the hallways, corridors and stairs are lit and kept clean and periodically decorated, and that all the owners should share the cost of this. Hence the sale of the flats as leasehold, not freehold, so that a positive covenant to keep the common areas of the property in good condition should be enforceable.

If you've ever wondered why there should be such a thing as a 999-year lease (which seems to amount to the same as a freehold), this is the reason. Often the properties sold on the basis of a 999-year lease have a corporate identity with neighbouring properties and are part of what is clearly a 'planned' estate.

Note: It is possible that there may be changes in the law on this topic. the Law Commission has looked into the matter of enforceable positive covenants between neighbours and thinks there should be more of them. It may be time to get that leaking gutter fixed and to put the front gate back on its hinges.

37   RIGHTS OF ENTRY

The Criminal Law Act, 1977, created two new criminal offences – using violence to secure entry to premises, and threatening violence to secure entry. Mostly the Act envisages situations arising between landlord and tenant (who are often neighbours), but if you are unlucky enough to live next door to someone who uses or threatens to use

violence to come onto your property to retrieve his kite,
ball or pet, to use your swimming-pool or to gatecrash
your party, it may come as some consolation to know that
he's committing an offence.

Under section 6 (1) of the Act, it is made clear that we
are dealing here with any person acting 'without lawful
authority'. It needs bearing in mind.

See also Section 32, Trespass, and Section 34, Occupiers'
Liability.

38 DEFAMATION

How far can either you or your neighbour go in verbal
abuse before breaking the law? We are dealing here with
audio-verbal abuse, the spoken word, slander. If you or
your neighbour reach the stage where you're writing
libellous things about each other, you had better consult a
textbook on libel or defamation or go to see a solicitor. But
remember: you can't get legal aid for a libel action, which
may be one reason why there are so few of them.

The law is quite strict in its definition of what does
constitute libel. It's not enough that someone has foully
and inaccurately called you bad names, or even that they
have circulated exciting but false rumours about the sort of
things you've been up to. You have to show that it was
done deliberately and maliciously and that you have
suffered (or may suffer) damage or loss as a result (but see
exception, below – Slander actionable without damage).
This is unlikely to happen in the case of a dispute between
neighbours, but it's not impossible.

A couple of years ago we became involved in an issue
with two neighbours who lived across the road. We had
complained to the housing association who owned the flat
in which they were living that their bikini-clad and tipsy
overtures to all passing males over sixteen and under
eighty were the sort of behaviour that other residents,
especially parents of young children, found upsetting. The
housing association must have passed on our complaint to
their tenants, perhaps even gingering it up a little – it's
amazing how things get distorted or exaggerated, isn't it?

A few days later we received an archly phrased letter from a firm of solicitors, threatening all kinds of action for defamation of character. Fortunately the solicitors had their facts wrong, and the whole thing blew over (after we sent an archly worded letter back to the solicitors), but the reason why it might have come to litigation was clearly because, had the housing association forced our merry neighbours to move, they could have claimed they had suffered loss.

It would be difficult to prove that loss arises from the usual critical exchange between neighbours – 'If you weren't bone idle, you'd do something with that bloody privet!' or 'I suppose it's too much to expect a tiny measure of sobriety, but if you could confine your drunken celebrations to the *inside* of your filthy hovel we'd all be eternally grateful!' Your neighbour may be neither idle nor a lush, but the fact that remarks are untrue will not be grounds for an action for defamation. They are what the law terms mere 'vulgar abuse'. In the ancient case of *Penfold v Westcote*, back in 1806, the defendant shouted: 'Why don't you come out, you blackguard, rascal, scoundrel, Penfold? You are a thief!' If he had omitted the word 'thief', all would have been well, but 'thief' (and 'thief' alone) made the remark defamatory. There's something quaint about the other epithets – 'blackguard', 'rascal', 'scoundrel'. Mere vulgar abuse seems to have gone downhill.

Slander Actionable Without Damage

The case of *Penfold v Westcote* illustrates another aspect of the law of defamation. Some cases of slander are actionable without proving damage:

i. where the defendant says something calculated to damage the profession, calling, trade or business of the plaintiff;

ii. where the defendant imputes that the plaintiff has committed a criminal offence, as was the situation in *Penfold v Westcote*;

iii. where the defendant imputes that the plaintiff is suffering from a contagious or infectious disease which is likely to prevent other people associating with him (an example today might well be AIDS);

iv. where the defendant imputes that a woman is unchaste or adulterous. Were we more litigious by nature, the courts would (perhaps should) be overwhelmed with such cases.

To sum up, in every action for defamation, you have to prove that the statement is defamatory, that the statement refers to you and that the statement has been published (i.e. communicated) to a third person.

39 INTIMIDATION AND HARASSMENT

There is a criminal offence of harassment, defined in the Protection from Eviction Act, 1977, section 1 (3):

> If any person with intent to cause the residential occupier of any premises –
> (a) to give up the occupation of the premises or any part thereof:
> or
> (b) to refrain from exercising any right or pursuing any remedy in respect of the premises or part thereof:
> does acts calculated to interfere with the peace or comfort of the residential occupier or members of his household, or persistently withdraws or withholds services reasonably required for the occupation of the premises as a residence, he shall be guilty of an offence.

This means that harassment can be committed by any person, including a neighbour. (I was once accused of this by a neighbour, who claimed that I was trying to hound him from his property so that I could buy it. I can't even afford a decent roof on *this* house (see Section 34, Occupiers' Liability – but it wasn't the same neighbour).

Note that the harassment must be committed against a residential occupier. This could include trespassers, service occupants (such as agricultural workers in tied accommodation) and service tenants, protected tenants, restricted tenants and unprotected tenants, lawful sub-tenants, tenant's licensees, joint tenants (flat-sharers) and deserted spouses by virtue of the Matrimonial Homes Act, 1981, section 1.

For the offence of harassment to be committed, it must be shown that the offender acted with intent to cause the residential occupier either to give up the occupation or to refrain from exercising any right or pursuing any remedy in respect of the premises.

Clearly, much of the above relates to disputes or difficulties between landlords and tenants rather than between neighbours, but it's not impossible to envisage circumstances in which neighbours might become involved. A row over a shared driveway could reach the stage where one sharer's life was being made a misery, and he felt he was being harassed to 'give up the occupation of the premises or any part thereof' (Protection from Eviction Act, 1977).

40 RACIAL HARASSMENT

There are no specific laws to deal with the racial harassment of one neighbour by another. The Race Relations Act, 1976, is concerned more with discrimination on a racial basis in housing or employment. Nevertheless, racial harassment is often a component of disputes between neighbours, a sad reflection of what a long way we still have to go before we stop looking for scapegoats, targets or excuses.

By the Public Order Act, 1986, section 18, 'Any person who uses threatening, abusive or insulting words or behaviour, or displays any written material which is threatening, abusive or insulting, is guilty of an offence if (a) he intends thereby to stir up racial hatred, or (b) having regard to all the circumstances, racial hatred is likely to be stirred up thereby.' This has to be a public offence, in the sense that it doesn't cover words or behaviour used in a private dwelling and seen or heard by others only in that or another private dwelling. If your neighbour racially abuses you over the garden fence, this probably wouldn't be an offence under the Public Order Act – it probably would be if he did so in the road outside your houses.

If you do feel you are being racially harassed by your neighbour, you need to take advice from your local Race Relations (or Community Relations) Office. This will be much cheaper than consulting a solicitor, and you will be going straight to the specialists. If you are a council tenant and feel you are being racially harassed by a neighbour, the best and simplest solution may well be to go to your local Housing Office (see Chapter 22).

41   NEGLIGENCE

The concept of negligence is one of the most important in law and is a factor in many of the cases that come before the courts. Whether we are concerned with road traffic offences, accidents in sport, dangerous or defective goods, occupiers' liability, savage dogs, shoddy repairs or accidents in factories, schools and building sites, negligence is almost certain to be an issue.

The law gives the word 'negligence' two meanings. The first is much the same as 'carelessness', as where someone is alleged to have driven carelessly and where the negligence is simply a component of some other offence, under, say the road Traffic Acts. The second is to describe a totally separate offence, or tort, as in the dear old case of *Donoghue v Stevenson* and the snail in the ginger-beer bottle.

We have already seen, from studying the latter case, that, where A owes a duty to B, and A breaks this duty by exposing B to an unreasonable risk of injury, and such injury results, A will be liable to pay compensation to B for the damage done. This is what the tort of negligence is all about.

The general principle behind the tort of negligence is the duty of care, and it's very similar to that in the law relating to occupiers' liability. In any situation where you can reasonably foresee that what you're doing may expose other people to risk of injury, you owe those people a duty *not* to injure them. It is an elastic concept, as far as the courts are concerned. There is a continual extension of the scope of situations that the principle is supposed to cover.

But note that we are here dealing only with situations where you may be exposing other people to *injury*. The tort of negligence doesn't cover annoyances: bonfire smoke, howling dogs, clucking chickens, car doors, stereo blasters, rotten fences that collapse on your prize blooms, shared pathways blocked through incompetence or slovenliness, shared gates left unfastened, straying children, all the panoply of neighbourhood life. The tort of negligence is concerned only with injury, which may, of course, include shock, as we saw in *Donoghue v Stevenson*.

The 'Neighbour Principle' Again

One of the questions posed in *Donoghue v Stevenson* was: 'Who, in law, is my neighbour?', and the answer was: 'persons who are so closely and directly affected by my act that I ought reasonably to have them in contemplation'. (See Section 3, Who Is Your Neighbour?)

Over the years, the courts have attempted to establish, in a series of judgments, where and when we ought to have other people reasonably in contemplation, where or when we should be considering people our neighbours.

In 1943, in *Bourhill v Young*, the House of Lords held that the estate of a dead motor-cyclist could not be sued for negligence by a woman who had suffered severe nervous shock and given birth to a stillborn child as a result of seeing the dead motor-cyclist. She had not been involved in the accident but had gone back to the scene of the accident and had been shocked at the sight. As far as the House of Lords was concerned, the motor-cyclist owed her no duty of care because she was not within his 'area of risk' at the time of the accident – she was not, in law, his neighbour. (Perhaps we should promote the idea of a new relationship, the neighbour-in-law.)

In 1970, in *Home Office v Dorset Yacht Co Ltd*, the House of Lords held that the Home office did owe a duty of care to people who lived in the neighbourhood of an open Borstal. A group of seven boys eluded their officers one night (it wasn't difficult – the officers had all gone to bed) and clambered onto a yacht moored nearby. They then damaged another yacht. As had been mentioned already on P.27, the House of Lords held that the Borstal officers should reasonably have foreseen that this sort of damage might occur if they didn't exercise sufficient supervision – i.e. if they were negligent.

For our purposes, whether or not the law would consider we owed a duty of care to a neighbour (who, remember, could be someone across the street or three flats above/below or next-door-but-one or a considerable distance away) would depend on what the problem was. A barking dog can be heard all over; an overflowing gutter may affect only the people immediately next door. Where somebody has been injured, the probability is that the law would look very carefully indeed to see whether the 'neighbour principle' applied. The factors involved are:

   i. the seriousness of the risk of injury, in the act or omission that preceded and maybe led to the injury;

   ii. the likelihood of injury;

   iii. the importance of the object to be attained.

In the case of *Bolton v Stone* (Section 26, The Meaning of Reasonable), where a passer-by was injured by a cricket ball, there was evidence that a ball had been hit out of the cricket ground only six times in the last thirty years. That was in 1951, long before Ian Botham had even been thought of. It was seventy-eight yards from wicket to fence, and the top of the fence was seventeen feet above the level of the pitch. So, although the court held that the cricket club did owe a duty of care to passers-by, they also held that the club had taken reasonable precautions and had not broken that duty of care.

Each case has to be treated on its own merits. The best defence against an action for negligence is to take precautions. If you leave an electric lawnmower in your garden, still connected to a supply of electricity, and your neighbour's child wanders in without your knowledge and is subsequently hurt, you would probably not be liable in an action for negligence, though you might fare less well in an action under the Occupiers' Liability Act if it could be shown that you knew that your neighbour's child frequently came into your garden. However, if, in the situation posed above, you knew that the child had come into your garden and you knew that the lawnmower was still 'live', an action for negligence against you could well succeed.

Contributory Negligence

It's possible that in the case of the lawnmower (above), a defence to an action for negligence would be to suggest that your neighbour was guilty of contributory negligence by letting his or her child wander unsupervised into someone else's garden.

Contributor negligence is never a total defence but is used to apportion the amount of damages between the two parties in an action. If you knock me off my poor little moped in your socking great flash car, and I'm not wearing a crash helmet, a court may well decide that I am fifty per cent (or more, or less) to blame for the injuries I receive. This is so even where the accident is totally your fault (which, of course, it always is).

Suppose, for example, I have a tree in my garden which is leaning dangerously towards your garden, its roots having been loosened in the dreadful gales of October 1987. You know all about the danger; I know all about the danger. We have discussed it, testily, several times. And yet you insist on sitting in your garden right on the spot where the tree would fall, if it fell. As luck would have it, the tree does fall, driving you several centimetres into your lawn. What's left of you may well be considered guilty of contributory negligence, because you consented to run the risk of injury.

Perhaps the most memorable case on the subject of contributory negligence is that of *Sayers v Harlow UDC* in 1958. The defendants owned and operated a public lavatory. The plaintiff was on her way to Olympia with her husband, but had twenty minutes before her bus was due. She decided to avail herself of the lavatorial amenities, put her penny in the slot (those were the days!), but, once inside the cubicle, discovered the inside handle was missing from the door. She was trapped. There was no warning notice and no attendant. The poor plaintiff went through the repertoire of banging on the door, shouting, and waving through the window to attract attention – all to no avail. This went on for ten minutes. (We are not told what her husband was doing.) The plaintiff then tried to climb out through the space between the top of the cubicle door and the ceiling. In order to do this she stood with her left foot on the seat of the lav and rested her right foot on the toilet roll and fixture, holding a pipe from the low cistern with one hand and resting the other on the top of the door. Thus positioned, she found it impossible to effect an exit. She then, in the words of the Law Report: 'proceeded to come down, and, as she was doing so, the toilet roll rotated, owing to her weight on it, and, upset her balance.'

The Court of Appeal decided two things. Firstly, the defendants were guilty of negligence and the damage was not too remote because it was reasonable for the plaintiff to see whether or not she could climb out of the cubicle. Secondly, the plaintiff was guilty of contributory negligence when she allowed her balance to depend on the rotating toilet roll. The plaintiff's damages were, therefore, reduced by a quarter – a lesson to us all.

PART III
THE NEIGHBOURLY MINEFIELD

This is the part of the book where we get down to it – the sordid details of inter-neighbour strife, hostility, friction and worse. We shall take one field of disaster at a time, dealing with the following topics:

pollution
animals
pets
pests
trees
drains and mains
landlord and tenant
gardens
light and privacy

amenities
building regulations
statutory nuisance
litter and untidy land
boundaries, walls and fences
squatters
rights of way

7   Pollution

42   POLLUTION – GENERAL

Pollution has been defined as 'the introduction by man into any part of the environment of waste matter or surplus energy, which so changes the environment as directly or indirectly adversely to affect the opportunity of man to use or enjoy it' (J.McLoughlin, *The Law Relating to Pollution*).

Ignoring the fact that the definition doesn't seem too bothered about the opportunities of women to use or enjoy the environment (see note, below), it does cover what most of us regard as pollution. For the purposes of neighbourhood pollution, the phrase 'surplus energy' is particularly apt. The stereo blaster, the car-door slammer, the DIY fanatic, the howling alsatian, all seem to have too much energy, and we often get more concerned about this relatively small-scale pollution, near at hand, than we do about nuclear dumping or holes in the ozone layer.

The reason why more neighbour disputes spring from incidents of pollution than anything else may partly be the difficulty of obtaining a consensus as to what constitutes the standard of environmental quality that we are striving to maintain. Your garden may be a showpiece; mine may be a haven for wildlife. You can't stand the windblown weed seeds and bindweed suckers that emanate from my wilderness; I am appalled at the chemicals and artificial fertilizers that you spray all over your smug little plot. McLoughlin, in the work cited above, points out that, although one minute we may be exasperated by pop music billowing from a portable radio in a neighbour's garden, the next minute we may feel entirely different if our neighbour has switched to a test match ball-by-ball commentary. All of a sudden we want to peer over the fence in friendly fashion and ask what the score is.

Note: My own feeling is that men are far more pollutive than women. You seldom see young women with stereo blasters in public places, and women less often need noise when they're in the garden. They tend to shut car doors more quietly, have fewer bonfires and, surprisingly, don't seem to find it so necessary to have large, noisy dogs. Women appear to see a garden as a place of peace and quiet, for relaxation, rather than as a kind of toy saloon bar/incinerator/football stadium.

43   AIR POLLUTION – BONFIRES

The commonest cause of air pollution for a householder is a neighbour's bonfire. It's amazing the odd hours bonfire-lovers keep. You may be peacefully in bed, dreaming that you are a kipper in a smoke box, and you awake to discover it's six in the morning and your pyromaniac neighbour is already stoking a four-foot-high pile of old nettles, rhubarb leaves and Sunday supplements or, worse, plastic sacks, old cushions and unwanted chipboard and polystyrene furniture.

At one time, a kind of folk myth grew up that there were fixed hours for bonfires, that you weren't allowed to start one before 9 a.m. and it had to be extinguished by 4 p.m. Sadly, this is untrue. There are no time restrictions on bonfires, so your neighbour may tend his acrid pile all day if he so wishes – and it's staggering how many of them do.

Faced with this problem, the first thing is to try peaceful and neighbourly intercession. Ask him to limit his bonfires. Suggest that he start a compost heap or take the sopping vegetation and tar-marinaded furniture to the local council tip, where it can be disposed of free of charge (address in telephone directory). Point out in what way his bonfire is causing you discomfort, annoyance or inconvenience: the washing on the line, the smoke curling in through your kitchen and bedroom windows, the fact that you can't see and are having to feel your way round your own garden. As in all neighbour problems, the best, cheapest, quickest and ultimately most satisfactory solution is if you and your neighbour can work something out together.

The National Society for Clean Air (address at end of book) publishes material which makes several important points about bonfires:

1. Avoid bonfires by composting as much garden rubbish as possible.
2. Dry non-compostable materials before burning.
3. Bonfires release polycyclic aromatic hydrocarbons into the atmosphere. Enough of these can become dangerous. Bonfire smoke contains seventy parts per million of the carcinogenic compound benzpyrene. Cigarette smoke contains only 0.2 parts per million of the same.
4. You shouldn't light a fire within an hour of sunset or leave it burning later than an hour after sunset – because weather conditions then cause smoke to hang in the air.
5. You shouldn't leave a bonfire unattended. If you've finished gazing, trance-like, into its flames, put it out.
6. A smoky bonfire could be actionable (more of this later).

If your direct intercession with your neighbour isn't successful, you can seek other remedies. At Common Law, you have a right of action against another for private nuisance if you have suffered unlawful interference with the use and enjoyment of your land. This interference would certainly include 'smoke' but has to have interfered with your enjoyment to an extent that is unreasonable. The nature of the area where you live and its general ambiance will be taken into account. We are back to the Belgravia/Bermondsey divide.

If your neighbour merely has the occasional bonfire, even as regularly as every Sunday, however inconvenient it may be for you, it may not constitute a legal nuisance. If, however, he lights a bonfire and keeps it going for a week or more (and the longevity of a bonfire often becomes a matter of pride for a fire fanatic), this could well be considered a nuisance.

Contact your local authority's Environmental Health Department (address and telephone number in telephone directory) and ask them to take the matter up. They may well groan, being almost certainly understaffed and underfunded and having what they consider more important things to do, since their field of responsibility is wide, but they are empowered to investigate your complaint and, if they are satisfied that a nuisance is being committed, can serve a notice requiring the nuisance to be abated, i.e. telling your neighbour to be more considerate in the number, size and duration of his bonfires.

If your neighbour persists, the local authority can apply to a magistrate's court for a nuisance order under the Public Health Act, 1936, section 94. If the magistrates are satisfied that your neighbour has behaved unreasonably, they can issue a nuisance order, restricting your neighbour's bonfires, imposing a fine and ordering a daily penalty for every day on which your neighbour breaks the terms of the order and the nuisance continues. It can be a hefty penalty. Ultimately the local authority has the power to abate the nuisance themselves.

It is possible to initiate the same procedure yourself, omitting the local authority, under the Public Health Act, 1936, section 99 (in a magistrate's court) or section 100 (in the High Court).

Some people favour more direct action, believing that

going to court never did much to improve diplomatic relations anyway, so you might as well resort to *force majeur*. Either way, it all ends in acrimony, and at least direct action has the advantage of speed. One man, whose wife suffered from asthma, became so enraged by his next-door-but-one-neighbour's bonfires that he connected his garden hose and sprayed the fire with a jet of water that curved over the intervening garden like a rainbow in the sky. It can't have been too pleasant for the people in the middle, caught in No-Man's-Land, between fire and flood, and with hatred on both sides.

A further word of caution about your own bonfire, which you light only occasionally, always at reasonable hours of the day, and on which you never burn unsuitable materials. By the Highways Act, 1980, section 131 (1)(d) and 161 (2), it is an offence ' ... without lawful authority or excuse, to light a fire or discharge a firearm or firework within fifty feet from the centre of the road in consequence of which the road is damaged or a road user is injured, interrupted or endangered'. Since the vast majority of inner suburban bonfires may well be within fifty feet (just over fifteen metres) of the centre of the road, it needs taking into consideration. Billows of smoke unsighting a motorcyclist or car-drive could have disastrous effects. Maybe the council tip is the best place after all.

Note: The law doesn't make any special provision for people who may be particularly affected by smoke, e.g. sufferers from asthma or bronchitis. The standard of care and consideration that the law reckons we should exercise toward each other is that of average person to average person. All you can hope, if smoke is a special problem for you, is that your neighbour is understanding. It's certainly worth telling your neighbour.

44   AIR POLLUTION – INDUSTRIAL

People sometimes turn wistfully to the Clean Air Acts when confronted by neighbour's bonfires, but, alas, in vain. The Clean Air Acts of 1956 and 1968 apply only to smoke emanating from a chimney.

Your local council has responsibility for the control of industrial smoke, grit, gas, dust and fumes. Generally speaking, it is an offence for 'dark smoke' to be emitted from a factory chimney, so the only problem is what constitutes 'dark smoke'. The darkness of smoke is judged by the shade it measures on what is known as the Ringelmann Chart. Dark smoke is that which is as dark as or darker than Shade 2 (Clean Air Act, 1956, section 2). If you are suffering from smoke such as this from neighbouring industrial premises, contact your local Environmental Health Office.

Note: The Ringelmann Scale was devised by Professor Maximilian Ringelmann of Paris towards the end of the nineteenth century. The chart consists of a number of squares crosshatched in black on a white background so that a known percentage of white is obscured in each case. The observer compares the emitted smoke with the squares and assigns a number on the scale ranging from 0 (white) to 5 (black). A diagram of the chart is contained in *Clean Air Today* (Department of the Environment, 1974).

If you live next to vast industrial premises, such as a steelworks, cementworks, chemical plant or power station, you need to contact HM Industrial Pollution Inspectorate, which is part of the Health and Safety Executive. The address and telephone number of your local inspector should be in your telephone directory. You may have to push hard to get their attention – there aren't many such inspectors.

It is an offence to burn the insulation from a cable with the intent of recovering metal inside, unless it is done at a place registered by the above inspectorate (Control of Pollution Act, 1974, section 78).

The law is in a state of flux concerning some aspects of pollution by smoke from industrial premises. It used to be the case that, even if you had been committing a nuisance – like making acrid smoke – for a long time, anyone who was newly arrived on the scene, e.g. a new housing estate bordering industrial premises, could object. More recent legal thinking seems to be that newcomers cannot object.

45   AIR POLLUTION – DOMESTIC

Certain areas have been established as Smoke Control Areas. If you and your neighbour live in such an area, it is an offence, under the Clean Air Act, 1956, section 11 (2), to emit smoke from a domestic chimney by burning unauthorized fuel. Your local council should have a list of authorized fuels, but they will include Sunbrite, Anthracite, Phurnacite, Coalite, Rexco, Homefire, Housewarm and washed singles and trebles of coal for use on specific appliances.

If you can show that your neighbour is burning unauthorized fuel in a Smoke Control Area, your local council may take legal action in the magistrate's court, and on conviction your neighbour can be fined.

Just for the record, it is also an offence to sell unauthorized fuel in a Smoke Control Area.

46   OFFENSIVE ODOURS

It is possible to be plagued by a strench so foul that you cannot use your own garden and are even invaded when indoors. It may well be that this would be considered a nuisance but, as always, each case would have to be treated on its own merits. It is never possible to say that any one thing is a nuisance. A fried fish shop has been held to be a nuisance in a residential area, because of the smell. It seems a fairly safe bet that the Belgravia/ Bermondsey Divide Theory would come into play here, though it's interesting to note that in this case the fact that the fish shop is useful to the neighourhood is considered no defence.

Another case was brought to court concerning a manure heap. It was on a site which was usually cleared regularly, but on this occasion clearing was delayed. The smell intensified. Other people began to take advantage of the site, dumping dead cats and dogs. Understandably, neighbours of the site complained. Although the heaps were considered a nuisance, the court did not grant an injunction, on the basis that the nuisance was only temporary and that there was no need to issue an order to stop. In other circumstances, people creating a temporary nuisance may be ordered to pay damages.

47   POLLUTION – INLAND WATERS

At Common Law, the riparian owner (a person whose property runs down to a stream or river) used to have the right to abstract from a stream all the water necessary for ordinary purposes, even if this meant there was no water left for anyone downstream. This is no longer true. By the Water Resources Act, 1963, all abstractions of water are controlled by the river authorities.

The odd thing is that, although you have no right to the water that percolates through your land (even if you have a well), you do have a right of action against your neighbour if his or her pollutants foul the water you draw from your land. In the case of *Ballard v Tomlinson* in 1885, the judge said: 'No man has a right to use his own land in such a way as to be a nuisance to his neighbour ... by sending filth on to his neighbour's land, or by putting poisonous matter on his own land and allowing it to escape on to his neighbour's land, or ... by poisoning the air which his neighbour breathes, or the water which he drinks.'

It's a strong statement, and not entirely undone by the Act of 1963. A riparian owner has a right of action against any owner upstream (or anyone else) who pollutes the stream. The culprit has committed a nuisance. It may be that a stream is polluted by sewage, carried to it by a local authority executing its responsibility under the Public Health Act, 1936. This is no defence. The 1936 Act specifically removes any such protection from a local authority guilty of polluting a stream or waterway. The only problem, if your stream is being polluted, would be if the local authority had given permission to the person discharging pollutant matter so to do.

48   PONDS, POOLS, DITCHES

Under the Public Health Act, 1936, section 259, it's a statutory nuisance for any person to reduce any pond, pool or ditch to such a state that it is so foul as to be prejudicial to health, or a nuisance. It is also a statutory nuisance for any person to choke or silt up any part of a watercourse so as to impede the proper flow of water, causing a nuisance or giving rise to conditions prejudicial to health.

In general, the pollution of a river, stream or ditch is a complicated matter legally. There may be several different bodies involved, and there are loopholes that have allowed industrial companies pumping or discharging pollutive effluent to escape liability. In some cases (say, to preserve the confidentiality of a secret industrial process), they are not even obliged publicly to reveal precisely what they are discharging into the river.

If you are a riparian owner, and 'your' stream becomes polluted, your best bet is to try to trace the source of the pollution and play it from there, taking legal advice where necessary.

49   CESSPOOLS

Any cesspool that is in such a condition as to be prejudicial to health is said to be a nuisance, but not a statutory one, even though it's designated a nuisance by a statute (Public Health Act, 1936, section 39 [1][c]). You have to admire the law for its fine disregard of logic, if nothing else. Brilliantly, the law has defined 'prejudicial to health' as 'injurious or likely to cause injury to health' and has remained happy with that definition for the last fifty or more years.

What it means is: if your neighbour's cesspool is overflowing, even if the overflow isn't reaching your land, you can take action against your neighbour for private nuisance. Before doing so, it's advisable to make sure that you aren't partly responsible, under the deeds of your house or cottage, for the upkeep and repair of the offending cesspool.

8 Noise

50 NOISE – GENERAL

As far as the police, the Citizens' Advice Bureaux, Housing Officers, Environmental Health Officers and almost everyone dealing with neighbour disputes are concerned, this is the big one. There are more complaints about noise than anything else, and the subjects of these complaints range from parties where vibrations from the travelling disco equipment shake an entire block of flats to the barely audible tapping, whistling or love-making which the complainant swears is deliberate and of evil intent.

What constitutes an acceptable level of noise is, of course, a very subjective interpretation. Local councils, who probably have more statistical data about noise complaints than anyone else, will tell you that all sorts of factors come into play: the generation gap, changes in lifestyle, unemployment for young people (their day begins in the early afternoon and doesn't end until 3 or 4 a.m.), twenty-four-hour television, more and more powerful record-players etc. A lot of difficulties are caused by the increasing use of old houses for multiple occupation. Where once one family used to live, there may now be three or more flats, or a whole multitude of bedsits. Such houses were neither designed nor built with sound insulation in mind. The cost of installing such insulation is prohibitive as far as most councils are concerned today. It is far cheaper to seek to rehouse tenants who are unhappy where they are or who don't fit in with the rest of the tenants in a building. This is assuming that there is any slack in the council's housing – often there isn't.

The Measurement of Noise

Sound levels are measured in decibels, abbreviated to dB. A *steady* increase in noise has a *rapidly* increasing effect on the human ear. Some noises are more intrusive to the ear than others. Decibels are therefore given an 'A' frequency rating, to give readings which take this variable into account. An increase of 10 dB(A) represents a doubling of loudness, so 80 dB(A) is twice as loud as 70 dB(A).

Here's a chart of some offenders:

Sound level in dB(A)	Source
120	Discothéque – in front of speaker
100	Pneumatic drill at 5 metres
90	Heavy goods road vehicle (from safety of pavement)
70	Vacuum cleaner at 3 metres
	Telephone ringing at 2 metres
	The famous Festival Hall Cough
50	Boiling electric kettle at 2 metres
40	Refrigerator humming at 2 metres
0	Total, blissful silence (rare)

So, as far as your poor ears are concerned, going to a disco is like surrounding yourself with sixteen power lawnmowers.

Given all this, the law makes provision for anyone aggrieved by noise to seek a remedy. The procedure is very similar to that for any other sort of pollution.

The first thing to do is to examine in your mind the noise that is disturbing you. Is there anything you could do about it yourself? Is the noise really unreasonable? There is obviously a great difference between a crying baby that your neighbour would love to be able to quieten but cannot, and banging and hammering in the middle of the night because your neighbour has decided that's a good time to install central heating. We have seen that there is no Common Law right to privacy (Section 27, Privacy), and it's unavoidable that from time to time you will be able to hear some of the activities of your neighbours, just as they'll be able to hear some of yours (active lovers, please note). This may well be why detached residences are regarded as so desirable by estate agents.

A great variety of cases have come before the courts, and in each one the particular circumstances surrounding the noise seem to be what matters. This includes the intention of the person making the noise. In one case a man who lived next door to a music teacher became exasperated by the regular and lengthy noises coming from the music lessons. He decided to throw a little concert of his own, beating on tin trays, blowing whistles and shrieking (you may have heard him giving recitals in some of the Modern Music series on Radio 3). The correspondence that flowed between the two parties in this case is of such a quality that it deserves to be quoted in detail.

51   THE DELIGHTFUL CASE OF *CHRISTIE V DAVEY*

The plaintiff, Mrs Christie, gave music lessons and held musical soirées, while other members of her family practised musical instruments. Mr Christie was, significantly, deaf. The defendant, Mr Davey, made no complaint for three years, then, in 1893, wrote as follows:

> During this week we have been much disturbed by what I at first thought were the howlings of your dog, and, knowing from experience that this sort of thing could not be helped, I put up with the annoyance. But, the noise recurring at a comparatively early hour this morning, I find I have been quite mistaken, and that it is the frantic effort of someone trying to sing with piano accompaniment, and during the day we are treated by way of variety to dreadful scrapings on a violin, with accompaniments. If the accompaniments are

intended to drown the vocal shrieks or catgut vibrations, I can assure you it is a failure, for they do not. I am at last compelled to complain, for I cannot carry on my profession with this constant thump, thump, scrape, and shriek, shriek, constantly in my ears. It may be a pleasure or source of profit to you, but to me and mine it is a confounded nuisance and pecuniary loss, and, if allowed to continue, it must most seriously affect our health and comfort. We cannot use the back part of our house without feeling great inconvenience through this constant playing, sometimes up to midnight and even beyond. Allow me to remind you of one fact, which must most surely have escaped you – that these houses are only semi-detached, so that you yourself may see how annoying it must be to your unfortunate next-door neighbour. If it is not discontinued I shall be compelled to take very serious notice of it. It may be fine sport to you, but it is almost death to yours truly.

That's one way of writing to your neighbour.

Mrs Christie made no reply. The defendant then commenced his impromptu concert on tin trays and the party wall, accompanying the bangings with shrieks, whistling and imitations of Mrs Christie's soirées. This provoked a letter from Mrs Christie's solicitors.

We have been consulted by Mr and Mrs Christie in reference to the outrageous system of annoyance which you have adopted towards them in hammering and beating trays against the party wall between your house and theirs, and making other offensive noises whenever any music is going on in their house. Your letter to Mr Christie on the subject was brought to us at the time; but the tone thereof was so extremely coarse and insulting that we advised our client to treat it with the contempt which it appears to us to deserve. It may be that, if you are not of a musical nature, the sound which may reach you from our clients' house owing to the thinness of the party wall (for which, by the way, they are not responsible), is not very agreeable to you; but at the same time you must remember that our clients have to carry on their profession, as well as yourself, and, moreover, we have yet to learn that it is an unreasonable use of a private house to play the pianoforte or sing. Your own complaint that the music interferes with the exercise of your profession is, we understand, quite unfounded, as we believe the fact is that you have converted the upper storey of your house into an office, where you could not possibly hear what is going on on the ground floor next door. On the other hand, your disgraceful proceedings are the cause of very much discomfort and annoyance to our clients, and seriously interfere with their professional pursuits and engagements, and, therefore, unless you at once give us an undertaking to discontinue them, you will compel our clients (much as they would wish to avoid quarrelling with their neighbours) to adopt the only remedy which appears open to them – namely, to take proceedings against you in the Chancery Division to obtain an injunction to restrain the continuance of the conduct you have seen fit to adopt.

Neither party, it appeared, was working towards a peaceful solution. Mr Davey replied:

Your favour of the 12th to hand in re Christie, in which you talk of 'outrageous system of annoyance, etc., hammering and beating trays etc.' This I emphatically deny. I have a perfect right to amuse myself on any musical instrument I may choose, and I am quite sure I should be the last person to do anything knowingly to annoy my neighbours. What I do is simply for recreation's sake, and to perfect myself in my musical studies. You express your opinion about my letter, which is quite contrary to my own. I see nothing coarse or insulting in it; but I look upon it as shewing my desire to be on friendly terms with my neighbours, for I wrote in quite a jocular manner. However, each one to his taste. Your third paragraph questions my musical taste. Well, I believe from my past musical training, that I am perfectly qualified to distinguish between music and noise. Now, seriously, I put it to you, is it not most excruciating to have constant repetitions of the five-fingered exercises, and only receiving the higher notes of the vocal efforts? I do not for one moment think that there are no beautiful gradations; but they don't reach me. I am quite thankful, I can assure you, for your eminently legal opinion as to your clients' non-responsibility for the thinness of the party wall. I do remember that your clients have to carry on their profession as well as myself, and this has made me shew more forbearance than I otherwise should have done. But, while making all allowances for the privilege of those who rent private houses, I have yet to learn that the same principle does not apply to me as well as to them. I now come to the most serious part of your letter, in which you say that my complaint of the music interfering is quite unfounded. You have the two opinions, mine and your clients'; one of us is evidently (to say the least of it) departing from the truth, and it is not I. the sounds reach up to my room most clearly, and my assistants are constantly complaining to me about it. We have the most difficult portraits to reproduce, requiring great thought and the most delicate treatment. This is my *spécialité*, and, if the thing were (I mean the noise) only now and then, I should not have thought of complaining; but it is morning, noon and night, and perhaps the thinness of the party wall acts as a conductor and carries this terrible noise right up to my studio. I am given to understand that your clients have no carpet on the floor, nor pictures on the walls, consequently there is nothing to deaden the sounds, as in other private houses. Your clients' predecessor was a very musical person indeed; but, his place being properly furnished, the sound did not reach here to any extent; but here everything is done to increase the sound, and I have yet to learn that I am compelled to be a martyr because my neighbour is musical. Lastly, you say that I interfere with your clients' professional pursuits. Just so; this is simply reversing my complaint, and what is sauce for the goose is sauce for the gander. I have not complained without reason, for I cannot sit downstairs either to read a book or converse with friends or clients, as the case may be, but what this atrocious hubbub drowns all efforts to hear, and is continued on to mid-night and after, and often commences a little after 8 a.m. When illness was in my house no cessation took place, and to my mind your clients have lately carried it so far as to shew that it is done maliciously; so you will, I have no doubt, see that, as I am the party wronged, and have the right of complaint on my side, I shall positively refuse to give any undertaking that I shall cease my musical performances. To shew my willingness to meet the convenience of my neighbours, I am perfectly willing to compromise the matter by their agreeing to have one part of the week and me the other. I will give them the choice, leaving the Lord's Day as it really ought to be, a day of rest, neither of us using it as a day of musical recreation, but absolute rest. Here is a case in point now – while I am writing this up in my studio there is someone next door making frantic efforts to reach an upper note. It is intolerable; the house is no longer a private house, but a public one, pupil after pupil coming and practising, and letting out their pianos for practising only, sometimes two pianos going at the same time. It is my intention during these winter months to endeavour to perfect myself on the following instruments – viz., flute, concertina, cornopean, horn, and piano, which my child is learning to accompany me. I used to play them at one time, both in a church band and an amateur troupe; but I have been out of practice lately, but hope soon to regain my former proficiency.

They clearly had a great deal more time to write letters in those days, but the correspondence between the two parties does reveal the classic mistakes to be made in neighbour exchanges. The tone is aggressive, self-righteous, sarcastic. Jibes and caustic comments are made – 'the privilege of those who rent private houses', 'Your clients' predecessor was a very musical person indeed; but his place being properly furnished ... ' – and there is no attempt to establish an atmosphere in which negotiations may take place. There is also the repeatedly inappropriate use of the word 'perfect' by Mr Davey, in what seems a most imperfect situation.

The very first letter from Mrs Christie's solicitors threatened High Court action. When the case reached the High Court, as it inevitably did, the court ordered the defendant to stop. Whether or not the music lessons were a nuisance was a separate matter – certainly the sort of noise he was deliberately creating did constitute nuisance.

Not only does the court examine the individual circumstances of each case, it also looks at what would be an appropriate remedy if an unreasonable amount of noise is being made. In 1980, in the case of *Kennaway v Thompson*, the plaintiff owned a house in the Cotswolds – yes, even in the heart of England's green and pleasant land it's possible to be plagued by noise. Next door to the house, on neighbouring land, there was a lake which a club started to use for motorboat races. At first the races were few and far between, but race meetings became more and more frequent, more and more popular, and by 1977 the lake had become a venue for national and international events. The plaintiff brought a successful action in nuisance, but the High Court awarded her damages rather than an injunction. The plaintiff appealed to the Court of Appeal because the remedy that she sought was an injunction – she wanted some kind of limit placed on the number of times the lake was used. She was successful – restrictions were placed on the number of times the club could use the lake and on the amount of noise generated by their meetings.

Having examined your own situation carefully and having come to the decision that the noise you are suffering is unreasonable, the next thing to do is to tell your neighbour. Try to do this calmly, choosing a time when both of you are least likely to fly off the handle, though this is hard if your nerves are fraught after a broken night's sleep. It may be that your neighbour has a reasonable explanation for the unreasonable noise: the cistern burst and water was pouring through the ceiling, old friends arrived unexpectedly and they were whooping it up but such a situation won't occur again, or, quite simply, they had no idea how penetrative the noise was.

Don't forget, if you're complaining because this is the forty-second time you've been disturbed by a particular noise or activity, your neighbour won't know that. If there's been no previous complaint, then, as far as he or she is concerned, this is the first time you've been bothered. If you then go in firing from all barrels, it may seem that you are over-reacting. The best thing is to complain early on, when you are at the beginning rather than the end of your tether, but when you can justifiably show that you have been inconvenienced.

If the situation is the other way round, and you're the one against whom a complaint is being made, try to listen to what your neighbour has to say. Again, is there anything you could do about the noise? Is your neighbour reasonable in his or her complaint? Would it have been better if you had remembered to warn your neighbour that you were going to be making an unusual amount of noise? Many people say they would much more easily have put up with noise if they had known why it was happening and roughly how long they would have to put up with it.

Let us assume that you have talked to your neighbour about the noise but that, sadly, it has not led to any improvement in the situation. You should now put your complaint in writing, without going to the lengths of *Christie v Davey*. Don't go over the top and fill your letter with vitriolic character assassination. Show clearly what noise you are complaining about, and request him or her to reduce the disturbance. Always keep copies of any correspondence you have with your neighbour. It is amazing how often there are subsequently differences of opinion as to what was said. Allegations fly thick and fast – the letter was rude, threatening, blasphemous, libellous (it can't have been if it was communicated only to the neighbour).

Once you've written the letter and sent it to your neighbour, allow a reasonable time for him or her to comply with your request. What constitutes a reasonable time will obviously depend on the source of the trouble. If you are complaining about chickens screeching early in the morning (they do screech: it's a myth that they cluck), don't expect your neighbour either to slaughter them immediately after the postman's delivered your letter or to build a new chicken house at the other end of the garden that very afternoon. On the other hand, if the source of the noise is a dog that gets left out all night and howls from dusk to dawn, it shouldn't take long for your neighbour to work out the simple solution – keeping the dog indoors. It may be that you have to give your neighbour time to reply to your letter or to come and see you to try to work out a compromise.

There are also subtle ways of bringing to the notice of dog owners the fact that their beasts are noisy. One family, troubled by the howling of their neighbour's dog every time the neighbours left it alone in the house, took the bold step of inviting the owners/neighbours in for a drink. The first thing the neighbours heard was the howling of their dog. It may not have completely solved the problem, but it did at least bring it to the attention of the owners, and that's the essential first step.

If the noise persists, you may have to take further

action, and you can do this formally, under the Control of Pollution Act, 1974, section 59. You don't have to go to a solicitor. You can go on your own to a magistrate's court where the justices' clerk or the magistrates will, if satisfied that there is a case to answer, witness the form of complaint that you will have been asked to complete. On the form you will have to show the times and dates of the nuisance, what sort of noise it was, how long it lasted and in what ways it constituted a nuisance to you.

Your neighbour will then be summoned to appear at the magistrate's court to answer your complaint. If you are taking this action on your own behalf, it is unlikely that you will back out at this stage, but if you have asked someone else to take action for you, this may be where your nerve fails. That's entirely up to you: you have to assess whether it's worth going through with the action for the peace and quiet you feel you're entitled to at home.

Many people, whether they're tenants or owner-occupiers, prefer to go to the local council when they wish to complain about neighbour noise. Again, talk and write to your neighbour first, but if that fails, contact your local Environmental Health Office. They will arrange for someone to come and visit you. If the noise is made at regular times and during normal working hours, try to arrange for the visit to take place at such a time, so that you can indicate what you're complaining about. If the noise takes place at night (a barking dog) or is irregular in its frequency, the council may suggest that you take recordings of the noise, to monitor the nuisance. This all takes a lot of time. In the first place, the council may have very few tape-recorders. The recordings have to be done on special machines with fixed recording levels (otherwise you could doctor the recordings to make the noise seem louder than it really was), and they cost over £3,000 each. There will almost certainly be a long queue of people waiting to use them: some councils get over 250 complaints a week about noise.

Secondly, once a machine is available, you will be asked to take recordings over a period of a week for about an hour a day. At the end of the week, the council will call for their machine, and then someone has to sit in a room at the Environmental Health office and listen to seven hours of tape, checking the noise levels. If the council is then satisfied that you are being subjected to a nuisance, they will issue a notice to your neighbour, requiring him or her to abate that nuisance. If the noise continues, the council will apply to the magistrate's court on your behalf, but you will probably have to attend as a witness, and you may have to wait for up to a year before the case comes to court.

Note: The law makes no special provision for people who have a greater than average sensitivity of hearing. If you are particularly susceptible to noise, or if you are a shift worker who is more likely to be disturbed by noise than others, this does not impose a special legal obligation on your neighbour to be quiet. As in the case of asthma-sufferers and bonfires, however, it is of course worthwhile informing your neighbour of the situation, in the hope that moral reason will work where legal 'reasonableness' doesn't.

It's also worthwhile checking the cause of the noise. It may be that your neighbour is guilty of converting his or her dwelling-house into business premises. With a considerable increase in the number of self-employed (and/or moonlighters), comes far greater risk of people using noisy machinery at home for business purposes. In some cases they need planning permission, in others they don't. The best thing to do is consult your local council, who will be able to give you guidance as to what constitutes 'conversion'. I hasten to add that typing or using a word-processor as a freelance writer, doesn't.

52 PARTIES

Parties are a frequent source of conflict between neighbours, the exceptions being where neighbours are all invited to the party. If you are giving a party and you know or expect that it will go on late into the night or early into the morning, it does help if you give notice to your neighbours. Over and over again, people who have complained about noise (parties, road works, building sites etc) say it would have been possible to put up with the noise if only they had known roughly how long it was going to last, or if they had had some warning.

Many people, assaulted by a noisy party that shows no signs of abating at one, two, three or four in the morning, turn in desperation to the police. The problem here is that noise itself isn't an offence. It becomes an offence when it creates a nuisance, but even then it doesn't become a crime and so, strictly speaking, doesn't involve the police.

It's all very unsatisfactory, because what the person who is being disturbed wants is an immediate end to the noise, an immediate solution to the problem. It's no good telling him or her to contact the council or to take action in the magistrate's court, to get an injunction or damages in a year's time. The party, the noise, the broken night, the lost sleep are taking place *now*.

There are, however, two straws to clutch at.

The first is that the police may intervene if they think it is likely that a breach of the peace will take place. This is because a breach of the peace is a crime. If the party has spilled out onto the road, or communal stairways and corridors in a block of flats, the police might well consider 'having a word' to quieten things down.

If you do phone the police in the middle of the night, don't be disappointed if they don't seem keen to get involved. They're well aware that people turn to them at such times simply because there's no one else to contact. You may, however, strike lucky, and they may say that they'll get a patrol to call in on the party. All the police can do, though is *ask* the merrymakers to turn down the noise.

In some areas, certainly in inner London, the local councils run what they call Party Patrols, under the auspices of the Environmental Health Departments. On Friday and Saturday nights, intrepid council officials, usually accompanied by a police officer, tour their boroughs, calling in wherever there has been a complaint about a party. They can ask the organizers to turn the noise down and, if the organizers won't comply, can serve a notice and then an order. Where they visit, they are effective, but, with over fifty calls on any one night, the problem is simply one of being able to get from one end of the borough to the other in order to visit each party.

It is, nevertheless, a useful service, and the council officials are brave people. Like all local authority services, it has been hit hard by cutbacks in expenditure. To find out whether such patrols operate in your area, phone your local Environmental Health Department, though they may well say that, for them to take any action, you must first phone the police.

53   BLUES PARTIES

These are an urban phenomenon. The idea behind a Blues Party is that a flat or house (it's usually a flat) is taken over for a night or an entire weekend. Often the occupiers of the flat are paid to go away. A party organizer then steps in, books a disco and proceeds to run a 'professional' party, charging for admission and drinks and whatever else has been laid on. The worst thing about these parties is that they can last for twenty-four hours or more. The police may try to do something to lower the noise level, but it's asking a lot of one officer to take on a hundred of more excited partygoers. Council Party Patrols will also intervene, with police accompaniment, and find that the best approach is simply to hang about outside the flat, thereby discouraging would-be customers and threatening the profits of the organizers.

Occasionally the organizers of such parties are brought to court for creating a nuisance. Often it's difficult to identify who is responsible for the organization of the party, and the defence is that it was simply a birthday party that got a bit out of hand (it's even been claimed that it was a child's birthday party). The trouble is that it takes months and months to bring the case the court, and it's quite possible that, even if the council win the action, the punishment will be the award of damages of less than £50. Since the profits made by a single Blues Party may be in the region of £1,500, it's hardly a deterrent.

54 INDUSTRIAL NOISE

If you have industrial neighbours and are disturbed by what you consider unreasonable noise, you should contact your local council. They are responsible for controlling noise-emission from industrial and commercial premises. The procedure for your council to follow is similar to that outlined above. If the noise amounts to a nuisance, they will serve a notice on the person responsible or the owner or occupier of the premises, under the Control of Pollution Act, 1974. The person on whom the notice is served has twenty-one days to appeal against that notice to a magistrate's court.

Subject to such an appeal, if the person responsible doesn't comply with the notice, the court has powers, on conviction, to impose a fine. This also applies to vibrations emanating from industrial premises.

We have already seen in Section 51, *Christie v Davey*, that the court is concerned in cases brought before it to examine the intention of the person responsible for the noise. It also looks at the question of whether or not the noise really interferes with the complainant's use or enjoyment of his or her property. In one case, the vicar of SS Mary and Mary Magdalene, Brighton, tried to get a court order banning noise coming from an electricity power station. The court refused to make an order, on the grounds that, although the noise annoyed the vicar and may have frequently caused irritation and annoyance to the congregation, it didn't stop him holding services in the church, it didn't affect the size of the congregation, and it did not generally distract the attention of ordinary healthy persons. Quite what this says about the state of health (mental, nervous, emotional or otherwise) of the then congregation of SS Mary and Mary Magdalene it's difficult to know.

There is one area where the Control of Pollution Act, 1974, as amended by the Local Government (Planning and Land) Act, 1980, offers a preventative measure. If the local council wishes to control noise from an industrial or manufacturing area for the benefit of local residents whose property borders the area, they may make a noise abatement order. The effect of this is to 'freeze' the level of noise, registering the existing level emanating from each factory, and forbidding any future increase without the council's permission. The idea is to prevent a deterioration of the situation.

55 LIGHT

Some people who live next door to industrial or commercial premises are faced with a problem of extremely bright lights being used to flood the premises at night. These are used for security purposes, to discourage would-be thieves. Unfortunately, these lights may also discourage sleep.

In one case, an elderly resident found it impossible to sleep in her bedroom because of the intensity of light at night coming from the car-park and surroundings of a large supermarket next to her house. She had been to her doctor, who had prescribed sleeping-pills, but was still unable to get a decent night's rest. She then visited the local Environmental Health Office, asking them to intervene.

This is a trickier situation than that for noise. As yet, the case doesn't have an outcome, but the thinking of the local Environmental Health Office is that there may be little they can do to help. It is possible that a magistrate's court would make some award against the supermarket, by way of compensation and in the hope that it might enable the resident to instal thicker, heavier curtains or some other barrier against the light.

A better solution might be for local authorities to think more carefully at the stage when they are considering planning permission, but, doubtless, they are having to weigh inconvenience to a few residents against what they regard as benefit to the whole locality, including employment prospects.

56   STREET NOISE

Although there aren't any rules limiting the hours of bonfires, the Control of Pollution Act, 1974, section 62 (3), does limit the hours during which mobile salespeople can operate loudspeakers to advertise their presence in a neighbourhood. The friendly travelling butcher, baker, candlestick-maker, fishmonger and, most particularly, ice-cream salesperson are permitted to operate a loudspeaker between the hours of noon and 7 p.m. only. and it must be used solely for the purpose of informing members of the public that they are in business to sell their goods from their vehicle, and not to give the entire neighbourhood a concert of electronic twanging. (Dvorák's 'Symphony From the New World', Vaughan Williams's 'Fantasia on Greensleeves', the final movement of Beethoven's 9th Symphony and, somewhat inappropriately, 'I Do Like To Be Beside The Seaside' are all current favourites in Catford.)

If such masterpieces are operated outside the permitted hours, or in such a way as to give reasonable cause for annoyance to you (one bar is more than enough for me, but I doubt that the magistrates would agree), an offence is committed.

If you are really plagued by the above, it might be worth getting hold of a copy of the Department of the Environment's Code of Practice which purports to give guidance to such traders on how to minimize annoyance or disturbance caused by such chimes. After all, it would be nice if someone read it. It's issued under the Control of Pollution Act, 1974, section 71, and it's called *Code of Practice on Noise from Ice-Cream Van Chimes Etc* (DOE, 1982).

There is a similar pamphlet for the guidance of model aircraft enthusiasts: *Code of Practice on Noise from Model Aircraft* (DOE, 1982). Recent developments in the hobby of flying model aircraft may lead to some interesting invasions of privacy – see Chapter 16, Light and Privacy.

9 Animals

In general the law reckons wild animals are free, independent creatures but recognizes three exceptions:
1. If you take or tame a wild animal, you may claim it as your property until it regains its natural liberty. This can be very important in the case of game birds or rabbits kept on what is grandly called a landed estate.
2. You have a right to the ownership of young wild animals born on your land, until they are old enough to run or fly away. This conjures up the wonderful vision of a court solemnly attempting to discover whether some young pigeons, say, are old enough to fly or not, with the court usher throwing them up in the air by way of experiment. Those that plummet to the floor of the court are yours, those that fly desperately round the court have obtained what amounts to their freedom.
3. If you own a garden, you have a right to hunt, take and kill wild animals in it. Our garden in Catford isn't really big enough to hunt anything in, though there is considerable danger of trampling each other to death if we are all in the garden at the same time.

In the case of dead wild animals, they belong to the person on whose land they lie, with the exception of animals from A's land killed on B's land or where a trespasser chases an animal from A's land and kills it on B's land. In both cases, the carcase belongs to the hunter.

This means that, if you have a large estate or any property big enough to contain wild animals, if the animals escape from your land onto somebody's else's, whoever kills them has the right to the carcase. If your neighbour kills them on his or her land, they belong to your neighbour. If a third party kills them on your neighbour's land, they belong to the third party.

You are not liable for any damage to your neighbour's garden or property caused by wild animals from your garden unless you have deliberately and actively over-stocked your garden with them. (This does not include dangerous wild animals. They come under different rules and regulations – see Section 60, Animals – Dangerous.)

Even though the law regards some wild animals, therefore, as having an owner, you may still be permitted to kill them if you have good cause, e.g. they are damaging crops in your garden, but the onus is on the killer to establish the reasonable necessity of his action. In *Hamps v Derby*, in 1948, a farmer shot some of his neighbour's homing pigeons, which were eating his peas. He was sued for trespass to the pigeons. It was held that the farmer had acted unreasonably, as he had not first attempted to shoo the pigeons away. The action for trespass was successful, because the defendant had not shown that he reasonably thought there was no other way of getting rid of the birds.

58   ANIMALS AND POISONS

You commit an offence if you knowingly put in your garden or outbuildings any poison, or fluid or edible matter that has been rendered poisonous, and cause loss or damage to your neighbour by killing or injuring pets or livestock (Protection of Animals Act, 1911). So it's no good leaving that doctored steak by the fence, in the hope that Wotan will shove his greedy face through, gobble it up and expire in mid bark.

There are four exceptions to the above rule:

i. if the poison was placed in your garden to kill insects, vermin, pests etc, in the interests of public health, agriculture or other animals, and you took reasonable precautions;

ii. if you have a licence to poison (sounds like an Agatha Christie, doesn't it);

iii. if you are using poisonous gas to kill rabbits, moles, foxes etc;

iv. if the use of the poison is approved by Government

order, to kill grey squirrels, coypu etc (Animals Act, 1971; The Grey Squirrels (Warfarin) Order, 1973).

59 TRAPS

In general, traps are illegal. It's unlikely, therefore, that a dispute with a neighbour would ever arise over the use of a trap – unless you really have gone over the top in your hatred for next door's Wotan. If your neighbour is using traps, he has to have a licence, the traps have to fall within Ministry of Agriculture specifications, and your neighbour has to inspect them regularly.

60 ANIMALS – DANGEROUS

In the old days, the Common Law very simply divided animals into two categories: *ferae naturae*, which meant fierce by nature, and *mansuetae naturae*, which meant tame by nature. The only problem that arose was deciding which was which. In 1940, for example, it was judicially noticed in *McQuaker v Goddard* that a camel is a creature 'tame by nature', a domestic animal. This was important, because Common Law makes the assumption that domestic animals are not dangerous (some other form of domestic animal must exist in Catford).

The position summed up by Lord Justice Scott: 'In English Law the keeper of a wild animal must keep it at his peril, so that if he lets it out and it causes injury to the person or property of any human being, the keeper or owner of the animal ... is liable in damage for the injury so caused; ... in the case of domestic animals, the presumption of law is to the opposite effect. There the plaintiff has to prove that the defendant was aware of the particular propensity to hurt human beings which ... the plaintiff suffered; unless he proves that knowledge, there is at common law no liability upon the defendant.'

In the case of animals fierce by nature, it was assumed that the owner knew of the dangerous propensities, and his or her liability arose out of that knowledge. It was called 'scienter' liability. Today what consitutes a dangerous animal is defined by the Animal Act, 1971 section 6: 'one which is not commonly domesticated in the British Islands' and ' ... whose fully grown animals normally have such characteristics that they are likely, unless restrained, to cause severe damage or that any damage they may cause is likely to be severe'.

The danger is not limited as coming only from those likely to attack human beings. The law is also concerned about the possible spread of diseases and attacks on property. This last remark is not a joke. It isn't a question of a rhinoceros charging into your new conservatory, or a pet goat eating your garden shed. Property doesn't just mean buildings.

In *Goadway v Becher* in 1951, the appellant owned a chicken farm. One day he saw a dog belonging to the respondent's stepson chasing his chickens. Although the appellant had a gun with him, he did not fire it but warned the respondent that, if he again found the dog worrying chickens, he would shoot it. On the next day (would you believe) he saw the dog among his chickens and killed it. The Wiltshire magistrates convicted him of unlawfully and maliciously killing the dog because, 'He did not exhaust every practicable means of stopping the dog from attacking the fowls.' On appeal, Lord Chief Justice Goddard reversed this decision. 'The question was not whether the appellant took every practicable means of stopping the dog, which had shown by its conduct that it was a fowl worrier ... the question was whether the appellant was acting reasonably in doing what he did.'

It has become more and more fashionable in recent years to keep exotic creatures as pets. Setting aside any moral questions as to whether a back garden in Orpington or Solihull is a suitable habitat for cheetah, chimp, chipmunk or chachalaca, from the safety point of view there is a great deal to be considered. If your neighbour keeps a dangerous wild animal, he or she has to have a licence issued by the local council (Dangerous Wild Animals Act, 1976, section 1). This applies to such creatures as poisonous snakes, alligators (some garden centres see these as a great attraction to the public –

beware if you live next door to a garden centre), apes, monkeys, elephants, tigers, pumas etc. Before granting such a licence, the local council will require a vet's inspection and will have to satisfy themselves that:

1. It is not contrary to the public interest on the grounds of safety or nuisance.

2. The applicant is a suitable person to hold such a licence and is over eighteen years old.

3. The animal will be protected in case of fire or other emergency.

4. All reasonable precautions have been taken to prevent and control the spread of any disease.

5. The animal can take reasonable exercise within the accommodation.

6. The animal's accommodation is escape-proof and adequate in all respects for the number and type of animals to be kept.

This last point brings us to a very important legal principle known as the Rule in *Rylands v Fletcher*, 1868.

61   THE RULE IN *RYLANDS V FLETCHER*

In the 1860s Fletcher employed an independent contractor to construct a reservoir on his land. He didn't know of, and couldn't reasonably have been expected to discover, the existence of disused mine shafts on the site. When the reservoir was filled, Rylands, who owned a coal mine on neighbouring land, found his coal mine was flooded.

The rule that came out of this case was formulated by the judge in the court of first instance (the Court of Exchequer), who said: ' ... the person who for his own purposes brings on his land and collects and keeps there anything likely to do mischief if it escapes, must keep it in at his peril and, if he does not do so, is prima facie answerable for all the damage which is the natural consequences of its escape.'

The rule is important because it is a rule of strict liability. It doesn't require proof of negligence, or lack of care, or wrongful intention on the part of the person being sued for damage caused. Rylands didn't have to show that

Fletcher was negligent or careless or in any way ill-motivated. It was enough that Fletcher had brought something 'likely to cause mischief' onto his land and that it had escaped and caused damage. Since 1868 the limits of the rule have been carefully defined, and there must now also be a 'non-natural' use of the land for the rule to be applicable.

'Things' construed by the courts as likely to cause mischief have included accumulation of water (where not by natural drainage), bulk storage of gas and electricity, deliberate fire, motor vehicles, guns, chemicals, explosives, sewage, vibrations, poisons and projecting poisonous trees. Not included are thistles which spread from one person's property to the next, destructive wild animals, trees and rocks that fall from natural causes, and walls and buildings that collapse during construction. There are also defences against the rule: act of God, damage caused by complainant's own fault, the 'thing' escaped through the actions of a third party, the 'thing' is used without negligence under statutory authority.

You may have noticed that the list of 'things' likely to cause mischief (above) are mainly inanimate objects, but the courts have also found people and animals to be 'things' within the meaning of the rule.

In *Attorney-General v Corke* in 1933, the defendant allowed caravan-dwellers to camp on his land. They escaped (shades of *The Grapes of Wrath*: it was clearly one of *those* camp sites) and committed nuisances on adjacent land. The defendant was held liable under the Rule in *Rylands v Fletcher*, and an injunction was granted to prevent further escapes and nuisance.

The implications are clear regarding responsibility towards your neighbour. You needn't worry about trees falling into his garden or on his house even, so long as you didn't have reason to believe that they might fall. You needn't worry about weed seeds blowing into his garden, not under the Rule in Rylands and Fletcher, though you could be liable in an action for nuisance. The most obvious areas of liability are: bonfires that get out of control, chemicals and poisons from garden spraying, and

dangerous wild animals. (For pets that are dangerous or
out of control, see Sections 63 and 64.) If your neighbour
chooses to keep tarantulas, scorpions, poisonous snakes,
Tasmanian devils etc on his land, he will be liable for any
damage these poor creatures might do.

62   ANIMALS – LIVESTOCK

The Common Law used to make no assumption about the
dangerous propensities of livestock. A complainant had to
prove that the owner, or person responsible, should have
known of the danger. Previous damage or injury usually
sufficed, but in most cases involving animals tame by
nature actions were brought in trespass, nuisance or
negligence, where the animal's docility or ferocity was not
an issue.

Nowadays the Common Law doesn't really apply, and
most cases involving straying livestock (the commonest
cause of neighbour dispute concerning livestock) come
under the provisions of the Animal Act, 1971. (See also
Section 70, Boundaries – General.)

The same Act defines livestock as meaning cattle,
horses, mules, hinnies (offspring of she-asses and stallions
– we don't get a lot of those in Catford), sheep, pigs, goats,
poultry and deer not in a wild state. It further defines
poultry as meaning fowls, turkeys, geese, ducks,
guinea-fowls, pigeons, peacocks and quails. Now you
know what you're dealing with.

For the purposes of the Animal Act, 1971, your
neighbour is a 'keeper' of an animal if he owns the animal
or has it in his possession or is the head of a household
where somebody under sixteen years old owns the animal
or keeps it in his possession. So your neighbour is
responsible for his loathsome son's beasts. Your
neighbour is still liable as keeper even if the wretched
thing has escaped, until someone else owns or possesses
it, but you don't become the keeper of the animal if you
take it into your possession simply to prevent damage or
to return it to its rightful owner.

In the case of trespassing or straying livestock, you have

to prove damage. There is a strict liability imposed on the person in possession of livestock, under the Animal Act, 1971, section 4, where trespassing cattle damage land or property or where others have temporarily to keep the cattle before handing them back to the owner. What you cannot recover is any damages for personal injury, so don't let your neighbour's prize bull tread on your foot.

If you have a large garden and are feeling particularly devil-may-care about relationships with your neighbour, you have the right to sell any straying animals that you detain after fourteen days, unless proceedings are pending for return of the animals or otherwise under section 4. Be careful, you could also be made liable for damage caused by failure adequately to care for or feed the animals. Don't let your neighbour's prize bull die in your possession – prize bulls are very, very expensive.

There are special rules about animals straying onto the highway. As late as 1947 it was held that the occupier of land was under no duty to fence that land to keep his animals from straying onto the highway, and that he wasn't liable for any damage such animals did once they got onto the highway. Now, by virtue of the Animal Act, 1971, section 8 (1), an occupier of land owes a duty of care in respect of his livestock if it strays from his land onto the highway.

When your neighbour chooses to ride his or her horse on the highway, however, the liability is slightly different. All he or she has to do is to exercise reasonable care to discharge the legal duty. If your neighbour plunges out on a Sunday morning on Black Beauty, and the noble beast puts its foot through the door of your car, you have to prove that your neighbour was negligent in his or her control of the animal. It may well be that your neighbour would have a perfectly good legal defence if he or she said that they'd never known Black Beauty to behave like that before. It's a bit like allowing every dog one free bite.

Once the animal has misbehaved once, it has a reputation as far as the law is concerned. In *Aldham v United Dairies (London) Ltd* in 1940, a pedestrian was walking along a pavement and, as she passed a pony attached to a milkcart, it bit her, dragged her down and pawed her with its feet. the pony had been left unattended for half an hour while milk was delivered to a block of flats. The pony had a habit of putting its forefeet on the pavement and (like so many of us) became restive when left unattended. This was a case where a domestic animal was known to be potentially dangerous, and the plaintiff (the pedestrian) won her case.

If your neighbour allows large numbers of livestock to roam all over the local roads, your best bet would probably be under an action for nuisance.

63 PETS – DOGS

In 1987 there were an estimated 12 million pets in British households, but let us attempt to deal with the main problem first – dogs.

Everywhere you go, you find people complaining about noise. It is the single most bitter complaint in all neighbour disputes. The principle cause of noise, in the ears of unhappy neighbours, is not stereo blasters or parties or banging doors or DIY drills and grinders – it is the barking of dogs. Politicians, sociologists and environmentalists are all looking desperately around to see what can be done to achieve some kind of truce between dog-lovers and dog-haters. At the moment they haven't come up with anything beyond vague hints that the dog licence should be increased from the paltry 37p that it's stood at since Victorian times. They have increased the licence fee in Northern Ireland and have used the extra revenue to provide dog wardens and initiate a programme of control – reports suggest that this has been a success.

But, in the meantime, in England, Wales and Scotland, nothing has changed and we all face a steady increase in the number of dogs around. The complaints about dogs fall into five categories: noise, mess, attacks, trespass and damage.

Noise
If you are disturbed by barking, howling, whining or

whimpering dogs, you need to follow the same procedure as that laid down for any other sort of noise (see Chapter 8 – Noise, above). First of all, try talking to your neighbour. Explain what the problem is, describe carefully, politely and in as much detail as you can, what it is that is upsetting you. Not all dog-owners are stupid or bigoted or totally blind and deaf to the shortcomings of their pets. Some may be prepared to listen and make genuine attempts to amend the situation.

If this doesn't work, if all you get are cross words and a sulky 'Come on, Prince, my little darling – we don't have to stay to listen to this nasty man/woman!', try writing a letter, again setting out as reasonably and simply as possible what it is you're complaining about. It's a good idea, if you think a letter from you is unlikely to work, to sound out the local area to see if you can get any support from others. Here you may be agreeably surprised. As in a great many things in life, there are a lot of disgruntled people out there, feeling trampled on but alone. You may find fellow-sufferers jump at the chance to add their names to the letter you wish to write. Your letter then carries far more weight. There is a chance that Prince's owner will stop the noise.

It has to be said, however, that this is only a chance. It's amazing how successfully dog-owners combine trucu-lence with paranoia. Nevertheless, having other people to back you up should help considerably if you seek to call in the local council with their noise-monitoring equipment (see Section 50, Noise – General). One of the categories of statutory nuisance is 'any animal kept in such a place or manner as to be prejudicial to health or a nuisance', but it's no good claiming that the noise of the dogs is getting on your nerves or giving you the shakes. They don't mean that kind of health.

There seems to be some confusion as to whether or not the barking of dogs is enough to constitute a nuisance. In *Galer v Morrissey* in 1955, it was held that the barking of greyhounds wasn't a nuisance, though their smell would have been. In *Coventry City Council v Cartwright* in 1975, however, the Lord Chief Justice said: 'I would have thought for my own part that a noisy animal could as much be prejudicial to health as a smelly animal.' It's nice to know that Lord Chief Justices aren't always wrong, and, indeed, there are those among us who would profoundly agree with the Lord Chief Justice in this case, and this is now the preferred view. It is generally reckoned that noisy dogs do come under the category of statutory nuisance.

Remember, an action in nuisance for noise will take a long time to come to court. Be prepared for a wait of up to a year, which is a long time to suffer Prince's nightly serenade.

Breeding and Boarding Establishments

If you are unlucky enough to live next door to a dog-breeding establishment or boarding kennel, you can try checking that your neighbour has the necessary licence from the local council. In the case of dog-breeding for sale, anyone who keeps more than two breeding bitches has to have a licence under the Breeding of Dogs Act, 1973, section 1 (9). If your neighbour hasn't got a licence, he or she may be fined on summary conviction in a magistrate's court. Only if he or she decides to shut down, however, will this do anything to abate the noise.

In the case of kennels, anyone who keeps a boarding establishment (for any animal) has to have a licence granted by the local council under the Animal Boarding Establishments Act, 1963, section 1. In determining whether or not to grant such a licence, the local council has to satisfy itself that there will be adequate accommodation, food, water, bedding and exercise for the animals and that precautions will be taken against the spread of disease. They don't have to consider the aural comfort of the neighbourhood.

Mess

There is no law that forbids dogs to make mess. This is understandable but, many feel, unsatisfactory. If your neighbour's dog comes into your garden and makes a mess, you may have grounds for an action for trespass. If your neighbour allows dog mess to pile up in his or her own garden, so that the place becomes offensive and/or a health hazard, you may be able to persuade your local council to take action for statutory nuisance under the Public Health Act, 1936. If your neighbour allows his or her dog to mess in the street, you need to know what your local by-laws are regarding this.

To find out what your local by-laws are, you may have to visit your town hall or local Environmental Health Office. It's no good looking hopefully up at the lamp-posts in your street. the odds are that, if notices were displayed there with details of the offence and the fine that could be imposed, local dog-owners will have torn down such notices. They do this wherever such signs appear – in parks, streets and open spaces. There is a kind of simmering anarchy among dog-owners, and they're very touchy when the faults of their fanged friends are indicated.

Attacks

The law distinguishes 'dangerous' and 'ferocious' dogs and regards the latter as more likely to cause harm or injury. It is an offence for any person in the street to 'suffer to be at large' any unmuzzled ferocious dog which causes obstruction, annoyance or danger to residents. It is also an offence to set on or urge any dog (or other animal, for that matter) to attack, worry or put in fear any person or animal. There are several Acts of Parliament that deal with this problem, notably the Town Police Clauses Act, 1847, Public Health Act, 1875, and Local Government Act, 1972.

The distinction between 'dangerous' and 'ferocious' is not clearly drawn. Your neighbour may have a dog that bites small children or postmen, but it could still be classed only as 'dangerous'. If a dog does bite someone, it may well be classed as dangerous, and a magistrate's court may order that it be kept under control. If the biting or attack is serious, of course, the court may order that the dog be put down (Dogs Act, 1871, section 2). Whether your neighbour's dog is allowed its one 'free' bite is a matter for the police to decide.

If you're attacked by your neighbour's dog, and you inform the police, they will probably visit your neighbour to check that the dog is kept under proper control. This will depend to an extent on where the attack took place. If it was in your garden or on the street, this will be regarded as more serious than if it took place on your neighbour's property, where your neighbour might argue that it was protecting that property. Even here, however, the 'common duty of care' of the Occupiers' Liability Act, 1957, would apply (see Section 34, Occupiers' Liability).

The law imposes a duty on a person in charge of any animal to exercise reasonable care. If you can show that your neighbour failed so to do, you have grounds for an action under the law of negligence. Most of the cases that have come before the courts have involved attacks that took place on streets or roads.

You are, of course, at liberty to take any reasonable measures to protect yourself from a dog that attacks you. If you wish to go further, however, note that it is an offence to beat, kick, ill-treat, override, torture, infuriate or terrify any domestic or captive animal.

Guard Dogs

If you or your neighbour keep a guard dog, you must clearly display a notice to that effect at each entrance to your property (Guard Dogs Act, 1975, section 1 [3]1). The Act further stipulates that guard dogs have to be secured so that they cannot roam the premises unless they are under the control of a handler, i.e. a person capable of controlling them.

Trespassing by Dogs

In law, an animal is considered to be as capable of trespass as human beings, but the owner of a domestic cat is not responsible for any consequences of the trespass. So your neighbour's cat may leap over the fence and do what it likes in your garden. What it likes is usually to scrabble in your flower bed, mess and then stroll impudently about. Occasionally, if a tomcat, it likes to yowl – a noise that can be as disturbing as a barking dog but which doesn't happen as often. The difference between cats and dogs is that, if you chuck a brick at the former, they flee and leave you in peace. Dogs don't.

Dog-owners may consider it a great injustice that, whereas cat-owners cannot be sued for any damage or mess done in a neighbour's garden, a trespassing dog does render its owner liable for its trespass if in doing so it causes damage to property, game or livestock (Animals Act, 1971, section 3). If a dog kills or injures livestock, the liability is clear, and it doesn't make any difference how much or how little control the keeper of the dog was exercising. The only defences open to the dog's keeper are if the damage to the livestock was entirely the fault of the owner of the livestock or if the livestock wandered onto land occupied by the dog's owner. In all other circumstances you are permitted to kill any dog that is worrying (or about to worry) livestock on your land if there is no other reasonable means of preventing or ending that worrying.

Note: A wide interpretation is put on the phrase 'injuring livestock'. It can include indirect injury, e.g. a dog barking at foals which then injured themselves, poultry ceasing to lay as a result of shock, or pregnant ewes subsequently aborting. Similarly, the phrase (worrying livestock' can have a variety of meanings – attacking livestock, chasing livestock in such a way as may be reasonably expected to cause injury, or simply being at large in a field or enclosure in which there are sheep. On this last point (the field of sheep), you needn't worry if you are the owner of a dog and it is a police dog, a guide dog, a trained sheep dog, a working gun dog or a pack of hounds, or if you happen to own the sheep as well.

Damage by Dogs
The Animals Act, 1971, does not take away the duty of care owed by dog-owners who take their dogs onto the highway, to take reasonable care to avoid damage to persons or property.

In the case of *Gomberg v Smith* in 1962, the plaintiff's van was damaged when the defendant's St Bernard ran out of a shop. The plaintiff brought a successful action for negligence, because the defendant hadn't exercised his duty to take reasonable care to control a dog on a highway. In what way the dog damaged the car, and whether it had been sipping its own brandy, we are not told.

In general, the law says that if you are attacked by a dog you may shoot it in self-defence. This seems a little sweeping. There's an appreciable difference between a tetchy pekinese and a blood-crazed Irish wolfhound. Also, the assumption that there we all are, walking down Penge High Street or wherever, gun at the ready in case we're attacked by a dog, seems happily somewhat wide of the target. It may not be the same in the country.

If you think your neighbour could really do with a crash course on how to manage his or her dog, or if you'd like to bring basic doggie etiquette to his or her notice, the Canine Defence League (address at end of book) promotes some excellent pamphlets that you could shove through your neighbour's letter-box, from a well-wisher.

64   OTHER PETS

It has already been noted, in the previous section, that, if your garden is plagued by the neighbourhood cats, there is little you can do about it other than throw stones. In fact, probably the best remedy in such a situation would be to get a cat yourself. Cats are very territorially conscious creatures, and the 'home-beat' mog would soon put an end to the depredations of your neighbours' felines.

There are no Acts of Parliament regulating the breeding of cats, hamsters, guinea pigs, budgies, tortoises, gerbils, stick insects etc, but the Animal Boarding Establishments Act, 1963, doesn't cover just dogs, so you may find some protection there if there is a cattery or Holiday Home for Elderly Rats next door.

Otherwise, if you're troubled or inconvenienced by next door's macaws, spider monkeys or plague of locusts, your remedy will lie in an action for nuisance, remembering that one of the categories of statutory nuisance is 'any animal kept in such a place or manner as to be prejudicial to health or a nuisance' (see Section 74, Categories of Statutory Nuisance).

It's worth noting that, under the Wildlife and Countryside Act, 1981, it is an offence to release or allow to escape certain creatures into the wild, among them budgerigars, fat dormice, Mongolian gerbils, Alpine newts, pumpkinseeds (Sun-fish), European pond terrapins and midwife toads.

65 PESTS

We need to look at four aspects of the problem of pests: verminous premises, verminous persons, protection of wildlife and plant pests.

Verminous Premises
What may be considered a pest in one part of the country may have protected status in another. It's not so much a question of the Belgravia/Bermondsey divide as that between Belgravia and Bodmin Moor. For example, under the Pests Act, 1954, section 1, the Minister of Agriculture Fisheries and Food, and the Secretary of State for Wales, were empowered, by virtue of Statutory Instrument, 1969, section 308, to make 'rabbit clearance orders' designating areas as 'rabbit clearance areas' in which all occupiers of land have to take all necessary steps to destroy the wild rabbits on their land, or prevent them from doing damage. Under the Animals Act, 1947, section 100 (2), the Ministry of Agriculture has powers to enforce the order if the occupier was in default. But the order didn't apply to the City of London, the Scilly Isles and the island of Skokholm. It conjures up pictures of the Stock Exchange or the Barbican overrun by little furry bunnies, with Securicor and the Agriculture Minister powerless to intervene.

The Ministry of Agriculture has further powers and is concerned to deal with many creatures it considers pests. You may have a different image of a pest: most householders apply the word to rats, mice and a few insects. The Ministry includes hares, squirrels, deer, foxes and moles and will act to prevent such creatures damaging crops, pasture, animal or human foodstuffs, livestock, trees, hedges, banks etc.

If your neighbour harbours any of these creatures on his or her land, and any of the above dangers exists, you may be able to persuade the Ministry to serve notice on your neighbour, requiring him or her either to destroy them or to take steps to prevent their escape from the land, i.e. similar to the requirements under the Rabbit Clearance Order, above.

However, for most of us the chief concern is rats and mice. Of course, you don't have verminous premises, but if your neighbour does, you should turn again to your local council and the Public Health Act, 1936. The local council will serve notice on your neighbour as owner or occupier, if they are satisfied that the premises are: (a) in such a filthy or unwholesome condition as to be prejudicial to health, or (b) verminous.

In fact, the local council has a duty to keep their area free from vermin as far as is practicable, by the Prevention of Damage by Pests Act, 1949, section 2 (1). Similarly, the occupier of land must at once give written notice to the local council if he or she knows that rats or mice are resident in 'substantial numbers'. One of the problems is that nobody knows what is meant by 'substantial numbers' – clearly, what the Pied Piper faced in Hamelin would qualify, but Samuel Whiskers and his family might not. If you are worried by the appearance of rats or mice in your neighbourhood, or traces of where they have been, it's a simple matter to phone your local council (Environmental Health Office) and ask them to take the necessary steps to remove the rodents.

Again, the procedure is similar to that for rabbit clearance. The occupier is required to take reasonable steps to destroy the rats and mice and to keep the land free from the same. If he or she doesn't, the council will probably step in and do the work themselves, subsequently recovering their reasonable expenses.

The only exception to the above is if your neighbour can

show that the horticultural use of his or her garden was for the purposes of a trade or business, i.e. comes under the heading of agricultural land for the purposes of the Prevention of Damage by Pests Act, 1949.

The term 'vermin' includes insects and parasites, and their eggs, larvae and pupae. This means that desperate measures may have to be taken to rid your neighbour's premises (or your own) of the subject of the complaint. If your neighbour's house is discovered to be verminous, the council may require that it is cleansed, disinfected and whitewashed, has the wallpaper removed or has anything else done to render it pure and wholesome. Your neighbour may then be required to paint, repaper or distemper his house, shop or office (they didn't know about vinyl silk at the time of the Act). If your neighbour has to leave the premises during fumigation, the council must provide free alternative accommodation.

In general, most complaints about verminous premises come from people who live next door to empty property, especially property falling into disrepair or decay. If you are in this situation, contact your local council and get them to trace the owner, as this is sometimes a difficult business. It may be that the empty property is registered in the name of a holding company which is part of a larger conglomerate, which in turn is owned by a multinational, and everyone is waiting to develop the site once several other adjoining properties have fallen into their hands. Let the council do this tracking-down – it can be time-consuming, costly and tricky.

The good old Public Health Act of 1936 also makes provision for the removal of verminous articles from premises or for their destruction, disinfecting, cleansing or purifying – there's a faintly biblical air about those last two terms. The local council must first receive certification from its officers that the article in question

(a) is in so filthy a condition as to render its cleanliness, purification or destruction necessary in order to prevent injury or danger of injury to the health of any person in the premises, or

(b) is verminous or, by reason of its having been used

by or having been in contact with any verminous person, is likely to be verminous.

If you are racking your brain to think of what could constitute such a verminous article, you're very lucky and clearly live in a jolly good, clean, posh area. One glance at the decaying old motor cars that people preserve as derelict shrines in their back gardens round here, and I'm only too certain what is meant by verminous articles.

You may also wish to consider (or not, if you are of squeamish disposition) the Rag Flock and Other Filling Materials Act, 1951, together with the Rag Flock and Other Filling Materials Regulations, 1971. Since such materials are seen by vermin as the nearest thing to a five-star hotel, premises using such materials for business purposes have to be registered or licensed, and anyone found using unclean flock or filling materials is guilty of an offence. When I gaze out of the window at the rotting old mattresses that are propped against the decaying old cars, I wonder if I shouldn't phone the council right now.

Verminous Persons (with apologies for inclusion under 'Animals')

The Public Health Act, 1936, says, with old-fashioned simplicity, that verminous persons may, on application, by consent or by order of the magistrate's court, be removed to a cleansing station. There the necessary measures may be taken to free such a person and his clothing from vermin. Females may be cleansed only by a registered medical practitioner or by a woman authorized by the District Community Physician.

It all smacks of *Dr Finlay's Casebook*, wooden-backed scrubbing brushes, carbolic soap and brown-glazed municipal tiles. You would need to be a brave person, or one at the end of all patience, to subject your neighbour to such a process. It would seem to remove all hope of amicable relations.

Protection of Wildlife

If you live in the country and are of a huntin', shootin', snarin' or trappin' disposition, it's a good idea to be aware of the provisions of the Wildlife and Countryside Act, 1981. The regulations concerning wild birds are complicated, ranging from those that are regarded as game and are protected only during the close season but can only be killed by persons authorized by the owner of the land on which they are found, to those birds that are protected at all times and to those that may be slaughtered by any authorized person at any time.

The simplest approach would seem to be to list wild birds which may be killed or taken in the garden by authorized persons at any time (except Sundays and Christmas Day in Scotland). This does also apply to the Scilly Isles and the City of London, though not the island of Skokholm, which is a bird sanctuary.

The birds that you or your neighbour are free to blast away at are: crow, collared dove, great black-backed gull, lesser black-backed gull, herring gull, jackdaw, jay, magpie, feral pigeon, rook, house sparrow, starling and woodpigeon. Anyone who wishes to rid station concourses of the poor crippled, mildewed, half-blind, disease-ridden pigeons currently infesting them has all my support.

You may think there aren't any protected species of wildlife in any of the gardens in your neighbourhood, but the list includes bats, badgers, dormice, hedgehogs, shrews, red squirrels, buntings, owls, tits and warblers.

Also, be warned that neither you nor your neighbour may use certain rodenticides (awful word). Even pests must perish without suffering. The use of the colourful yellow phosphorus and red squill is illegal, as is strychnine for the destruction of moles. Think how hard murdering would be these days for the likes of Dr Crippen. A hundred years ago, this land was full of poisoners, obtaining their supplies by pretending they were for the destruction of rats, moles etc. Now all they'd get would be some wholesome organic remedy which would probably ensure a long and healthy future for Mrs Crippen and her ilk. Life can be very hard.

10   Trees and Plants

If your neighbour's trees, shrubs or bushes overhang your property, you have the right to lop any overhanging branches at the point where they cross the boundary between your neighbour's garden and your own. Some authorities then suggest that all you have to do is throw the offending limbs back over the fence. Others put it more genteelly, saying you should hand them back, including any fruit attached to them. This seems more likely to lead to good relations, but perhaps the first and best thing to do would be to talk it over with your neighbour. Maybe he or she is in a better position to prune the branches: certainly there is then no fear of reprisals on the grounds that you didn't exercise reasonable care in the way you lopped – some plants or trees are delicate creatures whose limbs must be amputated with caution and sensitivity.

Note: Sometimes overhanging branches may interfere with a right of way or light. See Chapter 16.

We have already seen in the section on trespass that, if the roots of trees spread under a fence, hedge or wall and cause damage to a neighbour's building, the occupier of the property in which the trees stand may be liable to pay compensation for the damage and that it's no defence to say that the trees were in the garden before you bought the property. The only defence here might be if you could show that your neighbour built his house or other edifice in a silly position.

You or your neighbour, therefore, have the right to dig down and prune any roots that sidle under the boundary between your properties. Again, it might be a good idea to discuss any such action with your neighbour before beginning operations.

In *Butler v Standard Telephone* in 1940, it was held that there was a right to recover for damage done to the plaintiff's property by popular roots which drained a great deal of water from the plaintiff's land. The plaintiff's house bordered a sports ground on which a row of poplars had been planted, three feet only from the boundary fence.

You are expected to know this, as you cannot plead ignorance of the law as a defence. It is also no defence that any damage caused was purely the result of natural growth of the tree in question. You need to keep an eye on any trees or shrubs in your garden, therefore, and to be prepared to take remedial action where necessary.

Dangerous Trees
'Dangerous' here refers to species (yew trees on land adjoining land where livestock graze), condition or situation.

If you have a tree overhanging a highway, you may be liable for any damage it causes if you have actual or constructive knowledge that it was a hazard to traffic. 'Constructive knowledge' simply means that you ought to have known. You need to take this into consideration if you have a tree that interferes with your neighbour's vision and endangers his safe exit from his property onto the highway. the liability is strictly to do with a continuing state, not to any sudden intervening action by a third party or trespasser, or by some other natural happening of which you were aware, such as subsidence.

Many streets (usually called 'Avenue' or 'Crescent') in the outer suburbs of the large cities in Britain have grass verges between the pavement and the highway, and these verges are sometimes cultivated by the owners or occupiers of the houses in the street. If you wish to plant trees in such a verge, the Highways Act, 1980, states that you must first obtain a licence from the highway authority. To plant trees or shrubs without this licence is an offence. Even if you get a licence and plant your tree, it will be a term of the licence that you indemnify the highway authority for any damage, injury or loss arising out of the existence of the tree. Not only that: it is possible that the licence may be revoked if the tree subsequently becomes a danger, and in this case you will almost certainly be charged for any costs incurred by the highway authority in removing the tree. .

All of which suggests that, although it is a wonderful and good thing to plant a tree, you need to consider carefully before deciding where to do so.

If there is a tree in a dangerous condition in your garden, you can call the district council to deal with it. In the London area, this means calling your borough council; in the City of London (not abounding in trees, dangerous or otherwise), it means calling the Common Council for the City of London. You then ask them to make the tree safe. If they consider that the condition of the tree presents a danger to person or property, they will almost certainly fell it, and just as certainly seek to recover their felling expenses from you under the Local Government Act, 1976, sections 23 (1) and 44 (1). Better such expense than that your tree does some dreadful damage to your neighbour's person, house, garden, family etc. Should your dangerous tree fall into your neighbour's garden and demolish his or her greenhouse, pet labrador or favourite uncle, you will, of course, be liable in negligence for any such damage or injury, and you won't have done neighbourly relations any good.

If the dangerous tree is in your neighbour's garden, you can sneak on him to the same district or borough council. Having inspected the tree of which you are complaining, the council will inform your neighbour, if they think your diagnosis is correct, and require him to take such action as their notice will describe to make the tree safe.

Your neighbour has the right to appeal within twenty-one days on certain limited grounds – that he isn't the owner or occupier of the land on which the tree stands (not much chance there), or that the tree isn't likely to cause damage to persons or property, or that the job could be done more cheaply than the council suggest. If such a notice is served on you as a result of your neighbour's initiative, it's probably best to consult a solicitor but not to brood too much on how to get revenge on your neighbour for being such a dreadful sneak.

Trees and Preservation Orders
Should you or your neighbour possess a tree that is subject to a preservation order, certain complications ensue.

In the first place, the owner of such a tree must strive to do all that is possible to keep the tree alive and in good condition. One couple bought a property that had a fine tree complete with preservation order in the back garden. It was a new house, part of a new development. The builders had levelled the back garden and in doing so had piled up the earth a couple of metres round the base of the trunk of the tree. After a little while, the tree showed signs of ill health. Experts were called in who pronounced that the tree would die if the earth wasn't removed and the original expanse of trunk exposed. The couple now have a two-metre-deep crater all around their tree, imparting an odd look to their back garden and constituting a dangerous hazard to their young children and to any casual visitor.

People can become very emotionally involved with trees. Many people are horrified when a fine tree is felled, but there is usually nothing they can do about it. Your neighbour is entitled to cut down trees or plant trees on his or her own property with impunity, opening up a hideous view where once there was a fine prospect, or denying you the sight of a beautiful landscape that you have enjoyed for decades. The only exception to this is where a Tree Preservation Order is in force. These orders are made by the local planning authority, which is most commonly the local district council, under the Town and Country Planning Act, 1971. Such an order prohibits the cutting-down, topping, lopping or uprooting of, or wilful damage to or wilful destruction of a tree or trees, except with the district council's consent. This is one occasion where you cannot prune overhanging branches and hand or throw them back to your neighbour.

If you have such a tree in your garden, you should have

been informed of this during the legal negotiations that took place when you bought the property. It seems sensible to check that your neighbour is aware of the situation if the tree is near his garden or, especially, if any branches overhang it. You can't expect your neighbour to treat the tree with respect if he or she is unaware of the preservation order. Similarly, if you move into a house where there is a protected tree next door, it's reasonable to expect your neighbour to inform you of that fact. A great many neighbour disputes could be avoided or, at least, minimized by such basic foresight and communication.

There are exceptions to these rules. You or your neighbour may cut down, lop or top a tree subject to a preservation order if:

(a) the local planning authority consent to the action, or

(b) the action is immediately required for the purpose of carrying out development authorized by a planning permission, or

(c) the tree is a fruit tree cultivated for fruit production and 'growing or standing on land comprised in an orchard or garden', Town and Country Planning (Tree Preservation Order) Regulations, 1969.

You may also cut down, lop or top a tree under a preservation order if it is dead, dangerous or dying, or if such action is necessary for the abatement or prevention of nuisance, actionable in law.

Conservation Areas
Some areas are designated conservation areas – the idea here is to preserve the character of a neighbourhood and its style. If you and your neighbour live in such an area, there are restrictions on any building development, repairs and renovations, and, to a degree, all trees in the area are protected. In conservation areas it is an offence, punishable by 'substantial' fine, to cut down, lop, top, uproot or wilfully damage or destroy any trees unless you previously get the consent of the local district council (in London, this means the borough council), or give them at least six weeks notice by dropping a note in to them

stating what you intend to do, or send such a note by recorded delivery.

Again, there are exceptions to this. You can cut down, uproot, lop or top any tree that is dead, dying or dangerous or to prevent or abate a nuisance. You can cut down, uproot, lop or top any tree having a diameter not exceeding 75mm (which is very small – under three inches), or not exceeding 100mm (just under four inches) where this is necessary to improve the growth of other trees. Without these exceptions it is possible that anyone living in a conservation area would eventually disappear into an impenetrable forest.

67 PLANT PESTS

If your neighbour is a keen gardener, you are in luck. Your own plot won't be invaded by weed seeds or suckers from the pernicious ground elder or bindweed. Instead, you will enjoy the benefit of fragrances wafting over the fence from his or her blooms, and maybe the odd windfall from overhanging fruit trees. Be grateful you have such a neighbour.

If, on the other hand, your neighbour's garden is a wilderness, you may have grounds for complaint if you can identify certain prohibited species of weed growing therein.

The plants to look out for are spear thistle, creeping or field thistle, curled dock, broad-leaved dock and ragwort. If these are growing next door, the Minister of Agriculture or his minions is empowered by the Weeds Act, 1959, to serve notice, requiring your neighbour to prevent them spreading. If your neighbour fails to comply with the notice, he or she may be prosecuted and fined. The Minister also has powers to carry out the works in default, though it's unlikely he personally will nip down to attend to the matter.

11   Drains and Mains

Blocks of flats always share drains. Semi-detached and terrace houses usually share drains. Detached houses sometimes share drains. It is common for gas, water and electricity supplies to be brought through one person's property to reach another's. The person whose supply this is has no automatic rights over the other's property, but a special sort of legal right called an easement.

An easement is a privilege exercisable by you over your neighbour, compelling your neighbour to do, or refrain from doing, something on his own land, or to allow you to do something on your own land. This is where you are what is known as the dominant owner, and your land is the dominant tenement, and your neighbour is the servient owner, and his land is the servient tenement. If the easement attaches to your neighbour's land, the positions are reversed. Easements are generally regarded as 'privileges without profit' and do not belong to a person but belong (attach) to a piece of land or property.

Entitlement to an easement may exist either by grant, in the deeds of the property, or by what is known legally as 'long unchallenged use'. The process of acquisition of an easement over another's land by uninterrupted (and unchallenged) use is called prescription. In practice, under the Prescription Act, 1832, most easements may be acquired by twenty years usage (extended to forty years if the servient owner – the person over whose land the easement is to be gained – is a child or person of unsound mind). Forty years establishes an absolute right.

In most modern housing estates, when the plots are sold for the first time, the easements needed by one plot over another will be clearly specified in the conveyance or transfer to the first purchaser – you will know where you and your property stand. The same is true in the case of leasehold flats, where the lease should specify the owner's rights.

Any book which sought to give a detailed account of the laws and regulations concerning drains and drainage would run to several hundred pages. Suffice it to say here that, if all is going well with your drains, there's nothing to worry about. It's only when things go wrong that trouble may flare up between you and your neighbour, whether you have a shared or common drain or if your house drains separately into, say, a septic tank in an adjoining field.

The right to run a pipe through your neighbour's property and to make use of it carries with it the right to enter your neighbour's property to repair that pipe if necessary. It's advisable to ask your neighbour first, or at least give notice, and you are, of course, responsible for any damage you cause.

Beyond this, your rights will depend on the system of drains and sewers that serves your property – in particular, on whether you are making use of public or private sewers. A public sewer is one that is the responsibility of the water authority : a private sewer is one that isn't. Whether you have a public or private sewer will depend on several factors, among them where you live, what sort of dwelling you have (flat or house), how old your dwelling is etc. Your local town hall should have drainage plans for your area and should be able to tell you what your own situation is. Generally speaking, you are responsible for your drainage system until it reaches a common drain, the main sewer. If you live on a modern estate, you should check whether or not you have a continuing maintenance commitment, as many new estates are not served by a public sewer.

The Public Health Act, 1936, with touching simplicity, gives you the right as owner or occupier to connect your drain or private sewer to a public sewer, at your expense, provided that, where both foul and surface water sewers are available, you don't confuse the two and connect the wrong pipes. You are even entitled to dig up a stretch of road to lay or maintain such drains, after giving the council notice.

Repairs
Be careful over repairs. There is often doubt as to who is responsible for the upkeep of shared services. Sometimes the deeds to property state who has to pay; sometimes there is legislation. Often, however, there is nothing in writing, and you would be very unwise to make any assumptions where this is the case. It may seem fair and logical that everyone who uses a common drain contributes to the cost of repair, but you may find that your neighbours don't agree. If you go ahead and do the repairs or hire someone to do them for you, without getting prior agreement from these other users, you may well end up having to pay the entire bill. If you have any doubts, therefore, get your neighbours to agree to pay their shares first – before you have the work done.

Cesspits
In many rural areas cesspits are still in use, though their upkeep can be expensive and they are prone to backfire in the most unpleasant manner if something goes wrong or the country suffers a period of freak weather. Cesspits are often shared between two or more properties. Where this is so, the deeds or other documents relating to the properties should indicate who is responsible for bearing the cost of repairs, and in what proportion. If the cesspit needs attention, check first with your neighbours about sharing the cost of repair. It's another reason for trying to maintain reasonable relations with neighbours in the country.

It may be that your house has a cesspit and that you subsequently have a chance of joining up to a main sewer. If this necessitates running a pipe through your neighbour's property, he or she can object. You can insist on driving a pipe through his or her property only if you (or a predecessor as owner of your house) reserved the right to do so. It may be best here to resort to bribery, offering your neighbour money for permission to run a pipe over his property, since ultimately joining up to the main sewer may well increase the value of your own house. don't embark on this campaign of bribery without first consulting a solicitor. If your neighbour refuses even to be bribed, you can always hope that the cesspit blows back in his direction and thereby makes him change his mind.

Surface Water Drainage

Increasingly, people like to 'improve' their property. Such improvements take many forms: stone cladding, pebble-dashing, replacement windows, extensions, patios, pergolas, ponds. Not everyone realizes that most of these improvements are likely to effect the natural drainage system of the land on which their house stands.

The simplest way to explain this is probably to point out what happens if you pile earth up against the wall of your house. If that earth is above the level of a damp proof course, eventually damp will seep into the wall against which the earth lies.

Similarly, building a patio may result in the ground level of the patio area being raised, with corresponding changes to the surface drainage of the land.

It may be that your neighbour has carried out improvements to his property which affect this surface drainage in such a way that your property suffers – a building extension could result in a blocked drain, for example. If this is the case, you may have a remedy in Common Law or statutory nuisance, especially since it is presumed that uncontrolled water causes damage whether dripping from a projecting roof or flooding through a hedge. In an action for Common Law nuisance you may seek an injunction directing your neighbour to cease perpetrating the nuisance (which is probably what you would most want here) or you may seek damages. If the matter passes to the local council as being a statutory nuisance under the Public Health Act, 1936, the council may require your neighbour to instal proper drainage.

Much of this may well serve your neighbour right, since the construction or alteration of any drains or sewers requires the prior approval of the local council.

Note: Neither you nor your neighbour may empty into any drain, or public or private sewer:

(a) matter likely to injure the sewer or drain or interfere with the flow or affect prejudicially the treatment and disposal of its contents, or

(b) chemical refuse, steam or liquid above 43°C or 110°F, if it is dangerous, prejudicial to health or a nuisance, or

(c) petrol, motor oil or carbide of calcium.

Carbide of calcium is a substance that was used in car and bicycle lamps before more sophisticated methods were developed. When mixed with water, it gives off methane gas. If you were to empty carbide of calcium down your local drain, therefore, it's likely that you would become very unpopular with your entire neighbourhood, especially on a warm day.

And be careful what you throw into any stream, river or watercourse. You can be fined for throwing or depositing any ash, cinders, bricks, stone, dust, filth or rubbish. The last-named is hopefully a catch-all category: what people mostly hurl into streams and watercourses round Catford is old supermarket trolleys.

69   MAINS

The position regarding the installation and upkeep of drains is similar to that for supplies of gas, water and electricity. If these are brought to your home across, over or through your neighbour's property, you have an easement with which your neighbour must not interfere, and you, or more probably officials from the relevant authority, have a right to enter your neighbour's property to make any necessary repairs.

Electricity

Although not everyone in Britain has electricity, we all have a right to a regular and efficient supply of it (Electricity Act, 1957). If you have no electricity through no fault of your own, e.g. you haven't been disconnected for failure to pay for a previous supply, you and any five owners or occupiers along your street may requisition a supply by serving notice on your local Electricity Board under the Electric Lighting (Clauses) Act, 1899 – a situation where it would obviously pay to be on good terms with your neighbours.

The Electricity Board is responsible for all lines and cables up to and including your own meter, so if anything happens to the supply passing over or through your neighbour's property, that is a problem for the Board, not for you. Your neighbour cannot object to any of the main services crossing his land, though the various boards may seek his or her consent before installing them. In the background are the heavy guns of compulsory powers.

Gas

As for electricity, you have a right to a continued supply of gas, unless you haven't been paying your bills or there is a safety problem (Gas Safety Regulations, 1972). The supply and maintenance of all mains and service pipes up to and including the meter are the responsibility of British Gas; from thereon it's yours.

Gas services are less likely than water or electricity to cross your neighbour's land but, where they do, the position is the same as for electricity.

Water

The Water Act, 1973, imposes a duty on the various water authorities to supply water within their areas, and on local councils to check the sufficiency and wholesomeness of that water. Again, as for electricity and gas, you have the right to demand a supply of water adequate for the average domestic purpose. This means drinking, washing, cooking and sanitary purposes – it may not include your jacuzzi or heated indoor swimming-pool.

Once again there is a division between the pipes and equipment that are the responsibility of the Water Authority, and those that are your responsibility. The Water Authority is responsible for pipes and fittings from the main up to and including the stop cock which is situated under the pavement on the boundary of your property. The pipe that runs from the main to this stop cock is called the communication pipe. From here on, it is your responsibility and is called the supply pipe. It seems unlikely that you and your neighbour should ever fall out over a problem arising from this supply pipe since it will be only on your property.

Telephones

You or your neighbour cannot object to telephone wires going over your property, nor can you bring an action for trespass of air space. It is possible, however, that, if British Telecom or one of its rivals needs to stick a telegraph pole in your garden or on your land, you will get either a lump sum compensation or a small payment each year. But don't ever take umbrage and hack the pole down – it will be very costly. It is also possible that a telephone company might obtain an order for trees to be lopped or felled if they reached such a height that they caused interference to telephone wires.

12   Gardens

If you own the freehold of your garden, you have rights to airspace above it – to a height which is necessary for the full use of the land (which presumably means as high as trees, runner beans or shuttlecocks are likely to go). You cannot, however, do anything about civil or military aircraft or, as we have just seen, telegraph wires or pylons.

You also have rights to the materials beneath your garden to the very centre of the earth, except for gold, silver, oil and natural gas (which belong to the Crown) and coal and associated minerals (which belong to British Coal). In our garden, the sub-strata consist of broken lumps of concrete, the odd half brick, the decomposing remains of old woollies, bits of washing-machine motor and loads of thick, sticky, yellow clay, to all of which Her

Majesty and British Coal would be very welcome. If you are luckier and have a large garden on deposits of gravel or silver sand, these subterranean rights could be valuable.

The importance of this is that, if your neighbour tunnels under your garden, he is committing a trespass.

Gardens and Common Law Nuisance
Your neighbour may be engaged in some totally lawful activity in his garden but can still commit a nuisance if the consequences of his act are not confined to his own land but extend to the land of others by:

(a) causing an encroachment on his neighbour's land; or

(b) causing physical damage to his neighbour's land or buildings, works or vegetation on it; or

(c) unduly interfering with his neighbour in the comfortable and convenient enjoyment of his land.

As we have already seen in Chapter 10, Trees and Plants, an example of (a) would be where trees overhang or roots grow under a neighbour's land. It would also occur where a gutter, projecting roof or overflow pipe caused water to flow over a neighbour's land.

An example of (b) is where someone allows a drain on his or her land to become blocked or makes a concrete drive or path, as a result of which water flows from that person's land onto a neighbour's (see Section 68, Drains). It would also occur if noxious fumes caused damage to a neighbour's trees, fruit or plants.

Examples of (c) are where offensive smells, smoke, noise or vibrations invade a neighbour's land (see Sections 43, Air Pollution – Bonfires, Section 46, Odours and Section 50, Noise – General).

(a) and (b) are not too hard to prove. You need simply to show that your neighbour committed the act and that you suffered the consequent damage. There is likely to be solid evidence. You don't have to prove any malice afore-thought – though there may be plenty afterwards. It's the third category that's the commonest and the hardest to prove, since it's a question of degree whether or not the 'interference with comfort or convenience' is sufficiently serious to constitute a nuisance.

Gardens and By-Laws

Many by-laws affect gardens and gardeners, allotments and allotment holders. Since by-laws vary from area to area, it's a good idea to visit your local council offices to find out details for your own locality. Councils are obliged to make free access to by-laws at all reasonable hours, and you can obtain copies on payment of the appropriate fee.

It really is worth doing, since many districts have by-laws concerning the keeping of noisy animals, for example. Usually the terms of such a by-law are that no person may keep a noisy animal in a house, building or garden if it causes serious nuisance to residents in a neighbourhood. If there is such a by-law in your area, all you have to do is to get two other householders, living within hearing of the animal, to join you in signing a notice to be served on the offender – the animal's owner, not the animal. If the nuisance continues after a fortnight from the date of the serving of the notice, prosecution can follow, for a crime has been committed!

Rented Gardens

Unless there is something in a lease that says otherwise, you have the same rights as a tenant of a rented garden as an owner-occupier has in his or her freehold garden. Rather than having fewer rights, it's possible that the lease or tenancy agreement imposes certain duties on you, concerning good upkeep of the garden, regularly mowing the grass, keeping beds free from weeds, maintaining paths and drives etc. There may also be clauses about not cutting down trees or replacing dead fruit or ornamental trees and bushes, especially in a lease of some long duration.

Note: The law covering what happens if you bring anything into your garden that is 'likely to do mischief if it escapes' is covered in Section 61, The Rule in Rylands and Fletcher.

13   Boundaries, Walls and Fences

'*Nam tua res agitur, paries cum proximus ardet,*' wrote Horace in his *Epistles*. Roughly translated, this means, 'When your neighbour's wall is on fire, it becomes your business.' Discounting the fact that is seems jolly difficult to set fire to a wall, maybe Horace was on to something. Two thousand years later, Robert Frost wrote, in 'Mending a Wall', 'Good fences make good neighbours.' Certainly bad fences or no fences at all often make extremely bad neighbours.

And yet there is no legal rule that a boundary must be fenced, nor, even if it is known that a collapsing fence belongs to you, is there any obligation to repair it. This is true even if the previous owner of your property covenanted with your neighbour to build and maintain a dividing fence. That covenant is not enforceable against you. Unless there is specific ruling to the contrary in the deeds of your property, you may happily let wall, hedge or fence collapse, so long as it collapses onto your garden and not your neighbour's, and so long as you do not have any ferocious animals or livestock or there is no potentially dangerous fall between the level of your property and your neighbour's, or your property and the street.

Whose Fence is it Anyway?
The surest way of knowing whether any wall, fence or hedge belongs to you or your neighbour is to examine the deeds of your property. Often these contain a small plan which indicates who owns which fence. If there is no indication in the deeds, generally speaking a simple presumption is made: the wall or fence belongs to, and is the responsibility of, the person on whose side are to be

found the supporting posts or brick pillars.

The logic behind this is that these posts and pillars protrude from the line of the fence. It we were to locate them on our neighbour's side, the general line of the wall or fence would have to be several inches into our garden, since otherwise the posts and pillars would be located in our neighbour's garden and we should be committing a trespass. Nobody wants to give up even a few inches of the width or length of their garden, therefore we site the posts and pillars on our side of the fence or wall. Sadly, logic based on greed is often right.

Where there is a hedge, matters are more complicated. It's not difficult if there is a ditch as well as a hedge, because a similar presumption to that relating to walls and fences is made. The hedge and the ditch belong to the person on the opposite side of the hedge from the ditch. The brilliant legal reasoning behind this is that, when you dug the ditch, you piled the earth on your own property, so as not to commit a trespass, and then planted the earth with hedging, so that it would not slip back into the ditch.

If there isn't a ditch, or if there are ditches both sides of the hedge or if some smart alec has built a wall without supporting pillars, you may have to rely on the suspect memory and rambling verbosity of the oldest inhabitant of the village – never a happy state of affairs.

What Sort of Boundary and How High?

There are some situations in which you may not be allowed to fence. Many new estates have restrictions in the deeds against fencing at the front of property, where the design has been of an open-plan nature or where an initial restriction was placed on the developer when planning permission was first given.

Normally, however, the rule is that you may not build a fence more than one metre high at the front of your property or more than two metres high at the rear, without getting special planning permission. This is why prefabricated fencing units come in these heights, apart from the fact that you would need the strength of Superman to pick up a fencing panel more than two metres high, and erecting a fence on all but the calmest of days would be well nigh impossible.

It would be very unusual for there to be any restrictions as to what sort of wooden fence you were permitted to erect – larch lap, close boarded, blockboard etc. Correspondingly, you can't object to what sort of fence or wall your neighbour builds. Nor can you object if he or she chooses rather to plant a hedge and the blessed thing grows well above two metres high. If your neighbour chooses to play the Sleeping Macho (Beauty) and surrounds himself (herself) with an impenetrable hedge of thorns, there is nothing you can do about it. There are no restrictions on the height of hedges.

Many people are romantically inclined towards the idea of a walled garden. Suppose your garden is bordered by a wall belonging to your neighbour, and you have grown exotic fruit trees against it. Every summer and autumn you proudly pluck figs, apricots, quince and peaches, showing off like mad to your visitors. Suppose further, one dreadful day your neighbour chooses to demolish the wall and stick a grotty fence in its place, or, worse, nothing – or, worst of all, plants a *Leylandii* hedge. Provided he or she has not in any way damaged your fruit trees, there is nothing you can do about it, save raising a protest against any subsequent trespassing by branch or root from the *Leylandii*. They may suck the nutrients from the soil, they may block the light from your own trees – so long as they are planted on your neighbour's side of the boundary there is nothing you can do. The only way to avoid such a situation is to make sure you buy a property where *you* own the south- or west-facing wall.

Mysterious Moving Boundaries
Occasionally strange things happen to fences, especially when they are being repaired. They move. It's usually only a question of a centimetre or two, but nearly always at the expense of the non-repairer's property. If you should so suffer, take steps immediately to remedy the situation.

You have at least three ways of going about it. firstly,

Law and Your Neighbours

since your neighbour has committed a trespass, you are entitled to pull the offending fence down and hand it back to your neighbour. Secondly, you can get a court order requiring him to pull it down and either take it away or re-erect it in the right place. Thirdly, you may apply for an order for damages to cover any money loss you have suffered. This last doesn't really seem a very good remedy. You are dealing here with land, a commodity that is rising in value by some twenty per cent per year these days. It would be hard to negotiate a money payment that could adequately take this into account.

The other time when a fence may move is during the period when you are buying the property, especially if it is empty during the conveyance. A few years ago, my sister-in-law bought a cottage in the Fens. When she moved in, she was told by people in the village that the path to the side of her cottage was rightfully hers but that some years ago the couple who lived in her neighbouring bungalow had moved the fence so that the path appeared to be theirs. The properties shared the use of the path, but it was a question of who owned the path and who had merely a right of way over it.

It isn't pleasant to have to start neighbourly communication with a complaint, especially when the complaint is of a serious nature, amounting to theft of land. In the old days, in the far West, people were hanged for less. But the Fens lie on the eastern side of Britain, and it wasn't possible for my sister-in-law to raise a posse and initiate a 'necktie party'. She did, however, mention the matter to her neighbour, who denied there had been any such change of boundary. Other locals, no doubt impressed by the sudden arrival in the village of my sophisticated sister-in-law from the Big City, urged her to pursue a claim against the land barons of the little bungalow. She decided to take no action but to treat the path as though she now had the right of way over it.

Faced with such a situation, there are things that you can and should do. In the first place, it might be worthwhile contacting the vendor of your house, checking where the boundaries of the property lie.

Secondly, it's advisable to contact a solicitor and ask for a letter to be sent to your neighbour, explaining the situation. The problem is that, if you do nothing, after twelve years the non-disputed piece of land does become your neighbour's. As Trevor Aldridge says in his book *Homes*, it's one case where possession becomes ten points of the law. This is so even if the deeds to the property show otherwise. Usage overrules the evidence of the deeds.

The reasoning behind this is that the law feels that all legal quarrels must have some kind of time limit put on them. After twelve years there can be no more legal argument – the new line of the fence is held to be correct. The law, sadly, can do nothing about the ill will and resentment that may last until the grave.

71 HEDGES, WALLS AND FENCES THAT BORDER ROADS

Just as there is no obligation on you to build or maintain any fences or walls between your property and your neighbour's, so there is no need to build wall or fence between your property and the road.

Not surprisingly, the Highways Act, 1980, makes it an offence to build a fence or wall in a road. It takes all sorts to make a world, admittedly, but you'd have to be a very special person to nip out in the middle of the night and lay a few courses of bricks across your street. Only someone for whom the shattering of car headlamps and the crumpling of radiators meant a great deal would seem to be capable of such an act.

It is also an offence to plant a tree or shrub in, or within five metres of the centre of a road. Though it might add considerably to the ambiance of your neighbourhood to have a spreading chestnut tree sprouting from mid-street, you can well understand the difficulties that would ensue.

If you do decide to plant a hedge in your front garden, bordering the road or pavement, you should be aware of the following provisions of the Highways Act, 1980. It is an offence:

(a) to allow a hedge tree or shrub to overhang a road or

footpath so as to endanger or obstruct the passage of vehicles or pedestrians or to obstruct or interfere with the view of drivers of vehicles or the light from a public lamp (Highways Act, 1980, section 154 [1] 1);

(b) to have any hedge tree or shrub which is dead, diseased, damaged or insecurely rooted so that by reason of its condition it is likely to cause danger by falling on the road or the footpath (Highways Act, 1980, Section 154 [2] 1);

(c) to have a hedge or tree unless it is planted for ornament or shelter to a building, courtyard or hop ground which is causing damage to the road by excluding sun and wind from it (Highways Act, 1980, Section 136).

Walls, gates and fences must not be more than one metre high without planning permission from your local council, and, if you are building a retaining wall, you need to get planning permission anyway, for safety reasons. the only time you may have a notice served on you to build a wall or fence would be where there is something on your land (in your front garden) that could constitute a danger to the passing public, e.g. a large hole or a sudden change in the level of land.

72   DANGEROUS WALLS

You may have the misfortune to live next door to someone who regards his or her property as a kind of mini Fort Knox, a place that can never be too secure. It isn't enough for such people that they have guard dogs, alarm systems, floodlit front gardens, electrically operated wrought-iron gates and closed-circuit video cameras. They also wish to throw up more primitive defence systems, bringing the physiognomy of the battlegrounds of the Somme to Acacia Avenue.

The law always tried to cater for all tastes and anticipate all eventualities. By the Highways Act, 1980, section 164, therefore, it is an offence ' ... to have a fence adjoining the road which is made of or has barbed wire in it, and when the wire is likely to be injurious to persons or animals lawfully using the road'. If your paranoid neighbour *has* to have barbed wire, he or she has to keep it on the garden side of the wall, fence or hedge, away from passers-by.

The Common Law of nuisance also makes provisions to cover similar situations. Over the years a number of cases have established that it is an offence to build against the road a low wall surmounted by spikes.

73 PARTY WALLS

It may be that you are the joint owner of a party wall, one that you share with your neighbour. You have to imagine that the boundary between the two properties lies right in the middle of the wall. If it is a wall that is two bricks thick, each party owns one course of bricks. If it's only one brick thick, (a) each party owns half of each course of bricks, and (b) the wall probably isn't very safe.

The legal position is that each party has the right to have his or her side of the wall supported by the other half. Illogically, this doesn't mean that you have the right to demand that your neighbour keeps his or her side of the wall in good repair. If it appears that the wall is likely to collapse if your neighbour doesn't do something about it, you have the right to go onto your neighbour's property to repair his or her side of the wall. Repairs are usually at joint expense, so you should be able to recover the costs incurred in repairing your neighbour's side of the wall.

Party walls are tricky things, however, and you should first make some inquiries as to what sort of party wall yours is, since there are four sorts of party wall:

1. A wall of which two adjacent owners are tenants in common – technically now obsolete, but similar to 2 and 4, below.

2. A wall divided vertically into two strips, one belonging to each of the adjoining owners.

3. A wall which belongs entirely to one of the adjoining owners but is subject to an easement or right in the other to have it maintained as a dividing wall between two tenements.

4. A wall divided vertically into halves, each half being subject to a cross easement in favour of the owner of the other half.

If your party wall falls under category 2 above, neither

you nor your neighbour is entitled to support from the other. You may pull down the bit of the wall that stands on your land, provided the work is done reasonably and without negligence. You don't even have to give notice, but you should take care how you remove your half of the wall.

If your party wall falls under category 3, your responsibility depends on whether or not you are the owner of the wall. If you are, you don't have to take positive steps to keep the wall in repair, even if this means the things falls down and your neighbour cannot exercise his easement over it. You must not, however, knock the wall down. Natural decay is permissible; artificial aid to decay isn't.

If your party wall falls (or stands) under category 4, either you or your neighbour may use the wall for what are described as the contemplated purposes, and provided this is done without negligence, there will be no liability for any nuisance or inconvenience which arises.

Special rules apply in the Inner London boroughs, whether you are repairing, enlarging or building against party walls. If you wish to do any of these, you must give formal notice, so that your neighbour's interests are properly protected. It's common for both parties to make use of professional surveyors to achieve an agreement, even to the extent of bringing in a third surveyor to act as arbitrator where agreement cannot be reached. Check the rules in your own district.

14 Statutory Nuisance

People have been making nuisances of themselves ever since time immemorial, but it was probably easier to love your neighbour, or at least not hate your neighbour, when he was a couple of hundred kilometres away, the other side of an impenetrable forest or uncrossable swamp.

There is a story that at one time there were only two motor cars in the whole of Liberia and yet they managed somehow to crash into each other. Granted such coincidences may seem horribly common in this wicked world, the fact remains that the fewer people there are around you, the less likely you are to be disturbed, annoyed or harassed.

Industrialization and urbanization have changed our society beyond recognition, and the present century has done much to disrupt the social and residential patterns established by mill, mine and factory in the eighteenth and nineteenth centuries. A hundred years ago, people in a mill town, penned in back-to-back houses, lived very similar lives with very similar lifestyles. They got up at the same time, tramped to work in the same place at the same time, came home at the same time and fell into an exhausted sleep at the same time. There were no all-night parties and there was precious little energy left to annoy in any other way. Our flickering overview of the past leads us to believe that they all kept whippets and pigeons, all burned smoky fuel and all scrubbed their front steps at the same time, so what could there have been to complain to one another about?

Today – ah, today ...

The essence of all legal nuisance is to be found in a common law maxim: *'Sic utere ut alienum non laedas'* – 'So use your own property as to not injure your neighbour's.' And where you get Latin legal maxims, you may be sure there are disputes and cases going back hundreds of years.

Nevertheless, it remains true that crowding people into towns and cities and, more recently, breaking up established centres of work and providing the population with redundancy and unemployment on a large scale (as well as the cheap means to make an enormous amount of noise in hi-fi and stereo) have vastly increased the opportunities for people to commit nuisance by so using their property as to injure their neighbour's. Left to the old system of private nuisance, where an individual had to bring a costly and lengthy action in the High Court, either the legal system would have become completely swamped or people would have felt forced to take the law into their own hands.

To counter this, over the last fifty or so years, the category of 'statutory nuisance' has been established and developed, notably by the Public Health Act, 1936, the Clean Air Act, 1956, the Noise Abatement Act, 1960, the Deposit of Poisonous Wastes Act, 1972, and the Control of Pollution Act, 1974. The great advantage for the ordinary citizen is that, if you have grounds for believing that your neighbour is committing a statutory nuisance, you can involve your local authority, who may bring an action in a magistrate's court. Indeed, the Public Health Act, 1936, imposes a duty on local authorities to inspect their districts from time to time to detect statutory nuisances.

All this, and your Common Law rights unaffected – it's like a wonderful dream.

74   CATEGORIES OF STATUTORY NUISANCE

There are six categories of statutory nuisance defined by the Public Health Act, 1936, section 92. It's worth looking at each in turn, to see what protection it affords against unruly, untidy or unthinking neighbours.

1. 'Any premises in such a state as to be prejudicial to health or a nuisance.' (PHA, 1936, s 92 [1][a])

A great many subsequent cases have attempted to explain what this means. Although some of them conflict in their judgments, it would seem that it's possible to predict what is meant by 'premises in such a state as to be prejudicial to health' and what is meant by 'a nuisance'.

'Premises' includes 'messuages, buildings, land, easements and hereditaments of any tenure'. 'Messuage' is simply a posh legal word for a house and its associated outbuildings, garden and orchard. We don't get a lot of them in Catford. 'Hereditament' has three meanings:

   i. Corporeal hereditaments are tangible items of property.

   ii. Incorporeal hereditaments are intangible rights over land, such as easements.

iii. Units of land that have been separately assessed for rating purposes.

On the whole, you needn't worry too much about them. For a definition of 'easement' see Chapter 15, Rights of Way.

A street can be 'premises', sewers probably can't. Interestingly, land in its natural state can constitute premises. In *Leakey v National Trust*, 1980, soil, rocks, tree roots and other debris had slipped onto Leakey's, the plaintiff's, land from that of his neighbour, the National Trust, simply by the natural weathering process. It was held that the defendants were liable in nuisance.

'Prejudicial to health' is defined as 'injurious or likely to cause injury to health' by the same Act, but in a much later section (343 [1]). We can only marvel at the helpfulness of the great minds that drafted the Act and turn to subsequent cases to try to work out what the explanation means.

Whether your neighbour's premises are in such a state as to be prejudicial to health will be a question of fact in each case. In 1975, in *Salford City Council v McNally*, it was held that a house with rising damp, perished plaster, an unhinged and rotten back door, severe dampness and a cracked and insanitary water-closet pipe was likely to cause injury to health. If your neighbour's property is in similar condition, you may proceed to inform your local council with all speed – especially if your property is semi-detached, terraced or a connecting flat. Rising damp can travel horribly quickly.

Don't confuse, however, a house 'prejudicial to health' under the Public Health Act, 1936, with one 'unfit for human habitation' under the Housing Act, 1957, section 4: they are not the same. And a house can be unfit for human habitation without being prejudicial to health.

The important question as to what was meant by a 'nuisance' within this category was discussed in 1976 in the *National Coal Board v Thorne*. It's worth quoting at length from the judgment in the case:

> A nuisance cannot arise if what has taken place affects only the person or persons occupying the premises where the

nuisance is said to have taken place. A nuisance coming within the meaning of the Public Health Act 1936 must be either a private or public nuisance as understood by the common law ... [Remember: ' ... so use your own property as not to injure your neighbour's'] A public nuisance at common law has been expressed as an act or omission which materially affects the material comfort and quality of life of a class of Her Majesty's subjects. A private nuisance has often been defined in this way: private nuisances, at least in the vast majority of cases, are interferences for a substantial length of time by owners or occupiers of property with the use or enjoyment of neighbouring property.

What all this means is that if, say, your neighbour has a leaky overflow pipe or defective guttering, and the water drips onto your land or buildings, you will be able to take action under the heading of statutory nuisance. But if the water drips only onto your neighbour's own land – annoying and unsightly though this may be, and carrying with it the threat of lowering the value of property in the neighbourhood – you won't.

2. 'Any animal kept in such a place or manner as to be prejudicial to health or a nuisance.' (PHA, 1936, s 92 [1][b])

The rights and wrongs of keeping, breeding and boarding animals have been dealt with in Section 40, Animals.

3. 'Any accumulation or deposit which is prejudicial to health or a nuisance.' (PHA, 1936, s 92 [1][c])

A great many cases under this heading have reached the higher courts, and the crucial question is: 'What constitutes an accumulation or deposit?'

Before the Public Health Act, 1936, it was held that a pile of garden manure that gave off smells and attracted a great number of flies constituted an accumulation, as did a pile of cinders and ashes that emitted offensive fumes. You have to be careful here, however. In the important case of *Coventry City Council v Cartwright* in 1975, Lord Chief Justice Widgery (the same Lord Chief Justice who was so helpful about dogs – 'I would have thought for my own part that a noisy animal could be as much prejudicial

to health as a smelly animal') said that there had to attach
to the accumulation 'a threat to health in the sense of a
threat of disease, vermin or the like'.

Rubbish Tips
Many people live near official or unofficial rubbish tips, or
next to premises which are used from time to time to
deposit building rubble or bric-à-brac from some industrial
process or other. What the decision in *Coventry City
Council v Cartwright* suggests is that the unsightliness of
such premises, and the dust that surrounds them, aren't
enough to constitute statutory nuisance. There has to be
some unpleasant putrefying factor present, and, even
when this is so, it may be a defence for your neighbour to
say that the accumulation or deposit was necessary to
carry on his or her business and that it hadn't been kept
on the premises longer than necessary for that purpose.

In such circumstances, you may do better to nudge your
local authority towards the Town and Country Planning
Act, 1971, section 65, which provides that, if the amenity of
any part of a local authority's area is seriously injured by
the condition of any garden, vacant site or other open
land, they may serve a notice requiring abatement of the
injury. This obviously won't work against your neighbour
if he or she's running a business, but it's a useful catch-all
category for what is commonly called 'wasteland'. The
main drawback is that the penalty is a fine not exceeding
£50. It's hardly swingeing, and as that famous Law Lord
Duke Ellington said: 'It don't mean a thinge if it ain't got
that swinge.'

4. 'Any dust or effluvia caused by any trade, business,
manufacture or process and being prejudicial to the health
of, or a nuisance to, the inhabitants of a neighbourhood.'
(PHA, 1936, s 92 [1] [d])

This may at first appear more promising than the last
category, since it specifically includes 'dust', but we need
to discover what is meant by 'effluvia'. It includes spent
steam, but not that from a railway locomotive, though this
is unlikely to have the same importance now that it had in

1936, unless you live next to a preserved or narrow-gauge railway line. It also includes vapours. The leading case here is *Malton Board of Health v Malton Manure Co.*, though this case was decided some fifty-seven years before the Public Health Act, 1936, came onto the statute book. The Malton Manure Company made artificial manures so realistic that they gave off vapours that, even if they didn't make well people sick, certainly made sick people sicker. As such, these effluvia were held to be prejudicial to health.

There are strict limitations on this category, however, and it may well prove a sound defence if the defendant (i.e. your neighbour) can show that he or she has taken the 'best practicable means' to prevent or counteract the effects of any dust or effluvia. Also, you should note that 'effluvia' doesn't include smells, no matter how offensive. To counteract those, you would need to persuade your local council to take action under the Public Health Act, 1936, section 92 (1) (a): 'any premises in such a state as to be prejudicial to health or a nuisance' (see sub-section 1, above).

Of course, you don't really have to persuade your local authority at all. It's simply a question of complaining to them, giving them details of what it is you think constitutes a nuisance and letting them take it from there. But it doesn't hurt to keep an eye on how they are proceeding, and under what heading. It would be a different sort of nuisance if they proceeded under the wrong heading and lost the case, if your neighbour got off scot free and knew that you had shopped him and tried (unsuccessfully) to get him into trouble. Ill will would abound.

5. 'Any workplace which is not provided with sufficient means of ventilation, or in which sufficient ventilation is not maintained, or which is not kept clean or not kept free from noxious effluvia, or which is so overcrowded while work is carried on as to be prejudicial to the health of those employed therein.' (PHA, 1936, s 92 [1] [e])

This section deals with an employment situation, so it

isn't relevant to the matters that concern us.

6. 'Any other matter declared by any other provisions of the Public Health Act 1936 to be a statutory nuisance.' (PHA, 1936, s 92 [1] [f])

This is a catch-all clause that has been held to deal with wells, tanks, water-butts, ponds, ditches, watercourses etc which become blocked, silted up, foul, contaminated or whatever and thus constitute a threat prejudicial to health.

It also includes tents, vans, sheds or similar structures used for human habitation which become overcrowded or lack sufficient sanitary arrangements as to be prejudicial to health. Useful, therefore, if you live next door to a camp site, or if your neighbour has an excessively large family and is using the potting shed and the motor caravan as fourth and fifth bedrooms.

So much for the far-reaching Public Health Act, 1936, which did (and still does) a great deal to try to make urban life more comfortable and less unbearable. There are, however, other, later Acts which have added to the categories of statutory nuisance. Probably the next most important are those dealt with in Sections 75 and 76.

75   THE CLEAN AIR ACTS, 1956 AND 1968

A local authority is empowered by these Acts to make it an offence to emit any smoke in certain areas, called Smoke Control Areas. In such an area it becomes an offence to emit smoke from the chimney of any building, though it's a defence if your neighbour can show that the smoke came only from the burning of authorized fuel (see Section 45, Air Pollution – Domestic), and it's also a defence if your neighbour can show that, although he did burn unauthorized fuels, his chimney did not emit a substantial amount of smoke.

Be careful, therefore. Don't assume that, the moment a smudge of smoke appears from your neighbour's chimney, as he or she tries pitifully to keep warm on a bitter winter's day, you can bring the whole panoply of law down on his or her head. There has to exist a degree of live-and-let-live between neighbours. We are none of us perfect. Just because you and I are more nearly perfect than those dreadful people at No. 10 doesn't mean the local authority or the magistrate's court will smile benignly on us and rubber-stamp our every complaint.

And even if your rotten neighbour belches forth dark smoke from his chimney every time the sun isn't blazing, be careful. The Clean Air Act, 1956, makes the following provisions:

Smoke other than
  (a) smoke emitted from the chimney of a private dwelling, or
  (b) dark smoke emitted from the chimney of a building or from a chimney serving the furnace of a boiler or individual plant attached to a building or for the time being fixed to or installed on any land, or
  (c) dark smoke from industrial or trade premises within the Clean Air Act 1956 s 1
shall be deemed a statutory nuisance under the Public Health Act, if it is a nuisance to the inhabitants of the neighbourhood.

This does not, therefore, include the smoke from your neighbour's chimney. You don't have to show that the smoke is injurious to health, but it does have to be a considerable amount and has to interfere materially with the ordinary comfort of human existance. The only way in which this might be relevant for the ordinary neighbour situation is if your neighbour either burns old car tyres or polystyrene-stuffed furniture in the back garden or keeps more organic bonfires burning for a long time (see Section 43, Air Pollution – Bonfires).

76   NOISE ABATEMENT ACT, 1960, PUBLIC HEALTH (RECURRING NUISANCES) ACT, 1969, AND CONTROL OF POLLUTION ACT, 1974

Not until 1960 was noise considered a statutory nuisance. The 1960 and 1969 Acts didn't help much, because local authorities were given no power to deal with *anticipated* noise. If dear old Farmer Giles decided to stuff his pockets with Tin Pan Alley gold, by throwing open a neighbouring meadow to a Hard Rock or Heavy Metal entrepreneur, there was nothing that could be done, even though it was well known that several thousand megawatts of amplified skull-splintering noise would follow.

In the early 1970s, the Government appointed the Scott Committee to examine the problem of noise pollution, and their report was subsequently published under the title *Neighbourhood Noise*. This in turn led to the Pollution Act, 1974, which has done something at least to amend the situation. There are five aspects of the Act that we need to consider: noise nuisance generally, noise from construction sites, noise in streets, noise abatement zones, and noise from plant and machinery.

Noise Nuisance Generally
See also Chapter 8. Although it states that noise can include vibration, there is no definition of what noise constitutes a nuisance in the Noise Abatement Act, 1960, so the old Common Law test applies – ' ... so use your property as to not injure your neighbour's'.

To establish statutory nuisance, it does help if the local authority (who will be bringing the action on your behalf, if they believe there are sufficient grounds) has technical evidence. Mention has already been made of the tape-recorders some councils use to collect evidence of, say, a barking dog. If you want to know more about the measurement of noise levels, you should consult the Control of Noise (Measurements and Registers) Regulations, 1976, obtainable from Her Majesty's Stationery Office (HMSO). These are tricky regulations and have to be properly followed.

The idea is that a local authority will serve a notice on the offender, specifying that a noise level should not exceed a certain number of decibels. Suppose you live next to a pub that has a juke-box in one of its bars. It is possible that this interferes with your own 'reasonable enjoyment' of your house. It's possible it drives you halfway up the wall. It's possible that you are contemplating murder. If the council wish to take action for statutory nuisance, they must include in their notice to the publican a clear indication as to how much noise is tolerable from the juke-box, and from what precise place it is to be measured. In the case of *R(Regina, ie. the Crown) v Fenny Stratford Justices ex p Watney Mann* in 1976*, the local justices had ordered an abatement of noise nuisance under the Public Health Act, 1936, section 94 (2), saying that the sound from a juke-box should not exceed 70dB. They did not say, however, where the monitoring equipment measuring the sound should be placed. The entire noise abatement order was quashed.

If your neighbour receives a notice under the Noise Abatement Act, 1960, he or she has twenty-one days in which to appeal against that notice, unless:

(a) the noise is injurious to health, or

(b) the noise is of limited duration, i.e. the cause of the noise will disappear before the notice could have any practical effect, or

(c) the expenditure incurred in compliance with the notice would not be disproportionate to the public benefit resulting from compliance prior to the hearing of the appeal, i.e. the notice won't be suspended if the public are getting their money's worth from the notice.

In some cases the noise and disruption are such that a local authority may apply to the High Court for an injunction to stop the noise immediately and completely, pending a hearing. An interesting case is that of *Hammersmith London Borough Council v Magnum Automated Forecourts* in 1978. The defendants operated a twenty-four-hour 'taxi care centre' in the middle of a residential area. Local residents complained to the local authority about the level and duration of noise that this occasioned. The local authority served a notice on the company, including a statement that the notice was to remain in effect even though the defendant company was making an appeal against the notice to a magistrate's court. The company continued its operations. The local authority applied to the High Court for an injunction to force the defendant

* For full explanation of *ex p* (*ex parte*) see glossary.

company to cease operations immediately. The High
Court refused to order an injunction, but the Court of
Appeal reversed this decision.

Under the Control of Pollution Act, 1974, occupiers of
premises (you and me) also have the right to initiate
proceedings to abate noise. The statutory weapon is not as
powerful as that granted to local authorities, but you have
the advantage of cheaper and quicker proceedings in a
magistrate's court.

What you have to show is that you have been
'aggrieved' by the noise. Like so many legal expressions,
'aggrieved' has no precise meaning, though, with their
customary helpfulness, the legal profession used to
explain that you were aggrieved if you had 'a legal
grievance' – and they get paid for that sort of thing. Now it
is reckoned to mean, 'You have suffered a material
interference with your enjoyment of your property' –
whatever that means.

Whereas local authorities can move against an
anticipated noise, the private individual can't, though
magistrates can make an order against the repetition of
any offending noise. If your neighbour has such an order
made against him or her but won't do anything about it,
you can get the local authority to do what is necessary to
abate the noise, and they can subsequently recover the
costs incurred.

Construction Sites
By 'construction sites' is meant roadworks; building
maintenance, repairs or construction; demolition work;
dredging work and any work of engineering construction.

Under the Control of Pollution Act, 1974, section 60 (5),
a local authority can serve notice on a construction site
specifying the plant or machinery that can or can't be
used, the hours of working and the permitted noise levels,
and providing for any change of circumstances. One of
the considerations the local authority should have in mind
when deciding these specifications is the need to protect
any persons in the locality of the construction site from the
noise that may be created.

The poor old local authority is in a difficult situation here, however. On the one hand it wants to see its locality grow and prosper commercially, which frequently means construction work – shopping precincts, multi-storey car-parks, civic centres, sports complexes. On the other hand, it wants to have happy residents. The two are often not compatible.

Further, even where the local authority receives a complaint from someone who lives next door to a construction site, it doesn't necessarily wish to race into notices, orders and litigation. Local authorities have to watch their pennies, and they can't afford to have vast numbers of staff from Environmental Health and other offices spending all day every day pacing up and down the corridors of the High Court of local magistrates' courts.

If you complain, the local authority will probably send someone round to the building or constructions site, and that someone will have a word with whoever's in charge. Once the 'someone' has gone, 'whoever's in charge' will probably give orders for the work to start again, and the noise will come thudding back to you. Poor old 'someone' can spend all day playing Hunt the Noise. It's a bit like the scene in the panto where we all shout 'Behind You!', and Buttons (or the 'someone' sent by the council) always turns round too late.

Noise in Streets
The Control of Pollution Act, 1974, section 62, prohibits the use of loudspeakers in streets completely between 9 p.m. and 8 a.m. and at all hours for entertainment, trade or business – it's a pity these hours aren't used as a guideline to limit other types of noise. Exception is made for political activists at election time; police, fire brigade, ambulance services, water authorities and local authorities where carrying out their functions; and if the loudspeaker forms part of the public telephone system – though why anyone should wish to connect their telephone to a loudspeaker on top of their car I haven't yet been able to fathom – it sounds a bit yuppy to me.

Note: For the ill-deserved privilege of ice-cream vendors, see Section 56, Street Noise.

Noise Abatement Zones

Maybe we think we'd all like to live in a Noise Abatement Zone. Local authorities are empowered to create such zones, but then local authorities are empowered to do a great many things for which they simply haven't the resources. Also, the probability is that any Noise Abatement Zone wouldn't be the most desirable residential area. The Control of Pollution Act, 1974, section 63, isn't concerned with leafy suburbs or rural beauty spots: it's concerned with commercial premises, industrial premises, agricultural premises, places of entertainment, transport installations and public utility installations – in that order.

The whole idea behind a Noise Abatement Zone is that it is created where there is likely to be noise.

If you live in a Noise Abatement Zone and feel you have a justified complaint, the procedure you should follow is much the same as that for other examples of noise as a statutory nuisance (see this section, above).

Plant or Machinery

The Control of Pollution Act, 1974, section 68 empowers the Secretary of State for the Environment to regulate the use of noise-reduction devices on plant or machinery, but he doesn't seem to want to make many such orders.

15   Rights of Way

Rights of way don't often become a source of conflict between neighbours other than when they are blocked or obstructed. The main reason for this is that rights of way are usually clearly indicated on the deeds to property, and this lessens the chances of arguments as to who is allowed to do what. When you are buying a house, therefore, you, your solicitor or whoever else is handling the conveyance should become aware of any right of way over that property and of who has the authority to exercise that right of way, e.g. is it public or private.

Similarly, the deeds should show if you have a right of way over your neighbour's property, perhaps the right to have rainwater from your guttering discharge into your neighbour's pipe before it enters the main (public) drain, or to gain access to your own garden by using a neighbour's path.

Rights of way are what is known in law as 'easements'. As easement may be defined as a right to use, or restrict the use of, the land of another person in some way. When property is bought and sold, details of any easements, including rights of way, go into the contracts drafted for the purchase and sale. In fact, there is a standard set of printed terms covering rights of way, so there is no need to re-draft them each time any property changes hands.

You may also be able to discern rights of way simply by inspecting property. A right of way across the garden may be evidenced by a worn strip of grass, or the layout of paths and drives may suggest that one of two neighbouring houses must have a right of way over the other. Wires connected to a house may indicate a right to run an electric cable, for television or telephone, over a neighbour's property.

If all this is either readily apparent or carefully recorded in deeds, you may wonder how there could ever be disputes between neighbours concerning rights of way – after all, you can't make noise with a right of way, or set fire to it or, by its very nature, trespass upon it. But where any two people share something (and that, in essence, is what a right of way consists of – a sharing), you can be sure they will find grounds for disagreement if they really want to – and it's amazing how often neighbours really want to.

There are three ways in which trouble may arise: firstly when something needs to be done to the right of way, most obviously repairs; secondly when either the grantor or grantee of the right of way somehow obstructs or impedes it; thirdly if the grantee attempts to change the nature of the right of way.

77   REPAIRS TO RIGHTS OF WAY

In the absence of any contrary agreement or special circumstances, the law considers that it is for the grantee of the right of way to bear the cost of maintenance and repair. Suppose you have a right of way over your neighbour's land. This means that you are the grantee and your neighbour is the grantor (giver) of the right of way. In a rural area it may be that you have the right to drive cattle or livestock over it. If that right of way is over a path or metalled road, you as grantee will be responsible for any repairs the path or road may need. If you don't repair the path and it becomes impassable or in some way obstructed, you are foolish, because you have no right to make a detour round such an obstruction. If your neighbour (the grantor) causes the obstruction, that is a different matter, and you probably do have the right to make a detour.

In the case of a shared right of way, i.e. one that both you and your neighbour make use of, the situation is somewhat different. Suppose that a driveway runs between your house and your neighbour's, and that both of you use it to obtain access to a row of garages at the back of the properties (indeed, there may be several houses that have rights of way over the same drive or path). It's possible that the deeds to the properties in question will give clear indication as to who is to pay for what and in what proportion. If they don't, it is up to you and your neighbour to come to some workable, if not amicable, arrangement. Whatever you do, don't go ahead and do the work yourself or contract for someone else to do it on the assumption that your neighbour will be legally bound to pay his or her share. If you do this, the probability is that you will be saddled with total responsibility for paying any bills involved, and you may have established a dangerous precedent that it is down to you to undertake repairs whenever that becomes necessary.

In this, as in so many matters to do with neighbourhood issues, it is much better to talk to your neighbour first.

78   OBSTRUCTION OF RIGHTS OF WAY

Neither grantor nor grantee of a right of way is permitted to obstruct that right of way. For once, it is as simple as that. If your neighbour does obstruct your right of way, the first thing to do is to inform him and ask him to move the obstruction. It could be a dustbin, a pile of waste paper, some old furniture, a bicycle, a pile of wood, rubbish – anything. It could be something of obvious value or something that appears valueless. In the case of cowboy roof-repairers, it could be scaffolding poles. It could be something placed there in all innocence, in forgetfulness or in a clear attempt to stir up trouble.

Whatever it is and whyever it's there, don't see red, grab it and hurl in into your neighbour's garden; or worse, the dustbin; or worst, through your neighbour's front window. Point out the obstruction to your neighbour and ask him or her to move it. If he or she refuses, you may move it yourself, but you mustn't destroy or damage whatever it is that is causing the obstruction, and you should place it on your neighbour's land.

If the pile of wood, rubbish, furniture or dustbin reappears in the same place next day, go through the same process, but show your neighbour that you are complaining. If the obstruction persists, go to a solicitor to have a letter drafted, complaining formally. Many people respond to a solicitor's letter, promptly though somewhat joylessly. If your neighbour is of the more stubborn and anti-social variety, you may have to follow any solicitor's letters with legal action. If you and/or your neighbour are council tenants, it is a good idea to involve your local Housing Officer, since the right of way will presumably be vested in the local authority and it therefore becomes their battle.

79 CHANGES IN USE OF RIGHT OF WAY

With the passage of time, it may seem to make sense to modify or change the manner in which a right of way is used. Take nothing for granted, however – times may change, the law doesn't. A case in 1939 did allow that, where a right of way had originally been used for horse-drawn vehicles, it was legitimate to use it for motor vehicles, but in general the right of way must be used strictly in accordance with custom.

In cases that have come before the courts, it has been held that a right of way for agricultural purposes could not be used for carting building-materials; one for domestic purposes and for access to warehouses on land could not be used as a public approach to a railway station; one used as a carriageway could not be used for driving cattle but *could* be used as a footway. The principle behind this last case is the 'the greater includes the lesser', i.e. a right of way drafted to let you drive elephants over someone's land will almost certainly let you drive Shetland ponies or dormice over the same land.

16   Light and Privacy

Note: See also Sections 27, Privacy, 31, Rights of Light, and 35, Restrictive Covenants.

Like so many other problems between neighbours, disputes over rights to light and privacy occur only when some change takes place, upsetting the situation that has existed hitherto. Usually that change involves some extension to one person's house or the planting or cutting-down of trees.

Not many of us have the time or inclination to comb every edition of our local paper or visit our local council offices every month to check the applications for planning permission in our own neighbourhood. Thus the first hint

we may get that something is about to happen next door
or over the road may be when a lorry arrives and drops a
threatening load of sand, cement, breeze blocks and
bricks. We then realize our neighbour is up to something.
There follows a brief period of craning our necks over
fences and leaning dangerously out of upstairs windows
to see if we can discover what development our neighbour
has in mind. By the time we find out, it may be too late –
the building work is finished, a dark shadow falls across
our rose garden or strawberry bed, a vast new picture
window overlooks our hitherto secluded patio.

We hurry to the council offices and are told that our
neighbour had filled in all the necessary forms and had
planning permission (to be accurate, if the work was
extensive, we would probably have been informed of the
plans by the council before any work took place). It is, of
course, possible to put in an objection to this planning
permission, but the probability is that we won't be able to
prevent the building taking place. The best we can hope
for, if we can show that we have lost a beautiful view or
that our light will now be in some way obstructed, is a
reduction in rates – or, once the Poll Tax comes into force,
some compensatory payment. Desperately, we turn to the
law and learn that there is no such thing as a right to light
and no such thing as a right to privacy.

It's a sad scenario, but not necessarily correct in all its
details. Life is more complicated than this, and the law
does afford us some protection against neighbours who
wish to turn the neighbourhood into something resem-
bling Manhattan, the Barbican or a Giant Redwood forest.

80   RIGHTS OF LIGHT AS EASEMENTS

Your neighbour will not be entitled to build on his land,
depriving you of light, if you have an easement of light or
some other right, such as a restrictive covenant against
building. There are two ways in which you can obtain an
easement: it may be in the deeds to your property and will
pass to you when you purchase the property, or you may
acquire an easement through usage.

Let us assume that your house is more than twenty years old. If the window in question, the one that your neighbour is darkening, has been in the same position for twenty years and throughout that time has enjoyed light coming from over your neighbour's property, you have a right to that light, provided the window hasn't in any way been enlarged or its position changed. This doesn't mean, however, that if your neighbour builds something on his property that takes away most of your light you can force him or her to dismantle the obstructing edifice. You aren't entitled to all the light you previously enjoyed. The amount you may have is enough light ' ... according to the ordinary notions of mankind for the comfortable use of the premises as a dwelling, or, in the case of business premises, for the beneficial use of the premises for ordinary shop or other business premises' (P.V. Baker, *Megarry's Manual of the Law of Real Property*).

There's no system or light meter or any method yet devised that decides whether or not too much light has been taken away from a window. The test is: can the room lit by the window still be used for its normal purpose? The test is not 'How much light has been taken away?' but 'How much light is left?'

The law takes a different line if you are seeking to maintain light to a greenhouse, conservatory or (probably) solar panel: these are protected – your neighbour may not build to obstruct these. But if there are signs that your neighbour does intend to add to his property and that there might be a risk of your light being obstructed, then, as always, it's a good idea to talk to your neighbour and try to come to some agreement. The law doesn't want to see easements used to stifle all further development in your area. Indeed, in some more modern estates, there may be specific clauses in the deeds to the new properties denying the right to gain easements of light, for this very reason.

A right to light may exist even where the owner of the dominant tenement changes the nature of his or her property. In *Carr-Saunders v Dick McNeil Associates Ltd* in 1986, the plaintiff had changed an open-plan apartment

into six consulting-rooms. Subsequently the defendants
erected a further two storeys onto their neighbouring
premises. This reduced the amount of light to the
plaintiff's property. It was held that the plaintiff had
established an actionable nuisance, not because his rear
(modified) rooms were no longer adequately lit but
because the second floor as a whole (the floor occupied by
the plaintiff) could no longer be conveniently subdivided
in such a way that each area received an adequate amount
of light. The plaintiff was accordingly entitled to damages.

81   HOW TO PREVENT YOUR NEIGHBOUR GAINING A RIGHT TO LIGHT IF YOU'RE REALLY THAT MEAN

This may seem very much a spoilsport approach to life,
but it needs thinking about. Suppose you live next to a
building site and that houses are being built there. If these
houses have windows overlooking your property, then, in
time, unless you do something to stop it, these houses will
gain a right to light. This right is called a Lost Modern
Grant. It's a kind of modern equivalent of Ancient Lights
(see Section 31, Rights of Light). If the light to your
neighbour's window is unobstructed for twenty years,
you won't be able to plant trees or extend your own house
in a way that will obstruct your neighbour's light.

The way to get round this problem is to give your
neighbour permission to have a window overlooking your
property and to charge him or her a nominal sum for this
privilege – say £1 per year – on the understanding that you
reserve the right to withdraw this permission at any time.
So long as you keep collecting the £1, your neighbour will
not acquire any right to light. It's best to make this
arrangement formally and have it properly drafted. A
decent sort of person will make this arrangement soon
after the house in question is built, or even before it's built.
A real spoilsport waits eighteen years and then starts to
charge.

There is one other way of preventing your neighbour
acquiring a right to light. This is by application to the
Lands Tribunal, registering an obstruction notice. It takes

a long time to do this, it's very expensive, and it's a job for the experts.

Summary
1. There is no right to light or an unspoilt view unless you have made a private agreement with your neighbour or unless your property has acquired an easement.
2. You or your neighbour can, therefore, erect a building unless:

(a) building regulations prohibit new building, or

(b) planning restrictions prohibit new building under Town and Country Planning Act, 1971, or

(c) there is a clause in the deeds to the property, common in new developments, that prohibits further building.

3. Either you or your neighbour can acquire a right to light by

(a) uninterrupted enjoyment over a period of twenty years, or

(b) mutual legal agreement in the form of a restrictive covenant (see Section 35, Restrictive Covenants).

4. In some cases (very few) rights to light exist under the legal heading of Ancient Lights. This means that the right has existed since 'time immemorial', i.e. AD 1189. Not much good for Brookside, Coronation Street or Albert Square.

5. The maximum amount of light to which you or your neighbour may be entitled under any heading (Ancient Lights, easements, Lost Modern Grant) is that required for ordinary purposes.

82 PRIVACY

Contrary to popular opinion, there is no statutory or Common Law right to privacy. If you like to spend your autumn and winter evenings prowling the pavements of suburbia, gazing intently and critically into other people's front rooms, technically you are not breaking any law. Similarly, if you care to build a tree house in your garden and post yourself in it all day, with nothing but a flask of drink, a few rounds of sandwiches and a pair of high-powered binoculars, studying each and every move your neighbour makes, you are at liberty to do so.

It doesn't make for good relationships, however, and it's possible that your neighbour will be able to find some way of getting revenge – by taking direct action or by putting it about the neighbourhood that you are a Peeping Tom or some other kind of degenerate, or by involving the police, who may well dredge up some component of the Criminal Law which they are convinced you have broken.

One of the features of an easement is that the right must be sufficiently definite: it must be capable of reasonable definition. Although the law believes that the right to light may be sufficiently clearly defined ('enough light ... for the comfortable use of the premises as a dwelling' – see above), it doesn't accept that privacy can be so defined. There is, therefore, no such thing as an easement of privacy. The key case in this context is that of *Browne v Flower* in 1911, where it was held that the erection of an external staircase passing the windows of a flat, although it might amount to an invasion of privacy in lay terms, wasn't grounds for an action in law.

If, therefore, your neighbour is building an extension to the back of his or her house, and that extension will overlook your hitherto secluded patio, where you were want to sunbathe, barbecue and frolic, there is nothing you can do about it – unless, of course, there is something irregular or illegal in what your neighbour is doing. There would have to be, for example, some restrictive covenant or clause in the deeds to the properties concerned that expressly forbade extending your neighbour's property in this way.

The only consolation that you may find in all this is that your neighbour cannot object to whatever he or she sees taking place in your property. Unless you choose to act in a criminally uninhibited way (and it's certainly not within the province of this book to go into what is meant by that), you and your partner may do whatever you like. If this shocks or disgusts your neighbour, there's nothing they can do about it.

Note 1: This is the one occasion where it probably isn't better to talk about it with your neighbour first.

Note 2: Recent developments in the hobby of flying model aircraft pose an interesting problem regarding privacy. There are now model planes which are strong enough to have small cameras mounted on them. The idea is that it's a very cheap way of getting aerial photographs. It won't be long before someone comes along with a miniature video camera mounted on the nose cone of a model aircraft. As the law stands at the moment, your neighbour would be perfectly free to fly this aircraft over his garden, taking pictures of what was going on in your garden (no invasion of air space, you see). Fortunately, these aircraft make such an unpleasant, whiny little noise that it shouldn't be difficult to bring an action for nuisance on this ground or even to ask the council to deal with the matter on your behalf. If all else fails, build your own model aircraft and send it up to shoot your neighbour's down.

17   Building Regulations

Building regulations are almost impossibly complex things. They fill vast volumes with technical matters that it takes an expert to understand. It isn't proposed to go into any such detail here, but merely to give a brief outline as to how these regulations might bear upon relations between neighbours.

Note: 'Building regulations' normally means the Building Regulations, 1976.

The first point to be made is that building regulations are not the same as planning consent. Unlike Love and Marriage, or Rights and Duties, you can have one without the other. There are plenty of occasions where consent under the building regulations is required, while planning permission is not. Building regulations are devised to attempt to raise, or at least maintain, standards of building and safety when property is extended or in any way altered or developed. They apply across the board. Planning consent relates only to the one particular property that is being considered. It is granted or refused simply on the basis of whether or not the local council thinks the development proposed is desirable, doesn't present an eyesore, doesn't result in overcrowding, doesn't act to the detriment of the neighbourhood.

Among other matters, building regulations cover foundations, walls (are they reasonably insulated and properly constructed), chimneys (especially those built or adapted for central heating,), and roofs and guttering. You don't need to worry about building regulations if you are building a single-storey hut, shed, shelter or kiosk – unless it will contain a water closet or will be built of combustible material, or will be within two metres of an existing building, or will be built over a public sewer. You can do what you like with tents, marquees, caravans, tower masts not attached to a building, scaffolding, fences, walls, gates that aren't part of a building, and storage tanks (so long as they're not septic tanks). You may need to bother with building regulations if you are contemplating a summer house, poultry house, aviary, greenhouse, conservatory, orchard house, boathouse, coalshed, garden tool shed or cycle shed.

The point of all this is that, if you are contemplating some addition to your property, and relations with your neighbour are at a low point, you do need to make sure you obey all the rules relating to the planned addition. Check whether planning permission is needed. Make sure you conform to the building regulations. This will put you in a much more secure position if your neighbour decides to raise an objection.

Correspondingly, if your neighbour is developing his property in a way that seems to you unreasonable and deleterious to the neighbourhood, you may be able to scotch his or her plans by reference to the local council to see if he or she has obtained consent under the building regulations.

It's not a wonderful way to live, though, is it?

18   Litter, Untidy Land and Dilapidated Buildings

One of the many sources of bitterness between neighbours is differences in standards regarding the disposal of litter. There are those of us who seize upon every weed the moment it appears in the garden and scour front and back for windblown litter at least twice a day. There are those of us who make a pathetic attempt to spring-clean the garden once a year, occasionally remove rubbish and sometimes clear up after the dustmen. There are also those of us who do nothing, absolutely nothing, to tidy our property, maintaining it as a monument to old mattresses, sweet-papers, crisp packets, tea-bags, curtains, newspapers, take-away food containers, TV sets, washing-machines, car batteries etc, etc, etc.

Few people complain if they live next door to an excessively tidy person, even though it may make them feel uncomfortable, dirty and sluttish. The complaints are always directed at the slobs among us, those whose property presents a sore sight for eyes.

There is, of course, no law that says you or your neighbour must keep your property tidy. The law is concerned with only two aspects of untidiness: that which litters public places, and that which is so bad as to constitute a threat to health. It is no good going to the police or solicitors because you cannot stand the state of your neighbour's property. They may agree that it's dreadful but there's nothing they can do about it – and they won't thank you for wasting their time.

There remains the local council, who have some powers to deal with litter and rubbish, and several duties concerning the same.

Dilapidated Buildings

If you live next door to a building that is in a ruinous or semi-ruinous state or which is at least well on the way to such a state, you may be able to satisfy the council that it is 'seriously detrimental to the amenities of the neighbour-hood'. If so, they may serve notice on the owner requiring him or her to do one of two things: (a) repair and restore the building, or (b) demolish it and remove surplus materials from the site. The council's powers here derive from the Public Health Act, 1936 – it makes you wonder where we'd be without that particular statute, doesn't it? The owner then has twenty-one days in which to appeal against the notice. If he or she doesn't, but also fails to take the necessary steps to repair, restore or demolish, the council may step in and do the work themselves, subsequently recovering expenses reasonably incurred.

Untidy Land

If your neighbour's garden is in such a state of filth and congestion that it offends even us slobs, there are several ways of approaching the problem.

You can try talking to your neighbour, using friendly persuasion in the hope that he or she will see the light, book the skip, clear the rubbish. It often produces a far more positive response if you can get others living in the area to join you in this crusade. It also makes it a lot less personal. Some people are genuinely unaware of the facilities offered by councils, under the Control of Pollution Act, 1974, and the Refuse Disposal (Amenity) Act, 1978, to dispose of waste and rubbish. Most know that if you stick your daily household rubbish in a dustbin the council will come along every week and cart it away. They don't know that councils will call to collect much larger items (old bedsteads, chests of drawers, mattresses, lawnmowers, three-piece suites etc) if they are contacted and arrangements made. There is no charge for this service in most areas. Admittedly, most councils impose a limit of collecting only six such items at any one time, but you can always 'book' them again later. Your neighbour may also be one of those people who do not know of the existence of such places as council tips, to which they can take any amount of household or garden rubbish, again free of charge.

If you can summon up the neighbourly spirit, you might invite several parties to share in the cost of hiring a skip. They're often seen as communal bins anyway. Some of your neighbours may say 'no' (or worse), but it may be a quick and relatively cheap way of tidying up the neighbourhood. Everyone has his or her story about hiring a skip. One of my favourites is of the man who hired a skip and then watched, saying nothing, as his neighbour filled it with a privet hedge that he (the neighbour) had removed. At dead of night, the skip-hirer crept out and replanted all the privet bushes in his neighbour's garden. It's yet another example of how not to communicate with your neighbour. There can't be many people, who hire skips, with that amount of time on their hands.

It's a situation where you may need to exercise a little sensitivity towards your neighbour. There's a big difference between the ease with which a young couple with a car may make use of such facilities, and the difficulties an OAP or single parent, possibly without a car, would experience. I have frequently seen people pushing handcarts laden with household rubbish towards our local council tip, but how viable an alternative this is does depend, to a large extent, on how far you live from the tip.

If your neighbour is not in a position, for reasons of age, ill-health or whatever, to take advantage of the council tip, it might be an idea for you to offer to cart the rubbish away for him or her. Many of the people involved in trying to sort out neighbour disputes believe that a great deal of difficulty could be avoided if a more positive view of neighbourliness was adopted by all of us.

If, however, your neighbour is a hulking great brute, physically at the peak of fitness and with a vast car capable of transporting up to three tons of rubble in one journey, and he still won't do anything to tidy up his desecration of a garden, you will have to resort to calling in the council.

They are empowered, under the Prevention of Damage by Pests Act, 1949, to serve notice on your neighbour requiring him or her to remove the accumulated loathesome pile if it is causing infestations of rats or mice. They have another and wider power: they can serve a similar notice, under the Town and Country Planning Act, 1971, if they think that the said pile is a disamenity.

The twin notions of 'amenity' and 'disamenity' are interesting phenomena. The council is obliged by law to consider the beauty and other amenities of any areas under its control which are used for housing purposes. The council is also authorized to spend a certain proportion of its income (the local rate) on amenities. It's up to them how them spend this money and what they regard as an amenity. The point here is that you may be able to get the council to act against your neighbour's own private rubbish tip if they can be convinced that it constitutes a disamenity.

83 ABANDONED MOTOR VEHICLES

Some people collect stamps, some people collect beer mats, some people collect the shells of old motor cars. If you are unlucky enough to live next to someone whose idea of a colourful garden is one full of old Minis, Escorts or VWs, there's precious little you can do about it. My wife once lived next door to a family who had so many bits and pieces of old motors in their garden that a PH test of the soil revealed more oil than you would find in Saudi Arabia.

It's a different matter, however, if the old bangers (by which is meant the motors) spill out into the street. It is an offence, under the Refuse Disposal (Amenity) Act, 1978, without lawful authority:

'1. To abandon on any land in the open air, or on any other land forming part of a highway, a motor vehicle or anything which formed part of a motor vehicle and was removed from it in the course of dismantling the vehicle on the land; or

'2. To abandon on any such land anything other than a

motor vehicle, being a thing brought to the land for the purpose of abandoning it there.'

If, therefore, your neighbour is littering the street with bits of banger and smash, you can do something. Your neighbour may argue, wrench in hand, that he isn't abandoning or breaking them. In that case he may well be committing a different offence. The correct thing to do is to phone the council and let them know what is happening. From then on it is up to them to deal with the situation. But keep your eye on that wrench.

You may find that this takes time. Councils are sometimes slow, reluctant even, to act, and most of them are understaffed and underfunded. The problem is worst in inner city areas, where the home-based breakers and mechanics don't have enough space to keep the motors on their own land and where the streets are already overcrowded with parked cars.

Last year we were faced with a similar problem, though one which, fortunately, didn't in any way involve our neighbours. An untaxed vehicle was abandoned outside our house. In its windscreen was a tax disc that had expired a year earlier. We phoned the police, who made a note of the registration number so that they could track down the owner. Nothing happened for over a month, except that little children began to play in the car and managed to release the handbrake and roll it a few feet down the hill. We again phoned the police, pointing out that we thought the vehicle was a danger as well as a nuisance. They made a note of the registration number so that they could track down the owner. Nothing happened for over a month, except that one of the windows was smashed. We then tried phoning the council, who have a duty to remove a vehicle abandoned on open land or on the highway. They said they would attend to it, and we waited to see one of those stickers appear on the windscreen, giving notice that, unless an appeal was lodged, the car would be towed away on such and such a date. Nothing happened. We moaned about all this to a man who lived a few doors down the street – a man who believed in action. He immediately phoned a professional car-breaker, and within twenty minutes the abandoned car was towed away.

Now, presumably this was an unlawful action, and it certainly isn't suggested that you follow this example, but what seems worrisome is that in over four months the police and the local council hadn't been able to do anything, and that, once the car had gone, neither the police nor the council were the least concerned or perturbed or wanted to find out what had happened. And, of course, there was no action taken against the original owner who had dumped it.

PART IV

WHO CAN HELP?

Recent research undertaken by universities and government departments suggests that those of us who are
unhappy about our neighbours are in the majority. But
estimates vary as to just how much people feel they have a
real neighbour problem – it seems that the proportion is
somewhere between a third and a half and is rising. This
means that millions of people are seriously worried or
distressed by their neighbours.

Wherever possible, the law seeks to provide a
framework within which we can all live in close proximity
without making life intolerable for each other. The trouble
is, of course, that what the laws seeks to provide and what
actually happens are often two very different things.
Criminal Law may outlaw robbery, mayhem and murder –
but this doesn't mean that such horrors don't take place.
Indeed, not only do they take place but there is what
many would regard as an inadequate apprehension and
conviction rate of those responsible. The law is
overstretched. Life is very complicated. The chances of a
thief, vandal or confidence trickster getting away with it
are very high.

The same is regrettably true of thoughtless, insensitive
or bloody-minded neighbours. Anyone who has tried to
find someone capable of quietening a party at 2 a.m. or
persuading a neighbour not to park inconsiderately, or
convincing a neighbour that he or she should keep their
dog under proper control, may well have given up the
cause as lost.

It isn't. There are already many agencies that exist to
help you tackle a neighbour problem, and the signs are

that more funds and more effort may be put into this. It's clearly in everyone's best interest. A neighbourhood or community that is at war with itself or is torn by inner strife is going to be one that induces more stress, ill-health, injury, time off work and family upsets and takes up a great deal of important police, social workers', housing officers' and others' time.

Many people feel that what adds to the horror of having to dispute with a neighbour is the feeling that there's nobody to turn to or that, even if there is, there's nothing that can be done. We're all too busy nowadays – too busy getting on with our own lives, fastening the locks and chains on our own doors and watching the same soap operas on our individual televisions in our own little living-rooms. Living is still a precarious occupation, made all the more so if we should deign to complain. We accept shoddy goods, bad services, incompetent professional help, deceitful politicians – why shouldn't we also accept anti-social neighbours?

The first thing to do is to examine the agencies that already exist, to ascertain which would be the most likely to help in any particular situation and to see how they may be contacted.

19   The Police

Despite our many complaints, moans and grumbles about the police, they are usually the people we turn to when a neighbour dispute has flared into open conflict or has reached a smouldering intensity that we can no longer abide. Sometimes that happens in the early hours of the morning. The noisy party is well out of hand, stereos are booming, car doors are slamming, people are laughing hysterically in the road, sleep is impossible. We phone the police – simply because there isn't anyone else we *can* phone at 2 a.m.

At other times we feel we have put up with our neighbours' sullen, stupid and thoughtless behaviour long enough – for years and years we've let him or her get away with throwing rubbish all over the place, or playing that bloody TV at full volume all day, or spitting on our antirrhinums. Now we can stand it no longer. We feel prison is the only suitable place for someone so unthinking and unpleasant. We phone the police – simply because there isn't anyone else who deals in problems of right and wrong.

The police view of all this is that they would dearly like to see neighbours getting on well with each other but, unless a riot, crime or breach of the peace is likely to happen, it isn't any of their business. They also feel that they are called in as a last resort, when the dispute is completely out of hand. Some disputes flare up very quickly – especially those with an element of racial harassment or racism. Others are much slower to evolve, but, in either case, the police are involved too late or inappropriately. Usually they are called upon to deal with what is entirely a civil matter.

We may see the police as a twenty-four-hour-a-day agency to settle any and every problem, from murder to unwanted cooking-smells. The police see their role in dealing with neighbour disputes as limited to (a) defusing the situation, or (b) directing the parties involved to other agencies, or (c) preventing a breach of the peace.

Apart from noisy parties (to which the police are never invited but often summoned), most individual disputes arise out of long-standing rows, some of which have been going on for over thirty years. The origin may be long forgotten or have to do with what seems a minor irritation – a garden spade that was borrowed and returned in a dirty condition, or a stupid piece of parking one afternoon – but event has piled upon event, grudge upon grudge, resentment upon resentment, until breaking-point is reached. The police are still seen by many as arbiters of right and wrong, people who can make an authoritative and definitive statement about what should and should not be. So one party to the dispute calls in the police, and

PC Solomon, in all his wisdom, has the unenviable task of sorting out thirty years of ill will.

In some areas the situation is now greatly complicated by the possible added ingredient of racism, which the police often euphemistically refer as 'the racial angle'. An angry occupier may call his neighbour a 'black bastard' or 'white bastard' instead of simply a 'bastard'. Technically, what started as a civil dispute has now entered into other, more complicated issues, perhaps involving Community Race Officers, Racial Welfare Officers and Housing Departments.

Defusing the Situation
Some areas (inner city boroughs) have a designated officer of the Environmental Health Department (see Sections 50, Noise – General, and 52, Parties, and Chapter 21, Environmental Health Officers) whose job it is to be on call, all night if need be, to go from one noisy party complained of to another, trying to quieten things down. It's usually a 'he', and he's usually accompanied by a police officer (male or female) for protection's sake. The police like this arrangement because they see it as working more efficiently and effectively than if the police officer went alone. An Environmental Health Officer can serve a notice on the noisy party there and then, if the ravers don't comply with his request to make less noise, and the organizers of the party can subsequently be taken to court. The police, on the other hand, can do little on their own, since there is no crime of noise. They can take the initiative only where they have reasonable grounds for believing that a breach of the peace may occur – and that is not as easy to prove to a magistrate as we may think – or where they have reason to believe drugs are present.

To the police, the problem of disputes between neighbours, or mere bickering between neighbours, has become worse where local communities have lost their sense of corporate identity. They don't see the past as a series of Golden Ages where we all got on well with our neighbours – far from it – but older police officers recall times past when neighbour disputes were settled by the community, by someone being talked out of an unreasonable attitude or being given a thick ear, or the neighbourhood as a whole bringing pressure to bear on a particularly noisy or inconsiderate member. Police talk about a decline in 'local involvement' in their area. Many people would agree with this – we move house more often than we used to, we work further away from home, we have more disparate work patterns. People have to move to where the work is, rather than working in the local factory, as they did maybe less than a generation ago. There's also the problem that one person's wage may not be enough to run the house, so both partners are out at work all day. The late evening, when people are tired after a day's work, is not the best time to build up friendly relations with your neighbours. Now that so many people own a car, even the 'local' pub may well have ceased to be very local – young people in particular are prepared to drive a considerable distance to drink in the pub of their choice, and many couples drive twenty to thirty miles on a Friday or Saturday night for their evening out. With a high level of unemployment, especially among the young, there is a sharp divide between those whose days begin early in the morning and end early at night, and those whose days begin early in the afternoon and end very, very early in the morning.

The police also see a clear divide between young and old, in lifestyles and in attitudes to the neighbourhood. It's mostly old people who complain about dog mess, noise, litter and yobbish behaviour. Often these old people are genuinely frightened of the young and turn to the police for protection from what they fear *might* happen as much as to complain about what *has* happened. The police are having to grapple with very complex social issues and situations that may well be worsened by the general poverty of an area.

Although they are often called upon to deal with problems that are insoluble or which may be nothing to do with them, the police have a surprising amount of sympathy with people who complain about their neighbours, and they are well aware of the pressures people live under in the areas they police. One police sergeant I spoke to reckoned that tower blocks were 'the worst thing ever invented'. People living in them are isolated: they don't know who lives above or below them. It's possible to meet other residents of a tower block in a lift and not have the slightest idea whether or not they are near neighbours, whether they're the seemingly reasonable couple who don't give any trouble or the loutish family who apparently perform a nightly clog dance overhead, or visiting thieves.

The police are, therefore, having to defuse situations where there's little in the way of a neighbourhood feeling or spirit to fall back on. We may turn to the police: there are few other agencies they can turn to. One of the reasons why they are happy with their own Neighbourhood Watch schemes is that they have a number of helpful spin-offs in lessening animosity or tension within a neighbourhood. By participating in such a scheme, neighbours may develop a concern for one another, or the intensity of disputes between neighbours may be lowered. Members of the neighbourhood may share views and opinions more or may seek the involvement of their local police (whom they may know better) at an earlier time and more constructively than hitherto, before matters have got out of hand. They may even anticipate things going wrong – bad parking, noise, dog mess etc – and ask the local 'beat' officer to have a word with the potential offender while passing.

Clearly, it doesn't do to expect too much of the scheme. It has its limitations and works much better in some areas than others. Cynics may say that it works only in comparatively middle-class areas, where everyone has their own separate dwelling, their own garden, plenty of space, a pleasant environment and money in the bank. Under these circumstances it may seem much easier to get on well with your neighbour. In a poor, overcrowded, unattractive area, with inadequate space and facilities and with a high level of unemployment, people are under far more stress, tempers are likely to be shorter, noise far more obtrusive and breaking-point reached far earlier. Nevertheless, an increasing number of people, the police among them see *any* schemes which attempt to set up neighbourhood structures and encourage community feelings as being well worth trying.

Allied to the Neighbourhood Watch scheme is the policy in police forces of re-inventing the 'home beat' officer. He or she may link up with various other local bodies or individuals – caretakers in blocks of flats, officers or representatives of local tenants' associations. The role of the home beat officer is seen as largely preventative in terms of both crime and the petty civil unrest that may stem from problems between neighbours. There is a large element of counselling in the work of the home beat officer. He or she is seen by senior police officers as a 'go-between' and, therefore, as a person well placed to defuse problems. By getting to know their area, home beat officers also get to know the people who live in it, and are able to identify what may be called 'problem families'. It may be frowned upon by some to label people in this way, but the police experience is that there are often one or two families on estates or in streets around whom trouble seems to settle far more frequently than elsewhere.

This isn't necessarily a question of criminal activities, though there may be incidents of taking and driving away motor cars, a little receiving or thieving, or local vandalism. These families may pose problems for their neighbours because of the mess they make, the things they burn, the animals they keep, the noise they make etc. In areas where there are home beat police officers, it is much easier for neighbours so plagued to consult them and to ask them to intervene. The police accept this as part of the role of a home beat officer, and if the neighbour is worried that he or she may be seen talking to the police – thus arousing further malice in the offencers, they suggest writing to the local police station, outlining what's wrong. The station sergeant will then pass the complaint on to the home beat officer with instructions to defuse the situation as far as possible.

Directing Parties to Other Agencies
Because there is such a premium on police time, the police
would dearly love to see more agencies involved in trying
to settle neighbour disputes. At the moment there are few.
In the case of noisy parties, there is the Environmental
Health Officer in some inner city boroughs – council
officials in more rural areas tend to suggest that noise
simply isn't a problem in the country. Our own
experience, when we lived on the Kent/Sussex border,
was that the countryside is every bit as noisy as the city,
with ceaseless traffic on all but the tiniest of lanes,
helicopters spraying crops, combine harvesters, dogs by
the dozen, cows, shooting-parties, chickens, church bells
and aircraft (since most rural areas appear to be on the
flight path to some airport or other).

As far as possible, the police link up with existing
services and organizations within their own area. They
liaise with local tenants' associations, more to keep a
general eye on an estate than to deal with any specific
dispute. Representatives of a tenants' association may tell
the police if there seems to be a growing problem with
vandalism on their estate. If there are incidents of racism
on the estate, the local Housing Officers are likely to be
informed (see Chapter 22, Housing Officers). The police
regard tenants' associations as 'ginger groups' that seek to
get things done, but not necessarily, indeed only rarely, to
involve the police. The effectiveness of a tenants'
association, in police eyes, depends on the degree of
involvement of those in the area.

Preventing a Breach of the Peace
This is the most likely reason why the police would
intervene in a dispute between neigbbours – to prevent a
breach of the peace occurring. The offence dates back to
the Administration of Justice Act, 1260, but is now covered
by the Criminal Law Act, 1967. Under section 3 of that Act,
anyone is empowered to use ' ... such force as is
reasonable in the circumstances ... in the ... prevention of
crime, or in effecting or assisting in the arrest of offenders
or of persons unlawfully at large'. It's a vague, catch-all

concept which we may see as a dead liberty on the part of the old Bill but which the police know may well be very hard to prove satisfactorily in court.

The good thing about breach of the peace, where it's applicable to neighbour problems, is in the remedy or penalty that the court may impose. If two neighbours have been metaphorically at each other's throats for decades (and that in itself may pose problems for other neighbours), the court may decide that they shall both be bound over to keep the peace, with a sum of money held over as surety. The effect of this is to place a blanket embargo on stroppiness and antagonism between the two neighbours on pain of their appearing again in court and losing money. This may well bring some much-needed peace and quiet to the neighbourhood, at least for a while. Perhaps it would be better to call it 'breach of the peace and quiet'. A major difficulty for the police in all these situations is that whoever is being accused of behaviour causing or likely to cause breach of the peace must be found actually commiting the act – the police cannot rely on the statements of injured neighbours.

General Conclusions
The police feel they are called upon far too often to deal with matters that lie outside their province, particularly in complaints about noise. Here the police suggest a laid-back approach which may not cut much ice with those of us who are regularly victims to broken nights. The police believe in 'having a quiet word'. All will be different in the morning, they say, when the revellers will be silent, sober and hungover. They also offer the advice to the party-givers that they warn neighbours of a forthcoming party. It's not much help at 2 a.m., when you feel like lobbing bricks at the partygoers. The advice the police give to their own officers about noisy parties is, 'Don't ever go inside.'

In other matters the police can be very understanding and sympathetic to those of us with neighbour problems. Even in the matter of noisy parties they admit that, though their intervention may persuade people to turn the noise down, it'll be turned up again the minute the police are out of earshot. In general, they will help where they can, but they feel a great deal of preventative and educational work needs to be done by others to foster a closer and more sensitive atmosphere of neighbourliness.

Summary
1. Go to the police if the situation has got so far out of hand that threats are being made. You may first wish to try to calm things down yourself, placing your hands gently in your pockets (a sign that you are not considering thumping anyone) and talking gently and rationally to your difficult neighbour. On the other hand, bearing in mind that your neighbour may be a nut case, you may prefer to go straight to the police.
2. Go to the police if your neighbour starts damaging your property: taking a hammer or paint-stripper to your car, kicking the door of your flat, hurling your bicycle under a large passing lorry, poisoning your fishpond, setting his dog on your pet rabbit, shooting at your own dog. Sadly, all these things, and many more, have been done.

20   Solicitors

In the heat of the moment, people tend to see the police as the agency most likely to deal with their troublesome neighbour. On calmer reflection, they may think of turning to a solicitor. The former are the shock troops of social control, but the latter have all the pomp and majesty of the law behind them *and* may extract a heavy financial penalty from the errant neighbour. It would really seem to depend whether, in the hardest part of your heart, you wished to see your neighbour in gaol or bankrupt.

In the first instance, solicitors are there not to take people to court but to give them advice, and one of the

pieces of advice that many solicitors wish to pass on to us
is that the law cannot resolve animosity that arises
between neighbours. Indeed, our own legal system, based
as it is on an adversarial model, is particularly ill-equipped
to help neighbours get on well together. In English and
Scottish law there has to be a winner and a loser, because
our system seeks the outcome to a contest, not the
solution to a problem. Other countries, perhaps more
enlightened, have a more investigative approach which
seeks to bring the two parties together. In France there is a
person called the *Compasiteur Amiable*, whose job it is to do
just that. It is unlikely, however, say solicitors in England,
that going to law will do anything to lessen any rancour
that already exists between two disputing neighbours.

84 GOING TO A SOLICITOR

Having accepted all this, it may be helpful to see what will
happen if you feel forced to consult a solicitor about a
neighbour dispute.   There are hundreds of solicitors in
the British Isles. They are listed in Yellow Pages, and
there's almost certainly one near you. You can go in,
straight off the street, and ask to see a solicitor, but such
an unheralded approach may make them suspect that you
have just murdered someone. It's better to phone and
make an appointment. Don't write a letter asking for an
appointment. This would mean that the solicitor has to
write back, and that may well mean that you would be
charged for a letter. Solicitors' letters do not come cheap.

Having made an appointment to see the solicitor, the
next thing to do is keep it, punctually. Solicitors (in fact, all
lawyers) do not take kindly to being kept waiting or
worse, to being ignored altogether. Their time is valuable
in their eyes, expensive in yours. They are not, however,
unfriendly or inaccessible people on the whole. They exist
to listen to people's problems and to try to give them good
advice as to how to handle these problems.   If you do
consult a solicitor about your neighbour, he or she will
listen to what you have to say, asking the occasional

question, clearing the occasional point, trying to make the clearest possible sense of our long and rambling tales of woe, and will then tell you what they think you should do next.

85   SOLICITORS' ADVICE

This could be anything from moving house, consulting another solicitor, trying to make peace with your neighbour, changing your way of life, undoing some of the things you have just done, to leaving the matter in their own capable hands.

They will also, of course, tell you where you stand legally. It's very important to remember that solicitors know the law. They know how it works, they know what it says, they know its many foibles. In the case of neighbour disputes, one of the things they know is that county courts (where most neighbour disputes end up if legal action is taken) have a somewhat jaundiced view of such squabbles. In the hurly-burly of breach of contract, matrimonial causes, and landlord and tenant actions, county court judges put neighbour disputes well down their list of priorities.

If your case comes to court, be prepared for a long wait on the day appointed for the hearing. Neighbour disputes are usually heard last. This isn't mere bloody-mindedness on the part of the county court judges. It may be possible to estimate roughly how long other cases may take; it is extremely difficult to make any sort of forecast as to how long a 'neighbours' case may take. For example, in a case where there is a disputed boundary, a judge may have to visit the property in question – this will take a lot of time and incur a lot of expense.

This is another point that a solicitor may make about neighbour problems. Even if you have a sure-fire, water-tight, one-hundred-per-cent-guaranteed case, you may leave the court with what seems, at best, a Pyrrhic victory. In practice, lawyers will tell you, the winner of a case may recover as little as twenty-five per cent of what it cost him or her to bring the action.

86   SEEING A SOLICITOR

1. Make sure it's the sort of issue a solicitor could help you with – it's no good going to see a solicitor about a 'one-off' noisy party.
2. Check that there isn't some other (possibly cheaper) person who could be of more use – e.g. Housing Officer, Environmental Health Officer, Citizens' Advice Bureau, tenants' association etc.
3. If you're satisfied no one else will do, ask friends to recommend a solicitor.
4. Phone to make an appointment.
5. Do your homework – write down the salient points in the saga of you and your neighbour, and the order of events.
6. Keep your appointment with the solicitor – be on time.
7. Be honest with your solicitor – no exaggerations and no holding back.
8. Accept his or her advice on matters of law – but you don't have to agree with him or her otherwise.
9. Pay the bill.

87   LEGAL REMEDIES

There are other reasons why solicitors may counsel caution in going to court with a neighbour problem. Many of the disputes between neighbours need far speedier action to resolve them than the long haul of litigation can supply. The best legal remedy in cases of nuisance (noise, bonfires etc.) or where your neighbour is rapidly lopping a favourite tree or screening hedge is an injunction (in Scotland, an interdict). There are two sorts of injunctions: 'mandatory', which command that something be done, and 'prohibitory', which forbid something. You can also seek an injunction to prevent something being done – governments do it all the time. An injunction may be 'interlocutory', which is one granted provisionally before the hearing of an action, or 'perpetual', which is granted after the case has come to court.

Courts cannot, however, grant permanent injunctions, and judges are often hesitant about granting even temporary ones. There is, to the legal mind, something intangible about injunctions. Most judges are far happier to deal with neighbour disputes where the action is one for damages, where a cash value can be put on the wrong suffered.

The difficulty here is that there are some wrongs suffered that it is impossible to put into cash terms. Suppose a row of laurel bushes separates your property from that of your neighbour. The bushes are on your side of the boundary line, have been there for years, and afford both you and your neighbour what you regard as a pleasant screen, giving you both a measure of privacy. One day your neighbour takes offence at the row of bushes and decides to cut them down. No matter how fast you drive to your solicitor, no matter how quickly he races to court with an application for an injunction, the probability is that your neighbour will have levelled the hedge before the law can do anything to stop him.

So you take your neighbour to court. Even if you win your action for damages and trespass, what value will be put on the laurel bushes? The cost of replacement? What sort of replacement? Immature laurel bushes which don't act as a screen? No solicitor pretends to be able to guess what value should be put on a screen that has been lost, privacy that has been so rudely disturbed, or twenty years of growing.

88   THE SORT OF PROBLEM TO BRING TO A SOLICITOR

Solicitors are lawyers first, warm, kindly, understanding human beings second. They are, therefore, best at dealing with legal matters – the more legal the matter, the better they are at dealing with it. On the sort of wishy-washy issues of whether a dog is barking too much or whether your neighbouring violinist practices too much, they have to rely on Case Law to predict the outcome of a possible action. Since there won't be a case already heard that exactly fits the facts in your case, it's very hard for a solicitor to say with any certainty what would happen if your case came to court. On matters of noise, smoke or other aggravations covered by Statute Law, it's much better to go to the local council, especially if you can get other residents in the neighbourhood to support your complaint.

On the other hand, if your complaint is in the nature of a boundary dispute or the interpretation of some legal document (say the terms of a lease), a solicitor is definitely the person to go to. There are all sorts of complications about title to land of which we poor laypeople are entirely ignorant. In some cases, whether it's wise to go to law or not may depend on whether your property is in an area of registered or unregistered land – and there are some particular regional variations. For example, the area in Essex between Southend and Benfleet, which includes Hadleigh and Canvey, is one where most rights to title are possessory – they arose from squatting. This was due largely to the massive slaughter in the First World War of the previous legal owners.

Similarly, in what amounts to the old London County Council area, boundary disputes, problems about party walls and building development, are governed by the London Building Acts, tricky things that need a solicitor and a surveyor to interpret. Outside the old LCC area, according to at least one solicitor, 'It's a pure punch-up in the courts, and the new building regulations have done nothing to sort out the problems.'

Perhaps the simplest way of looking at the question of whom to consult, is to say that, the bigger the problem, the more sensible it may be to go to a solicitor.

Summary
Go to a solicitor if the problem
(a) is anything to do with a document: a lease, restrictive covenant, deeds to property etc;
(b) centres around property – remember, the law is much more certain about property matters than it is about personal matters;
(c) is about long-term interests;
(d) concerns a matter of legal principle, e.g. the repair and maintenance of shared walls, paths and driveways;

(e) involves a considerable infringement of your quiet enjoyment of your own land. (See Section 50, Noise – General.)

21   Environmental Health Officers

By virtue (and that seems an appropriate word for so good a statute) of the Public Health Act, 1936, section 9, local authorities have a duty to cause their districts to be inspected 'from time to time for the detection of statutory nuisances' (see Chapter 14, Statutory Nuisance). Under the Control of Pollution Act, 1974, local authorities are empowered to deal with the noise problems. The person whose job it is to see that these duties are carried out is the local Environmental Health Officer. He or she runs a special department, usually understaffed, always under-funded, and together these people have the uneviable task of trying to keep their locality reasonably quiet, smoke-free and happy.

89   HOW ENVIRONMENTAL HEALTH DEPARTMENTS WORK

Suppose you have a complaint about one of your neighbours, and you believe that the cause of your complaint comes within the responsibility of the local council – suppose it is an example of statutory nuisance. This is roughly what happens:

You communicate your complaint to the council. It's possible to do this by phone or letter, but you may be able to explain more graphically and dramatically by putting in an appearance at the Environmental Health Office (EHO).

Having been made aware of the facts (as you see them), the council (in the person of one of the staff of the EHO) considers whether it is appropriate for them to take any action. What they may well do is invite both you and your neighbour to come together, maybe on neutral council territory, to see if the problem can be amicably worked out.

If your neighbour responds to the council's invitation, it may well be that he or she will first want to put the 'other' side of the story. Environmental Health Officers say there are nearly always two sides to a complaint and, like the police, that many of the disputes between neighbours that come to their attention have been going on for years.

If your neighbour has responded to the communication from the council, the officer working on it will try to negotiate a settlement between you and your neighbour. There isn't any statutory duty on them to do this, but most EHOs want their locality to run smoothly and with as little friction as possible.

If the council decides that action should be taken against your neighbour, they may serve an abatement notice which states three things:

(i) what the nuisance is considered to be, and

(ii) what steps must be taken to stop it, and

(iii) the time limit within which these steps must be taken.

If your neighbour fails to take the appropriate steps within the time limit, technically the council can take your neighbour to the local magistrate's court to get a nuisance order. The difference between a notice and an order is a simple one: a notice informs your neighbour that a nuisance he is committing has been noticed and asks him to stop; an order orders him to stop or suffer the legal penalties.

In practice, however, councils are reluctant to go this far. It all takes a great deal of time. In the first place twenty-eight days notice has to be served on your neighbour before any further action can be taken. It may take the court up to three months to fix a date for the hearing, and that date will almost certainly be many more months away. Lastly, the council's legal department (who may have far weightier problems than yours on their hands) takes up to six months to process the information and prepare their case against your neighbour. The whole thing can take up to a year to come to court.

It's not often that this provision is used. Councils hope that you and your neighbour will have come to some sort of truce before matters reach this stage. They have many reservations about going to such lengths, among them that, even if the court makes an.order, it's the council that has to check that the order is being complied with, which means tying up more staff in a great deal more work. Furthermore, the council has the unenviable and difficult (often impossible) duty to recover its costs in such an action.

EHOs say that all this sort of thing is very time-consuming for local authorities and that the sort of problem they are dealing with will probably affect only two people – people who may never grow to love one another. They also have to be prepared for many wasted journeys. To take action, the local authority has actually to hear the noise complained of. This means that officers may have to visit the premises several times to establish that a nuisance is taking place. Often they arrive, listen, hear nothing and are then told by the complainant 'Oh, he isn't doing it today/tonight.' The officers can leave recording-equipment for the complainant to make his own recordings of the noise but, as we have already seen, such machines are expensive, noise has to be recorded over a long period (at least a week) and there is a long queue in many localities for the use of such machines. And then someone at the council offices has to listen to a week's worth of recordings to estimate whether or not a nuisance is being committed.

Nevertheless, don't be disheartened – councils will act where they feel you have a genuine grievance. One Environmental Health Officer described a particular case which had come to court in which a professional pianist was giving his neighbour a hard time by practising up to 2 a.m. – not only that: he was playing a lot of Wagner. The neighbour complained to the council. The council tried to reason with the pianist. The pianist took little notice. In came the officers of the Environmental Health Department, people trained in accoustics and noise-control. They offered advice to the pianist as to how he could reduce the amount of noise that was getting through to his neighbour. And still the pianist played Wagner. A notice was served: the melody lingered on. The case eventually came to court, and the magistrates laid down conditions under which they considered piano practice was reasonable. The Environmental Health Officer believed that these conditions were adhered to by the pianist.

90 PROBLEMS DEALT WITH BY EHOs

Except in the most remote of rural areas, most EHOs say that the greatest problem is that of noise, and that it is growing alarmingly. In one Outer London borough, with a reputation for poise, stability and 'niceness', the number of complaints about noise in 1987 was thirty per cent higher than the number in 1986. Particular problems about noise related to construction sites and the use of industrial plant and machinery. This was a locality where noisy parties and untrained dogs didn't present an enormous problem, maybe because most people had a reasonable amount of space to live in. Inner city boroughs have worse tales to tell.

But even in the desirable suburbs inhabited by the Tom and Barbara Goods of this world, noise can become a problem. Most EHOs say that, at first instance, they would like to see people attempting to sort out their own problems far earlier. People are too tolerant for too long and then go over the top, demanding that the council bring in the SAS, the marines and a gunboat to deal with what may have started out as a very minor problem. Many EHOs also say that neighbours seem far keener to use professional bodies than to talk to each other about a problem. Not only is this often a more unsatisfactory way of attempting to resolve a dispute between neighbours but any time spent by the local EHO is trying to deal with such disputes pushes other work into second place. It's the other work, which is often to the benefit of the whole environment and may well be of a preventative nature, that EHOs regard as the more important. Legally all local authorities have to investigate the one-to-one complaint situation, but already some local authorities are saying they won't, simply because they can't.

Local authorities have considerable powers, on paper, to deal with noise problems. Under the Control of Pollution Act, 1974, they may serve a Prohibition Notice on anyone causing a noise nuisance if the level of noise constitutes a statutory nuisance. Failure to comply with the notice may result in fines of up to £200 for a first offence plus up to £50 per day for each day if the noise continues thereafter.

The trouble is that there is no fixed level above which noise constitutes a statutory nuisance. So it's up to the poor Environmental Health Officer to decide according to volume, frequency and persistence of the noise, whether or not it would constitute a nuisance in the eyes of the law. In making your complaint, therefore, you are asking a lot of the EHO. It's understandable if he greets your complaint with less than boundless joy.

Traffic Noise

This isn't a 'neighbour problem' but a neighbourhood one. Local authorities are getting more and more complaints about traffic noise. If you are faced with this problem, you may be able to get a grant to help towards the cost of noise insulation for your house if the increase in noise is due to a new road being built or to substantial alterations in the amount of traffic using an existing road. Local authorities in fact have a duty to let people know about their possible right to such a grant.

Smoke

This is another common cause of complaint to EHOs. Contrary to popular belief, there aren't any restrictions on when your neighbour can light a bonfire. There are rules about how near a road a bonfire may be, and too many, or too lengthy, bonfires may well constitute nuisance. The general attitude of the law is that you mustn't have a fire that causes a nuisance. We are back to the notion of what is reasonable, and it's up to the local authority in many cases to decide. On the whole, however, most EHOs are unlikely to do anything about your neighbour's bonfires other than sympathize. They certainly won't want to get involved in a psychological analysis of the state of your neighbour's mind and his or her bottomless capacity for evil. And it's no good complaining that your neighbour lights the bonfire when your washing is hanging on the line. This may be inconsiderate, stupid, unneighbourly – it isn't illegal.

If you live next door to a demolition site, however, you may get a more positive response from the EHO. Environmental Health Officers in town and cities say that a common cause of trouble and complaint is the bonfire that crackles and flares away on a demolition or building site. It is an offence to cause smoke on a demolition site unless burning timbers infected with dry rot, e.g. that would otherwise constitute a danger if carried away, the danger coming from wind-blown spores of dry rot fungus. If fires are lit on demolition sites, the local authority usually takes statutory action, serving notices on the demolition company and (if necessary) including recurring nuisance notices, which make any subsequent fires an offence. It's a catch-all method of dealing with the problem. The local authority does, however, need to obtain evidence of subsequent fires, and this is where local residents can play a part. If you've complained about such fires to the local authority but the fires recur, don't assume that the local authority has done nothing about it – they can't afford the staff to monitor demolition sites all day every day. If a recurring nuisance notice has been served and you report another fire, the local authority should then be able to take further action, bringing the offending company to court.

The difficulty is, of course, that the EHO is often having to deal with a problem when it's too late. Nero may have fiddled while Rome burned – had he wanted to slap a nuisance notice on the incendiaries, he may well have been too late. All members of a demolition squad have to do, when the council officer arrives, is to feign ignorance of the law, apologize and take steps to extinguish the fire. By the time your complaint has reached the EHO, and the council officer has reached the site, the demolition squad may well have burnt most of the rubbish anyway. There is perhaps a need for a change in the law here.

Dog Mess

Increasingly, people are beginning to see direct and immediate action as the best way to deal with this problem. A ready supply of small plastic bags, a scoop and the necessary courage to confront your neighbour (face to faeces, as it were) whenever his or her dog fouls your garden or the pavement directly outside your house may be all you need. Dog-owners (like dogs) may become very aggressive in manner when approached in this way, but over a period of time it does seem to pay dividends.

If you aren't up to what the French call *action directe*, and the offending matter accumulates, you can contact the EHO, who have powers to serve a notice on your neighbour under the dear old Public Health Act, 1936. Certainly, the council will act if they consider there is any possibility of a threat to health.

Elderly People

This is not to suggest that elderly people constitute a nuisance, but EHOs are faced occasionally with the problem of an elderly person who cannot look after his or her property. The house or flat may get into a verminous state or may be a haven for a dozen or more ex-stray cats, all of whom are housebound. Living next door to such a person does pose a real problem. We don't like to interfere: some would say we carry the doctrine of non-interference too far. In time, we become increasingly and distressingly aware that all is not well next door.

The EHO, informed of such a situation, will contact local social services. Together they will approach your neighbour, who may well be unaware of the health danger that he or she is both running and causing. In practice, your neighbour will not be bundled away to a Home for the Chronically Incompetent. The council, through its several offices, will do what it can to clean up the premises and make sure all is well. The worry is, however, that within a couple of months the unhealthy status quo may well be restored. EHOs say that this problem, too, is on the increase.

Vermin

In the case of vermin, local authorities, through their EHOs, operate free services to deal with rats and mice, cockroaches and bedbugs – all of which can spread diseases. You are unlikely to be able to distinguish cockroaches or bedbugs on your neighbour's property (unless you are flying a model aircraft with a powerful telephoto lens on the nose cone), but if you see rats or mice next door, you can report the matter to the council if you can't deal direct with your neighbour.

Wild Animals

If you're alarmed at the sudden appearance of snakes, eagles, alligators, chimpanzees etc in your neighbour's garden, you can check with your local council. To keep such creatures, your neighbour must have a licence issued by the local authority, and that licence won't have been issued unless the authority (on the advice of a vet) is satisfied that the animal concerned is looked after and kept securely in the right conditions. It's worth checking, since a licence costs £120 a year and it's quite possible, therefore, that your neighbour hasn't applied for a licence in the hope that he or she will get away with it. This could mean that the creature isn't being kept safely or humanely.

91 GENERAL ADVICE OF EHOs

Environmental Health Officers are very much in the front line when it comes to neighbour disputes. It's part of their job to see that the environment in which we live is at least reasonably pleasant, and various acts of Parliament impose strict duties on them to protect us from noise, smoke, effluvia, vermin and industrial waste. At the moment, it would seem that few of them have the resources to deal with a rapidly growing problem. There are three ways in which they feel we could help ourselves and, in so doing, help them.

The first is by talking more with our neighbours. Without that communication, problems grow out of all proportion, misunderstandings arise, compromises that might easily be reached are never even considered, and resentment smoulders until it bursts into a flame of violent anger. A lot of time, trouble and expense could be saved, and a lot of problems could be dealt with far more speedily and effectively, if we talked more with each other. We don't have to live in each other's pockets, but, where neighbours are used to talking before trouble arises, it does seem to help once they do.

Secondly, EHOs feel that people should be more considerate. Children do make noise when they're playing in the garden or on the designated play areas of council estates; it isn't possible to use an electric drill silently; bicycles are not easy things to store. It may be hard to keep in touch with what is or isn't reasonable behaviour, but we must all try.

Lastly, some EHOs despair at the 'Englishman's-Home-Is-His-Castle' syndrome. People seem increasingly to hold the view that 'This is my property and I can do what the hell I like to it and on it.' A problem of this magnitude needs to be tackled nationwide.

22   Housing Officers

92   ROLE OF HOUSING OFFICERS

Local authorities are the landlords of all the council flats, maisonettes and houses in the country. Some of the council estates they administer are huge, housing thousands of people, sometimes in high-rise blocks of flats or other, less than desirable surroundings. This can lead to problems, and it is the job of Housing Officers (sometimes called Housing Assistants) to sort out many of the problems that arise among and between council tenants, many of them disputes between neighbours. They tend to get involved mainly where the matter complained of is a breach of the original tenancy agreement between council and tenant.

Housing officers are not given any special training in handling such disputes, though many think it would be a good idea if they were. Without any such training, the problem is that, although Housing Officers may attempt to resolve conflicts between neighbours, the focus is rarely upon changing the relationship between the complainant and the alleged 'offender'. Such expertise as Housing Officers have, they pick up as they go along, though they do have the advice of senior, more experienced staff.

Most of the complaints they receive come under the broad heading of nuisance, and of these most relate to noise. Whatever the complaint, the initial procedure is much the same – the Housing Officer is called upon to investigate. This requires visits to both the complainant and the alleged perpetrator of the nuisance – the Housing Officer has to be very careful at this and, at all stages, not to take sides. This would apply even where the party complained of was not a council tenant. In a situation where an owner-occupier or private tenant lived next door to a council tenant, however, it's extremely unlikely that the Housing Officer would ever take action against the council tenant. If the council tenant is at fault, they might well point this out and try to get the council tenant to end the nuisance, but Housing Officers work for the local authority and for the council tenants, not against them. Housing Officers try to see disputes as problems that require solutions, not as contests that need winners and losers. The hope is always that it will be possible to resolve the problem amicably.

If this isn't possible, the next step is for the Housing Officer to write a follow-up letter to the perpetrator. The letter sets out the general nature of the complaint that has been made, draws attention to the relevant conditions of the tenancy (i.e. that part of the tenancy agreement the council feels the tenant is in breach of) and seeks co-operation from those concerned. It may also say that the situation will continue to be monitored. If the nuisance ceases, no further action is taken. If it doesn't, the tenant who is complaining will probably be asked to 'log' further occurrences, recording the date, time and description of any further incidents.

If there is no improvement, it is possible that the Housing Officer will eventually consult the local authority solicitor to see what can be done. Some feel there are fewer and fewer options open to the council. Before the Housing Act, 1980, council tenants had slightly less security of tenure when they were the alleged perpetrators of nuisance. Before the Act, all the local authority had to do was to satisfy themselves that a nuisance was being committed. Having done so, the local authority could apply to the county court for a possession order against the perpetrator of the nuisance. Now, however, the local authority has to prove to the court that they have just cause to be granted a possession order. This usually means that the complainant has to be prepared to go to court and stand in the witness box and say, 'This is what happened.'

93   PROBLEMS DEALT WITH BY HOUSING OFFICERS

Although the majority of the cases that come to their attention relate to noise, council tenants give Housing Officers a wide variety of problems to solve: keeping uncontrolled pets, running businesses from council properties, late-night visitors causing disturbances, the repair and parking of motor vehicles, even the warming-up of a motor-vehicle engine so that the exhaust fumes blow towards a neighbour's property.

Lorries Parked in Residential Areas
Some tenants have neighbours who work as lorry-drivers. There may well be special sites set aside in the area where lorries can be parked legitimately and without causing a nuisance, but these cost money. Some lorry-drivers pocket

the £5 a night parking allowance given them by their firm, and park in the road outside their own house. The trouble is that most lorries are too big. They take up a great deal of parking space that the private motorist could otherwise use, and they may well cause other kinds of obstruction.

If this happens to you, contact your local Housing Officer. He or she will, in turn, probably contact the lorry-driver's employers, who may well be able to have a helpful little word.

Noise

This has already been covered in Chapter 8, Noise, but one or two points need to be made here. From the Housing Officer's point of view (and this applies as much to cases concerning owner-occupiers), there is a great difficulty in persuading complainants to see the matter through to the end. Nine times out of ten, complainants about noise withdraw before the issue is settled, often through fear of reprisals.

Housing Officers are also having to tackle a situation where a great many people are under the misapprehension that, as landlords, a local authority can go in next door and *make* their neighbours quiet. Further complication comes from the fact that the local authority and the Housing Officers are seen as being responsible for moving in the guilty or noisy tenants in the first place, so they're the ones who ought to do something about it.

Many Housing Officers say that people would much rather go through the council than deal directly with their neighbour because they feel increasingly that their neighbour might turn to violence. It's safer to go to the council. It avoids face-to-face confrontation.

Some situations where noise creates disputes between neighbours can be tackled by installing improved sound insulation. Houses that have been converted into flats are particularly subject to noise problems. As a house occupied by one family, it may not have mattered that bedroom was on top of living-room with poor sound insulation in between. As separate dwellings, it does matter. Housing Officers may suggest carpeting (with finance from social services) or putting layers of felt or old newspapers under the carpet. Full-scale sound-proofing is prohibitively expensive for most local authorities and rarely solves the problem anyway.

Business Operating from Residential Premises

If a tenant wishes to operate a business from council property (or if an owner-occupier wishes to do so from his or her own house or flat), he or she should first obtain planning permission. Without this permission, enforcement action can be taken requiring the business to cease. If you're faced with a neighbour who is operating such a business, and it's causing you discomfort, it's worth checking that your neighbour has the necessary planning permission. You can do this at your local council offices.

You should note, however, that action here may well be a lengthy matter, as the person complained of (your neighbour) has the right to appeal to the Department of the Environment. This can lead to delays of six to nine months.

Once your neighbour's appeal has been dismissed, the council can proceed against him in the magistrate's court. If the case is proved, your neighbour may be fined. Most councils won't take this sort of action, for a simple, if slightly odd, reason. An enforcement notice forbidding the use of the premises for business purposes has to be served on the owner of the freehold of the property concerned. The local authority owns the freehold of council houses and council flats. The outcome would, therefore, be one council department taking action against another.

Racial Problems

To the person suffering racial abuse or harassment, nothing is so important, so destructive or so unpleasant. The fewer black people in the neighbourhood, the more personal and painful it seems. Housing Officers say that racism can be easier to deal with than many other problems, because it is a crime and they are presented with a situation where there is a very obvious villain and victim. This is so only where the racism is public and open, however. Blatant racism among neighbours is easier to tackle than the furtive variety.

If you are the victim of racial abuse, you should inform your local Housing Officer. Provision is made by most local authorities to transfer tenants where incidents of racism occur. Many local authorities publish guidelines about racial harassment, recommending that attacks of a racial nature should immediately be reported to the police and the council, and that assistance be sought from the local Council for Community Relations. However, local authorities also point out that they are not in such a strong position when dealing with racial abuse or attacks from owner-occupiers on council tenants. Here you really have to bring in the police, though you may get a better response if you proceed via your local Council for Community Relations or similar body.

Some councils also give top priority to the removal of sexist or racist graffiti, pledging to remove it within twenty-four hours of its discovery. To do so, they need tenants to report incidents of such graffiti as quickly as possible.

Sexual Discrimination or Abuse

In principle, many local authorities make similar pledges to deal as quickly and effectively with incidents of sexual harassment as they do racism. If you are a tenant on a council estate and feel that you are being subject to sexual harassment, get in touch with your local Housing Officer. It might also be an idea to see what literature the council publishes on this subject. From it you should be able to gauge how rigorously they will deal with your complaint.

Car-Parking

Councils try wherever possible to provide adequate parking spaces for their housing estates. Often, sadly, the provision isn't adequate, and, even where it is, it relies on the good sense of the motorists using the estate. If you are regularly inconvenienced by the stupidity of your neighbour – a person who parks wherever it's convenient for him and without a thought for anyone else, take the registration number of your neighbour's vehicle and report him to your local Housing Officer.

Some local authority housing estates are plagued by the 'indiscriminate riding of bicycles and motorbikes'. Offenders are usually young people, often those bored out of their minds. It's a real problem for old people, who are frightened as well as annoyed by the noise, and who may read threats into the situation, feeling that they are under some kind of attack.

One way to avoid this sort of problem might be to set up different sorts of council estates, each one housing different sorts of tenants – the classic example of this is the Sunset Home environment for senior citizens. A lot of tenants are in favour of this, young and old, but it's a piece of social engineering that doesn't meet with everyone's approval and, anyway, most councils don't have the right sort of housing stock or the financial resources to put such a scheme into operation.

Car Repairs
On some council estates this is reckoned to be the biggest problem, manifesting itself in oil slicks in the road and on the pavement, noise, pavements being obstructed by engine hoists and other pieces of machinery, roads being filled with old bangers in various stages of demolition. Sometimes it is a 'genuine' case of a family working on their own car simply to give it a new lease of life and some much-needed repairs, but more often it's a case of a small, unofficial business.

This creates more problems, as financial matters now enter. It may well be cheaper for the person repairing the cars to hire machinery on a twenty-four-hour basis rather than over the weekend. This means that, to get the most cost-effective use out of the hired machinery, work may well continue throughout the night, and friends with similar work to do on their cars may be invited round for a kind of Engine-Swapping/Panel-Beating/Arc-Welding Party.

If you're faced with this sort of situation, contact your

local Housing Officer. Most local authorities instruct their
tenants not to carry out car repairs on estate roads,
courtyards or parking bays. Routine maintenance (the
changing of tyres or spark plugs) is permitted, but even
draining the radiator to refill with anti-freeze, or changing
the oil, would be allowed only if the site was properly
cleaned afterwards. Oil shouldn't be slopped over roads
and pavements, for obvious safety reasons as well as those
more aesthetic ones, nor should it be poured down drains
or gullies. It is an offence to pour petrol down drains.

Pets

Not many people complain about cats, hamsters, gerbils,
budgies, canaries, guinea pigs, goldfish, terrapins, newts,
white rats, stick insects etc. Lots of people complain about
dogs – the noise and the mess.

Despite appearances to the contrary on occasions, local
authorities want their tenants to be as happy as possible
and to be able to live life to the full. If a tenant wants a dog
or cat, the council tries not to be obstructive, but their
recommendation is that no one should have a dog or a cat
if they haven't got a garden (or ready access to one)
wherein the animal can exercise and 'do its business'. Not
everyone takes notice of this advice. In some blocks of
flats, the keeping of animals is prohibited. If you're
plagued by an alsatian above and a Rottweiler below,
contact the Housing Officer. It may also be worth while
letting him or her know if you're afraid of reprisals from
the dog-owners. Dog-owners can be strange people: they
surround themselves with fierce beasts when they've got
more than enough aggression on their own account.

If you're plagued by noise or mess from next door's
Great Dane, see Section 63, Pets.

The Mentally Ill

In the last few years it has increasingly been the policy to
close down hospitals and other institutions that have
catered for the mentally ill. The current trend is to return
these patients 'to the community', and this has given local
authorities quite a headache. Whatever the rights and

wrongs, advantages and disadvantages of the policy, it has meant that some tenants see their local authority as dumping someone who can't cope with normal life (whatever that means) next door.

Worried tenants contact the Housing Officer, saying, 'Why did you put this person here?' There follows a list of complaints – that the person is dirty, keeps funny hours, is obsessed with certain practices, takes exception to something we've been happily doing for years etc.

From the local authority's point of view, it's a very difficult situation to deal with. They can try to get help from the institution where the mentally ill person was formerly a patient (if that institution is still in existence). They can also hope for support and expertise from their own Social Services department, but this won't necessarily solve the problem. Social Services have an obligation to their own client – in this case the ex-patient. Even with the best will in the world and adequate resources, it will take a long time to educate us all so that we accept such people totally into our neighbourhood.

94   PROBLEMS FOR HOUSING OFFICERS

You have to remember that Housing Officers see themselves, in the first instance, as arbitrators. They won't necessarily be on your side from the word 'go'. Indeed, the first thing they will want to do is to talk to both you and your neighbour. Their experience is that there are nearly always two sides to a problem. Of course, we know that this isn't so in your case. We know that right is totally on your side and that your neighbour, of whom you are complaining, is a thoughtless blockhead. The Housing Officer, however, will almost invariably want to hear your neighbour's point of view.

It may be that the Housing Officer will decide to advise your neighbour of the conditions of tenancy. Since these conditions are drawn up to suggest criteria for a reasonable standard of and approach to living, the idea is that it's an impersonal way of pointing out to your neighbour what it is that he or she is doing wrong. Don't forget, there is always the possibility that your neighbour isn't aware of the harm he or she is causing, or that there is anything in his or her conduct to which people could take exception. By going through the conditions of tenancy, a Housing Officer may be able to bring your neighbour's shortcomings to his or her attention and suggest a course of action to remedy the situation.

Having heard both sides, the Housing Officer may then give you some disappointing advice. Wherever possible, councils want to avoid rows between their tenants. They are in a no-win situation: if it comes to an out-and-out confrontation, the council is bound to lose, because they represent both complainant and offender, victim and villain, winner and loser. So the advice of the Housing Officer may well be to ignore the shortcomings of your neighbour wherever possible, to walk away, to turn the other cheek, to find some alternative route home. Let us assume that this is unacceptable to you.

What happens next very much depends on circumstances. If the matter is not too complicated, it may be that a solution can be found by bringing in either the caretaker to the estate where you live or, if it's more serious, the local beat PC. The caretaker or a maintenance team would be brought in if all that was needed was better lighting on the stairs or a properly fitting door or an eye kept on where your neighbour parks his or her car. The council does, however, have to be sure that they don't expose their caretaker to reprisals.

If the problem isn't that simple, the council has to take further action. In matters of racial or sexual abuse or harassment, they may well seek to rehouse the offender or even bring in the police. In matters of nuisance, particularly noise or smoke, they will almost certainly ask you to keep a diary, because, if the case ultimately comes to court (and the local authority would be loathe to see it come that far), you are the one who will have to stand up in the witness box and say, 'This is what I suffered.' It is as well, therefore, to have all the facts clearly and conveniently at your disposal. If this is suggested to you, check that the Housing Officer doesn't merely see the diary as a way of keeping you occupied, hoping that you'll believe that something is being done simply because you're writing something down. About fifty per cent of those asked to keep a diary do so, but nothing like that many cases come to court.

If the Housing Officer is satisfied that your complaint is justified and that you do have a legitimate grievance, he or she and the council are in the unenviable position of having to decide what to do about it. If your complaint is against an owner-occupier (not a council tenant), the council is freer to take action, though apparently in a less powerful position. If your complaint is against another council tenant, the council may well be in a predicament.

You may feel that the best solution would be for them to transfer your errant neighbour, but in most cases today that isn't even an option, since there isn't any slack in the housing supply. In some parts of the country there has been a virtual end to the building of new council homes, so it isn't possible to rehouse people with fundamental needs (e.g. a large family in small house or flat), let alone those with a social need. A corollary of this is that more and more people are having to accept property that is barely acceptable to them. They are, therefore, more likely to find fault with it, which includes a greater likelihood of bad relations between neighbours. A person who has moved into a house or flat under protest is hardly likely to be tolerant of the shortcomings of others in the neighbourhood.

What Housing Officers have found is that, where plans are underway to regenerate an estate, tenants tend to come together far more and work together to solve the sort of problems that had hitherto been the cause of friction between them. If there are plans for a major facelift of a council estate, the number of complaints by neighbour about neighbour falls dramatically.

95 ACTION THAT HOUSING OFFICERS CAN TAKE

It's unlikely, however, that you are in the relatively happy position of awaiting a major facelift of your area. You're much more likely to be faced with the possibility of your wretched neighbour continuing the nuisance of which you so justifiably complain. If the nuisance is repeated, the Housing Officer has the authority to warn your neighbour of a possible loss of tenancy – which means eviction. The Housing Act, 1980, section 4, states that the council may regain possession of a secure tenant's home if ' ... the tenant or any person residing in the dwelling has caused a nuisance or annoyance to neighbours, or has been convicted of illegal or immoral use of the property'.

In serious cases, the Housing Officer will almost certainly have to report to a sub-committee of the local council, sometimes called a Tenancy Contraventions Sub-Committee. This committee has three possible options: to monitor the situation, to recommend what is known as a 'management' transfer or to serve a notice seeking possession. The last is a rarely used option. It creates two immediate problems: it's costly, and the council is almost certainly under the obligation to house your neighbour and his or her family once they become homeless.

Transfer has its supporters and opponents. Supporters of transfer say it's a logical way of dealing with the problem because, in nine cases out of ten, you and your neighbour won't get on so long as you continue to live next door to each other. Opponents of transfer say that, by transferring your neighbour to alternative accommodation, all that's happening is that the problem (i.e. your neighbour's unsociable behaviour) is simply being shifted elsewhere, and in a short while some other poor tenant will be complaining, just as you did. (It would, however, be difficult for the pestered tenants successfully to take action against the council in this case unless the transferred neighbour was guilty of some crime.) In a recent study undertaken by the Applied Psychology Division of Aston University, the conclusion was reached that, 'For those tenants with a history of nuisance, transfer and eviction do not seem to provide the answer.'

In the final analysis, it's quite likely that the Housing Officer will hope to negotiate some kind of agreement between you and your neighbour, but if you show good cause as to why they should do so, the council will back your case and take it to court. Indeed, some Housing Officers say that it's the more serious problems that are easier to deal with – it's the minor irritants that are tricky.

Summary

If you are a council tenant, contact your local Housing Officer if you are having any of the following problems with one or other of your neighbours:

(a) noise or other nuisance caused by dogs or other pets;

(b) cars parked thoughtlessly or dangerously (e.g. denying access to emergency services);

(c) car repairs taking place on the road, the pavement, estate courtyards or parking bays;

(d) vehicles abandoned outside your house;

(e) nuisance caused by other tenants or owner occupiers carrying on business on residential premises near you;

(f) nuisance caused by noisy neighbours – but do try sorting it out privately first;

(g) nuisance or worry caused by harassment from other tenants – if you are being threatened, however, don't hesitate to call the police as well.

Note: There are indications that people are increasingly frightened of being threatened with violence if they dare to complain about a neighbour. It's difficult to tell whether such fears are justified or not, though Housing Officers say they reckon there are more weapons about, particularly knives. At the same time, most Housing Officers don't think relationships between neighbours are any worse than they've always been. Some say people sit on their resentment for too long and then over-react. They also think that unemployment plays its part in rows between neighbours: more youngsters are seen to be 'hanging about' and are believed to be looking for trouble. Older people are in their homes for a much greater part of the day: often listening, watching and waiting for trouble.

Like the police and Environmental Health Officers, Housing Officers believe we would all do better if we communicated more easily and more readily with our neighbours wherever it's possible.

23   Mediation Schemes

Faced with a neighbour problem, some people turn to their local branch of the Citizens' Advice Bureau. What happens next depends very much on the staff of your CAB. Some are reluctant to get involved in disputes between neighbours. On the whole, they do regard it as their job to give advice rather than to take sides or try to resolve a specific issue. Hence, if you go to them with a problem about noisy parties or car-parking or racial abuse, bonfires or DIY or dog mess, they may simply refer you to some other agency.

There is, however, an interesting, and some would say much-needed development taking place – in some areas under the auspices of the CAB, in others from initiatives taken by church groups or other volunteers within the community. This development takes the form of Mediation Centres where disputes between neighbours can be settled.

The idea originated in the United States, where both the use of counselling and the notion of neighbourhood are perhaps more widely practised and better regarded. In the States many communities have a mediation service that may deal with a variety of problems – those between friends, husband and wife, different sections of the community and neighbours. Mediators in Britain are not always happy with the description of their work as 'counselling', preferring to describe it as a mixture of 'listening and prompting'.

96   TYPES OF MEDIATION CENTRE

There are at present basically two types of Mediation Centre. The first seeks to set up a grass-roots neighbourhood project where members of the local community can find ways of dealing with their own problems, including that of disputes between neighbours. The second seeks to provide a community with an agency that will deal with problems arising in the community, often an agency staffed voluntarily by 'experts'. So far, there are far more examples of this second model.

The first models for any such schemes in many areas came from the police (Juvenile Panels or Bureaux) and the Probation Service. They are becoming increasingly widespread, but you'll be lucky if there is one already established in your neighbourhood. Schemes which deal with civil matters, particularly neighbour disputes, are still few and far between, but there are signs that more and more are being established or at least considered, and early reports suggest that, wonder of wonders, they do work.

97 HOW THE MEDIATION CENTRE WORKS

No matter who runs the mediation scheme, elements common to all seem to be the technique of intervention and the principle of bringing people together. Mediators recognize that the solution of a single problem that exists between neighbours isn't likely to be the end of the story. You and your neighbour probably won't live happily ever after unless something happens to change the quality of your relationship. This isn't to suggest that you have demonstrably to love your neighbour. It may be that the final solution to the problem of co-existence is that you never speak to each other again – that may be a great improvement as far as you and your neighbour are concerned.

Perhaps the best approach here is to outline how one such agency might tackle a neighbour dispute, in this case an agency that works in close co-operation with a local CAB. (Note: There aren't many such agencies!)

Suppose you have a complaint about one of your neighbours and you go to the CAB. They pass you on to the Mediation Centre, who then listen to what you have to say. The first advice may well be that you should go and have a quiet word with your neighbour, in the hope that matters can be speedily and amicably settled. No matter what agency you are dealing with, all believe that the only hope of establishing good relations between neighbours lies in the two parties themselves reaching a settlement.

Let us suppose, however, that you believe the situation is past that, and that you tell the Mediation Centre you won't go and have this quiet word with your totally unreasonable neighbour. The Mediation Centre will then write to your neighbour (enclosing a stamped addressed envelope for his or her reply), inviting your neighbour to come to the office (neutral territory) to discuss the problem with you and with two mediators.

The next step is largely up to your neighbour. If he or she refuses to take up the invitation or phones the Centre with a mouthful of abuse at the ready, the mediators simply point out that all they wished to do was help achieve a peaceful and friendly settlement of the dispute without either party having to go to a solicitor. This sometimes helps to convince the reluctant neighbour that it might be a good idea to submit to mediation.

If your neighbour still refuses, there is nothing further the Mediation Centre can do to help. If, however, the mention of solicitor sends a chill financial wind into the living-room of his or her life, a meeting is arranged for you, your neighbour and the two mediators at the Mediation Centre.

Don't worry. It isn't like a court. You won't have to wait in a freezing ante-room, staring across at your horrible neighbour – you wait in separate rooms. Both parties have the procedure explained to them, and both are interviewed separately, with the same amount of time given to each. Both parties are then brought together with the mediators.

The next step is to get you to tell your neighbour what you said to the mediators in your interview. Once you've done that, your neighbour tells you what he said to the mediators during his interview. The role of the mediators is a skilled and subtle one – they have to hold back, hoping that you and your neighbour will gradually work towards a compromise or other satisfactory settlement.

If you do, what is agreed between you and your neighbour (who is now less than horrible) is recorded and read back to you both. It is entered into the records of the mediators, and you and your neighbour are given copies which you are asked to sign, though they are not legally binding in any way. (It's different in the States, where the mediation service is part of the court system.)

In the experience of mediators working in this way, the system has a lot to recommend it. In the first place, it's a free service. It also works towards a solution that the parties to the dispute themselves have arrived at. This is very important – solutions imposed by the law or the local authority are often unsatisfactory in the long run. Rancour is still prevalent. There is nearly always a feeling (on the losing side) that justice has not been done. This is true, because very, very few cases of disputes between neighbours have all the wrong on one side and all the right on the other. (In practice, the mediation service avoids the few cases that are as cut and dried as this, because they aren't suitable for mediation.) There is nothing the law can do to make two people who hate each other get on well together – but the mediation service can show warring neighbours a new way to approach their problems.

The service is also adaptable. On occasion the routine may be changed to fit the problem of the parties concerned. One Mediation Centre cited a case where they had to deal with a very obstinate complainant. The cause of the complaint was a shared gate. A complained that B never shut the gate and that, as a result of this, dogs came into A's garden. The simple solution, which presented itself during the mediation session, was that a spring should be put on the gate, so that the gate shut itself. A then wanted to know who was going to pay for the spring. The mediators felt A should – A wasn't so sure. In the end a compromise was reached. A paid for the spring, B took the trouble to fix it on the gate. The problem was solved.

98 WORK UNDERTAKEN BY THE MEDIATION SERVICE

Apart from their reservations about taking on a case where there are clear right and wrong sides (e.g. racism, sexual harassment, gratuitous violence), matrimonial disputes (the province of Marriage Guidance Counsellors), cases involving the mentally ill or criminal actions, Mediation Centres are prepared to tackle a wide variety of problems: barking dogs, boundary disputes (the CAB offers a voluntary surveyor's aid scheme), bonfires, noise (TV, radio, hi-fi, youngsters) and shared drives and paths (and gates, see above).

If you are lucky enough to have such a scheme operating in your area (and the number of centres is increasing), it may well be worthwhile contacting the mediation service before resorting to other more drastic and more expensive courses of action. The crying shame is that there aren't many more of these centres and that mediation, practised in every village in China and in most schools in the United States, is overlooked here.

PART V

THE WAY AHEAD

24   Where Do We Go From Here?

Suppose you have a noisy neighbour. You have tried speaking to him or her, politely asking for a reduction in the noise. It hasn't worked. You have tried complaining directly. That hasn't worked, either. You have been to the council, to the local Environmental Health Officer. Here you found sympathy but not much else. The council sent out one of their standard letters – they may send up to a hundred each week. It had no effect. You went back to the council. They sent a stroppier letter. It, too, had no effect. You have been asked to keep a diary noting the occasions when the noise disturbs you and are now booked to borrow one of the council's recording machines but will have to wait many weeks before one becomes available.

You have tried phoning the police, in the heart-rending small hours of the morning, when they are cosy and warm in their canteen, being paid for being awake, while you are cramming your fingertips in your ears in a desperate attempt to create an artificial silence. The police, too, have been sympathetic. They have said that they'll pass the message on to their patrols, but they haven't promised to do much else.

You have even taken the seemingly enormous step of going to a solicitor. Here, again, you found sympathy – maybe more expensive sympathy than that offered by the council or the police. But the general advice of the solicitor is that your best bet is to tackle your neighbour directly. Either the problem isn't one that litigation will solve or, if it is, cost and time factors (not to mention the strain of nagging doubts as to what the outcome of the case might be) make the whole idea unadvisable and unattractive.

It isn't really any wonder then that there are signs that a kind of lethargy or paralysing pessimism has descended on many of us when faced with neighbour problems. We feel we can't deal directly with our neighbour and we have tried calling in the experts. The only immediate practical solution they offered was to instal double glazing or move the bedroom to the back of the house.

Under these circumstances it's easy to start blaming the council and muttering, 'They ought to do something'. Councils often wish they could. There's nothing most paid council officials would like better than to see everyone in their borough or district happy. They spend the whole of their working life trying to make our environment a clean and pleasant place to be in. One official from an Environmental Health Department whom I spoke to explained how he and the rest of the department had spent an entire week clearing a local street that had ben used by lorry-drivers to fly-tip rubbish from a building site in the City of London. Every night lorries turned up, smashed the street lights so that they couldn't be identified and filled the street with rubble. The darkened streets became dangerous as well as unpleasant for the local residents. There was an increase in the incidents of mugging and assaults. Tackling this problem became a priority for the EHO, taking up time and resources that could have been used to tackle neighbour disputes. It cost the council over £6,000 to clear the street, and within three days it was again full of debris. For residents of such a street, the inconvenience that you or I complain of (living next to a barking dog, for example) must seem very small beer indeed. The sad and awful truth is that neighbour and environmental problems have reached such epic and epidemic proportions in Britain that few councils are able to carry out their statutory duties, let alone help and advice where no such duty exists.

The police are in a similar position. They respond to some calls for help in neighbour disputes, but only where there seems a real possibility that things will get out of hand if they don't, and that usually means where there is a possibility of violence. We may think it monstrous that we are kept awake for most of the night by a noisy party next door. We may regard such behaviour as criminal. The police don't. Their view (and it may well be mistaken) is that many such complaints spring from resentment that we weren't invited to the party, or that the complainant is an ex-boyfriend of the girl giving the party, or that things will seem very different in the morning when the party is over and normal relationships can be restored. The trouble is that what passes for normal relationships may well be unfriendly, bitter and acrimonious.

If we feel deeply aggrieved, we can always go to the law, but this is expensive, carries an element of risk and takes a long time. It's also a bit like taking a sledgehammer to crack a walnut. In moments of calm, we can appreciate the kind of figure we'd cut in court, standing there, Ringelmann Chart in hand, solemnly complaining about a bonfire, or the decibels of a lawnmower or dead leaves from a neighbour's tree that fall into our fishpond. If pushed hard enough, lawyers will do almost anything (legal) to help a client, but many of them shake their heads in a most unpromising way when listening to tales of woe about neighbour trouble.

Where do we go from here?

In the long term, what is needed is probably a massive attack on the problem from several fronts. Some people think that schools could have a part to play. There is little or nothing in our educational system that seeks to promote neighbourliness as such. It may be that the general ethos of any particular school seeks to encourage a policy of consideration towards others, but even this may not go much further than frequent requests to children to behave in the bus queue and not to drop litter.

This isn't to blame schools. They have quite enough to do as it is, and it would be almost impossible for them to squeeze more into an already overcrowded and increasingly imposed curriculum. Somewhere, though, we may have to decide which we consider more important: computer literacy or concern for other people, history (how we used to live) or good neighbourship (how we ought to live).

In the long term, too, much could be done with improved design and planning – of houses, estates and neighbourhoods. It does seem ridiculous that two or more families should be deprived of sleep by one baby (or the poor mother or father having to walk up and down trying to pacify the baby), simply because there is inadequate sound insulation between one flat and another or one terrace house and another. How many architects have to live in such conditions?

And, as we convert more and more houses to multiple occupation and cram more and more people into any given area, it seems shortsighted that we don't give more regard to the problems created by lack of space. There is a lot of talk about inner-city deprivation: probably the biggest single deprivation in inner cities is lack of space. Despite the horrors of the back-to-back houses of Victorian times and the high-rise blocks of flats of the 1960s, it's possible that there are more people in Britain today with restricted or no access to a garden of their own than ever before.

Admittedly, lack of garden is seldom recorded as a source of neighbour dispute, but it can play its part in exacerbating an unpromising situation. For years we have known what lack of space does to rats and other creatures, and rats don't have the problem of parking cars, storing bicycles, drying washing or exercising dogs.

It's significant that problems between neighbours in rural areas tend to be different from those in towns. There are far fewer complaints about day-to-day thoughtlessness – you don't get the people at No. 8 complaining that their neighbour deliberately warms up his car engine with the exhaust pipe pointing towards them. In the country, where there is plenty of space, problems tends to be less to do with people, more to do with property, and often of a proprietary nature. People row about the location of fences, hedges, ditches, the encroachment of branches over boundaries, the roaming of cattle and horses. It's much more like the days of the Old West – as if all that was needed was to bring in Gary Cooper or Henry Fonda in the last reel to shoot, or at least arrest, the offenders.

Long-term solutions are all very well and have the bonus of including preventative measures, but they have two drawbacks. In the first place they are long term, and we want relief from our dreadful neighbour right now. In the second place, you don't remove the source of neighbour disputes simply by making the world a better place to live in. It helps, but it isn't the complete answer. There are many people, living next door to each other, who wouldn't be able to co-exist peacefully if they had a thousand hectares each, a hundred per cent sound insulation, triple garages and boundary walls ten metres high. One Environmental Health Officer told me of a complaint he had recently had to deal with that concerned neighbours living in large detached houses with vast gardens. The complaint was about the noise made by a swimming-pool pump. In the average miserable English summer, the pump was turned on about half a dozen times. Nevertheless, the EHO was expected to make sure that the swimming-pool owners either turned the pump off or somehow kept it quiet. And when he failed (as he was bound to do since the people with the swimming-pool were every bit as obstinate as the complainants), the matter was taken to the Ombudsman, and the poor EHO was reported to the Chief Executive of his council for dereliction of duty. There is little that education, design, planning or resources can do for people who have reached that state of hostility.

In some ways, the short term offers more hope. The most interesting, and potentially the most useful, development is the idea that mediation can be used as a means of solving neighbour problems and, more importantly, of establishing better communication between neighbours.

Mention has already been made of the mediation and reparation centres that are being developed in various parts of the country, and that one of the main emphases of their work is to bring people together to examine a problem that exists between them. Much of the work of these centres has to do with disputes between neighbours, between people who are going to remain in contact with each other and who, unless something is done to change their day-to-day approach to each other, will continue to get on each other's nerves.

What is hopeful about mediation as a means to solving neighbour problems is that it looks at the wider issues, the background to the present complaint, and that it seeks to facilitate both neighbours arriving at a mutually satisfactory solution – one that has a far better chance of surviving in the long term. What makes this difficult to achieve, of course, is that we allow our resentment to build up to such an extent before we make our complaint that we are enraged and feel that only a full-scale legal confrontation can possibly do justice to the situation. We want to see the judge put on a black cap, to see our neighbour dragged in chains down to the cells, to have him put away for the duration. We want to win: we don't want a compromise.

This isn't the place to go into a psychological analysis of the revenge syndrome, but it may be the place to say, yet again, that the earlier we communicate our complaint to our neighbour, the easier it may be to find a solution to the problem. It's perhaps too early to say whether mediation will provide a widespread and long-term means of tackling a great many neighbour disputes. An obvious difficulty is that, if we as complainants are reluctant to go to mediation, how much more reluctant will our neighbour (the thoughtless, noisy, anti-social blockhead) as offender be. And there are still many occasions where mediation wouldn't be the right avenue of approach to a problem – where there is a dispute about a boundary, for example, or where a neighbour allowed his or her property to become overrun with rats or other vermin. (The burghers of Hamelin didn't invite the Pied Piper to act as arbitrator.) There is also the danger that mediation becomes a somewhat glib approach, seeking a slick, wordy solution to a series of problems as though they are unrelated.

Part of the attraction of mediation can be that it seems quick and cheap when compared with a more formal legal solution. There needs to be a careful examination of each situation to see whether or not mediation is an appropriate approach. Early indications are that it works best on complex situations, where both parties have got themselves into a mess and where both parties would like to get out of the mess.

Nevertheless, by placing the emphasis on co-operation and a sense of the community, mediation may be our best immediate bet to tackle what has already reached a desperate situation for a great many people. It doesn't take great resources. There isn't any long waiting period. It doesn't cost any money. At its best, it also holds out the hope of making a real and lasting change in the situation that exists between you and your neighbour – not seeking to make you bosom pals but to help establish, by negotiation a *modus vivendi* that will work for you both.

It may not appear the most attractive of propositions at first sight, but the alternatives all have drawbacks, and some people are moved to very desperate straits indeed by problems with their neighbours. Many seriously consider moving house – quite a few do actually move, but there's no guarantee whatsoever that they find 'better' neighbours in their new surroundings. To uproot the whole family because someone cannot keep his (and it's usually a 'he') stereo/car/labrador under control is deeply upsetting and can do a great deal of damage to one's sense of security. It has to be said, however, that there may be occasions when it is the only way out.

What cannot be said too often is that the best way to tackle a problem that you have with your neighbour is by approaching him or her directly. If this isn't possible, then, if you're lucky enough to have one in your area, try involving a mediation agency. They will tell you if they can't help or if they think you need a different sort of solution.

If your problem is about rights of way, light, boundary disputes, shared paths and driveways, the ownership of a strip of land, the responsibility of repairing walls or fences

– go to a solicitor. The law is always much happier to click into action when faced with an argument about property, and you need a legal and permanent solution to any such problem.

If you are being threatened with, or subjected to, violence – go to the police. Where they think it's appropriate that they should act, they can do so effectively and with far more sensitivity than many of us give them credit for – but they really don't like trying to find out whose dog is barking at four in the morning.

If you are being racially abused, threatened or harassed – go to the police and/or your local Community Relations Officer. If you're a council tenant – go to your Housing Officer. The probability is that you won't have to move house, but your racist neighbour will, a much more satisfactory arrangement.

Almost finally, whatever action you contemplate, whoever you go to see, you are always in a much stronger position if you can persuade some of your other neighbours to join you. The thoughtless bloke at No. 10 is far more likely to mend his ways if he receives a letter signed by several of his neighbours, or if a small posse gathers on his doorstep. The police may move more swiftly if they receive a bunch of complaints about the same fire/car/party. An Environmental Health Officer may give a complaint preferential treatment if it comes from a whole neighbourhood.

And finally – give it a go, don't suffer in silence. The more of us who manage to raise the problems that so many of us are faced with, the more chance there is of success. Something has got to be done, soon, and on a massive scale. Too many people are unhappy.

Useful Addresses

The Ramblers' Association,
1/5 Wandsworth Road,   01-582 6826
London SW8 2LJ   01-582 6878

Open Spaces Society,
25A Bell Street,
Henley-on-Thames,   Henley-on-Thames
Oxon RG9 2BA   (0491) 573535

The Noise Abatement Society,
6 Old Bond Street,
London W1X 3TA   01-493 5877

The National Society for Clean Air,
136 North Street,
Brighton BN1 1RG   Brighton (0273) 26313

National Canine Defence League,
6a Pratt Street,
London NW1   01-338 0137

Lands Tribunal,
5 Chancery Lane,
London WC2   01-936 7200

Law Centres Federation,
Duchess House,
Warren Street,
London W1   01-387 8570

Sources

Aldridge, Trevor M., *Questions of Law: Homes, Buying, Selling, Owning, Renting* (Hamlyn, 1982)

Your Home and the Law (Oyez, 1979)

Arden, Andrew, and Partington, Martin, *Quiet Enjoyment* (Legal Action Group, 1985)

Artis, Denise, *Odour Nuisances and Their Control* (Shaw & Sons, 1984)

Baker, P.V., *Megarry's Manual of the Law of Real Property* (Stevens, 1975)

Chapman, R.M., *You and Your Home* (Shaw & Sons, 1984)

Clayden, P., and Trevelyan, J., *Rights of Way: A Guide to Law and Practice* (Open Spaces Society/ Ramblers Association, 1983)

Cumberbatch, G., Graham, N., and Tebay, S., *Disputes Between Neighbours* (Aston University, 1986)

Curzon, L.B., *A Dictionary of Law* (Macdonald & Evans, 1983)

Dias, R.W.M. (ed.), *Clerk and Lindself on Torts* (Sweet & Maxwell, 15th edition, 1982)

Dias, R.W.M., and Markensinis B.S., *The English Law of Torts* (Etablissements Emile Bruylant, 1976)

Dunbar-Brunton, James, *The Law and the Individual* (Macmillan, 1979)

Eddey, K., *The English Legal System* (Sweet & Maxwell, 1987)

Evans, *The Law of Landlord and Tenant* (Butterworths, 1985)

Furmston, M., and Powell-Smith, V., *You and the Law* (Hamlyn, 1987)

James, P.S., *Introduction to English Law* (Butterworths, 11th edition, 1985)

Jones, M.A., *Textbook on Torts* (Financial Trading Publications Ltd, 1986)

McCloughlin, J., *The Law Relating to Pollution* (Manchester University Press, 1972)

Major, W.T., *Mastering Basic English Law* (Macmillan Master Series, 1985)

Marshall, T., and Walpole, M., *Bringing People Together: Mediation and Reparation Projects in Great Britain* (Home Office, London, 1986)

Martin, E.A. (ed.), *A Concise Dictionary of Law* (Oxford University Press, 1983)

Mitchell, Barbara, *Landlord and Tenant Law* (BSP Professional Books, 1987)

Niekirk, Paul H. (publishing ed.), *Halsbury's Laws of England* (Butterworths, 4th edition, 1973)

Onions, C.T. (ed.), *The Shorter Oxford English Dictionary* (Oxford University Press, 1983)

Rozenberg, J., and Watkins, N., *Your Rights and the Law* (Dent, 1986)

Sandys-Winsch, Godfrey, *Garden Law* (Shaw & Sons, 1982)

Saunders, J.B. (ed.), *Words and Phrases Legally Defined* (Butterworths, 1969)

Smith, P.F. (ed.), *Evans: The Law of Landlord and Tenant* (Butterworths, 1985)

Tettenborn, A.M., *An Introduction to the Law of Obligations* (Butterworths, 1984)

Tyas, J.G.M., *Law of Torts* (M & E Handbooks, 4th edition, 1982)

Walker, D.M., *The Scottish Legal System* (W. Green & Son Ltd., 1981)

Walsh, Clifford and Jowett, Earl, *A Dictionary of English Law* (Sweet & Maxwell, 1977)

Webster, Charles A.R., *Environmental Health Law* (Sweet & Maxwell, 1981)

Wilson, W.A., *Introductory Essays on Scots Law* (W. Green & Son Ltd., 2nd edition, 1984)

Glossary of terms

Ancient Lights: (Not as Ancient as they used to be). Originally, windows through which light had been enjoyed – without consent or permission – for so long that 'the memory of man ran not to the contrary'. Since 1832, for upwards of twenty years without interruption.

Chattels: There are two sorts – **Chattels Personal** are any kind of property other than **Chattels Real**. Chattels Real are rights derived out of land and buildings (real estate) which at Common Law devolved on the personal representatives of the deceased owner, and not on the heir.

Damages: Money paid as compensation by one person to another for injury, loss or damage caused by breach of legal duty.

Defamation: Damaging someone's reputation by falsely communicating to a third party matters bringing that person into unjustified disrepute: libel when written or given permanent form, slander when spoken.

Defendant: The person against whom legal proceedings are brought.

Easement: A right attaching to a piece of land (the **dominant tenement**) entitling the owner thereof to exercise some right over adjacent land (the **servient tenement**) owned by someone else.

ex parte: On behalf of. A judicial proceeding in which an

application is made by someone who is not party to the proceeding, but has an interest in the matter.

Hereditament: (Impress your friends with this now seldom used word). A term for every kind of property that could be inherited – both land and the rights and profits issuing out of it.

Injunction: An order of the Court that any person shall refrain from doing something (**restrictive injunction**) or shall do something (**mandatory injunction**).

Litigant: A party to a civil lawsuit – one who has come to law.

Lost Modern Grant: system that existed from 1623 to 1832, whereby the courts assumed that an easement had been created after twenty years but that the original deed of grant for the easement had been lost.

Messuage: Simply, a house and its surrounds (orchard, barn, outbuildings, garden, etc.).

Plaintiff: The party who complains and brings an action.

Precedent: A previous case that lends weight and support to the decision made in the particular case in hand.

ratio decidendi: The reason for deciding a case one way rather than another – the basis of the actual decision.

Restrictive Covenant: An agreement that restricts the use of a particular piece of land to the benefit of another piece of land.

Squatter: Someone who wrongfully encloses a piece of wasteland, builds on it and lives there. More commonly, someone who enters another's premises and takes up residence there.

Tenement: **Dominant** – tenement of land in favour of which and for the benefit of which an easement exists over a servient tenement. **Servient** – land subject to an easement.

Tort: A harm or wrong that does not come within the province of the criminal law.

Table of Cases

Table of Statutes

ORDERS AND REGULATIONS

Index